Terror in Our Time

D0483153

Written by two leading scholars, this book is an accessible over-view of the global political consequences of the 9/11 terror attacks.

The War on Terror has defined the first decade of this century. It has been marked by the deaths of thousands of people, political turmoil, massive destruction, and intense fear. Regardless of the name it goes under, the long War on Terror will continue to affect lives across the world. Its catalyst, 9/11, did not have to happen, nor did the character of the responses. This book offers a set of compelling arguments about how we got here, where we are, and where we should be heading. It is organised around 12 penetrat-ing and readable essays, full of novel interpretations and succinct summaries of complex ideas and events. In their examination of those aspects of global order touched by terror, the authors argue that the dangers of international terrorism are not overblown. Future 9/11s are possible: so is a more just and law-governed world. Terrorism cannot be disinvented, but with more intelligent policies than have been on show these past ten years, it can be overcome and made politically anachronistic.

The book will be essential reading for all students of interna-tional security, terrorism studies, war and conflict studies, US for-eign policy, and international relations in general; it will also be of considerable interest to general readers concerned about world affairs.

Ken Booth is Senior Research Associate in the Department of International Politics, Aberystwyth University, where he was previously EH Carr Professor and Head of Department. He is a Fellow of the British Academy and editor of the journal *International Relations*. Among his many books are *Theory of World Security* (2007) and the edited volume *Realism and World Politics* (Routledge 2011).

Tim Dunne is Professor of International Relations in the School of Political Science and International Studies, University of Queensland, where he is also Research Director of the Asia-Pacific Centre for the Responsibility to Protect. He has written and edited several books, including *Worlds in Collision* with Ken Booth (2002). He is currently an editor of the *European Journal of International Relations*.

Terror in Our Time

Ken Booth and Tim Dunne

Routledge
Taylor & Francis Group

LONDON AND NEW YORK

First published 2012
by Routledge
2 Park Square, Milton Park, Abingdon, Oxon, OX14 4RN

Simultaneously published in the USA and Canada
by Routledge
711 Third Avenue, New York, NY 10017

Routledge is an imprint of the Taylor & Francis Group, an informa business

British Library Cataloguing in Publication Data
A catalogue record for this book is available from the British Library

Library of Congress Cataloging-in-Publication Data
Booth, Ken, 1943–
 Terror in our time / Ken Booth and Tim Dunne.
 p. cm.
 Includes bibliographical references and index.
 1. Security, International. 2. Terrorism.
 I. Dunne, Timothy, 1965– II. Title.
 JZ5588.B665 2011
 363.325—dc22
 2011015873

ISBN13: 978–0–415–67830–8 (hbk)
ISBN13: 978–0–415–67831–5 (pbk)
ISBN13: 978–0–203–69725–2 (ebk)

Typeset in Joanna by Swales & Willis Ltd, Exeter, Devon

Printed and bound by Edwards Brothers, Inc.

Contents

Prologue

The iconography of 9/11 was constructed in real time by the instantaneous words and pictures of the world's media.

On September 11, 2001, two hijacked aircraft, a short time apart, hit the Twin Towers of the World Trade Center, one of the most recognisable buildings in the United States. Soon after this attack in New York, another hijacked aircraft hit the Pentagon in Washington DC, and a fourth was brought down in a field 130 km south of Pittsburgh. Within four minutes of the second aircraft hitting the North Tower, CNN had broken into an advertisement; the global coverage of 9/11, still on-going, had begun. On screen and in our minds remains the contrast of a sunny autumn morning scarred forever by death and destruction under a spreading pall of smoke. Out of a clear blue sky came terror.

But wait.

It was not a 'clear blue sky', metaphorically speaking. The skies had been pregnant with terrible potentialities and presentiments of 'spectacular' terrorism for many years: the terrorist hijackings of aircraft in the 1970s; the radicalisation of Islam; the release in 1974, a few years after the World Trade Center had been built, of the scarifying film *The Towering Inferno*;[1] the Rushdie affair; the formation of al-Qaeda in 1988; the speech in 1990 by the first President Bush talking of living in 'the age of the terrorist'; the *National Review* headline in the same year warning 'The Muslims are Coming! The Muslims are Coming!'; the claim in 1992 by

John S. Esposito that the 'Green Menace [of Islam] will replace the Red Menace of World Communism'; the attack on the Twin Towers in 1993 by terrorists; the Nairobi and Dar es Salaam bombings in 1998; the Taliban's nurturing of al-Qaeda in Afghanistan; the attack on USS *Cole* in October 2000; Usama bin Laden's 'Messages to the World' to fight a jihad against Western targets; and on and on.

The writing was on many walls, and had been for years.

While eschewing the idea that a desperate attack on the symbols of US global power was inevitable, the chain of causation that can be constructed in hindsight leads us to think that it was an outrage waiting to happen. It had been gestating in long-term historical trends within radical Muslim communities and in global geopolitics, in certain religious eschatology, in the streets of the Middle East, in fantastical imaginations, in the extremism of groups acting in the name of religion, in new styles of militancy, in the radicalisation of young Muslim men in Europe and elsewhere, in technological possibilities and nightmares, and in feelings of humiliation and revenge. 9/11 was not a virgin birth of spectacular terrorism.

In the ten years of almost constant fighting and continuous terror since 2001, the imagery of the bolt from the blue that September morning remains as powerful as ever. It is kept alive by current news stories, by personal hurt, by the media, by politicians, and by religion. Many people in the West remain in shock, crystallised by the iconography; in other parts of the world, others remain shocked and awed by the nature of some of the counteractions to what happened. The costs, everywhere, have been enormous, and most importantly in lives that have been forever lost or broken. When the reckoning is done, it is our view that in the democratic world these will be seen as ten largely wasted years. It could and should, by now, be feeling different.

It is not our intention in this book to criticise all that has been done by Western governments in the decade we will call '9/11 + 10'. We recognise successes in counter-terrorism and record some excellent contributions to knowledge from researchers; yet in our examination of what world leaders and individual societies have made of the years since 9/11 it is difficult to avoid an overwhelming sense of disappointment and frustration. Alternative responses were available. Terrible mistakes could have been avoided. We could have done so much better. We might next time, on the day after, if we reflect wisely on 9/11 + 10.

Acknowledgements

We have incurred a number of debts in writing this book. We want to thank, for commenting on one or more chapters: Richard Devetak, Ed Frettingham, Robert Gleave, John Heathershaw, Faaeza Jasdanwalla, Nida Shoughry, and Harmonie Toros; for his outstanding service as a research assistant and indexer, Alexander Pound; and for their enthusiastic backing, Andrew Humphrys at Routledge and Caroline Watson at Swales & Willis.

Ken Booth wants to thank the organisers of the conference 'Terror and the challenges to the nation-state', at the Instituto de Filosofia da Linguagem, Universidade Nova de Lisboa, Lisbon, for the opportunity to present some of the preliminary arguments; and the founders of Critical Terrorism Studies at Aberystwyth University, Jeroen Gunning, Richard Jackson, and Marie Breen Smith. Tim Dunne wishes to acknowledge the institutional support he has received from the University of Queensland and the School of Political Science and International Studies.

Given the controversial nature of many of the issues discussed in this book, nobody mentioned here bears any responsibility for what we have written.

We also want to thank our many colleagues and friends who have not contributed directly to this book but whose ideas have shaped how we think about all the issues it contains. Finally we would like to thank our close friends for backing the work we have put into this book, and our immediate families for their love and support – thank you to Caroline, Eurwen, Lola, Rob, Seb and Tom.

Part I
Terror and danger

1 9/11 + 10

Where do you stand in relation to the big questions about terrorism? Do you think there are circumstances in which a terrorist should be tortured, in the hope of extracting information that will save innocent lives? Should the civil rights of those in suspect communities be impinged in order to further the security of the majority? Are the risks of terrorism exaggerated? What are the fundamental causes of terrorism? What kind of world order produces this kind of violence? Who is winning the 'War on Terror' after ten years? Can terrorism ever be defeated? This book will help you to put these questions in context and, we hope, lead you towards wise answers.

What if?

Our subject matter, of course, is the real 9/11 + 10 (our shorthand for the decade since the terror attacks by 19 hijackers on the United States on September 11, 2001): but we also should consider a radically different, counterfactual 9/11 + 10.

Consider these alternative historical possibilities. What if '26/11' as it is known in India – the terror attacks in Mumbai in 2008 that killed 126 people – had taken place during the six-month stand-off between India and Pakistan during the first half of 2002, when up to 800,000 troops were massed on both sides of the Kashmir border? Might the terror attacks have been enough to tip these two adversaries into full-scale (and possibly nuclear) war? What would the Russian government have done if all 646 hostages had been killed after the 57-hour siege in a Moscow theatre in October 2002 (116 were killed in a rescue mission that was designed to save them)? What would have been the reaction if Umar Farouk Abdulmutallab had succeeded in exploding his terrorist device on the Northwest Airlines flight from Amsterdam to Detroit in December 2009, and 289 passengers had been killed? Even this terrible total would have been exceeded had an earlier plot not been thwarted, this time to blow up multiple airliners over the Atlantic: had this occurred, collecting evidence and assigning blame would have been extraordinarily difficult with wreckage scattered over thousands of miles of ocean – much of it lost forever. In 2010 in Times Square, New York, car bombs left at the heart of busy tourist areas were detected without causing harm: what if they had gone off? The most recent terrorist 'spectacular' (known) to have been averted, in December 2010, was the result of the discovery of printer cartridges converted into small high-explosive devices and smuggled in two cargo flights originating in Yemen and bound for Chicago; detonation over the eastern seaboard of the United States was planned, thereby hoping for heavy casualties on the ground.

If these plots had been successful, this book would have been very different. We would all be *feeling* radically different about terrorism in our time – except al-Qaeda and its sympathisers, for whom these acts of brutality would have represented successes. The anxiety that took hold in America after 9/11 would have been shared by more people, in more places.

Sheer good luck is one major reason why we are able to discuss the historical 9/11 + 10 as opposed to a potential decade of terrorist spectaculars and the spread of the sort of desolation in their aftermath shown on the book's front cover. When the IRA failed to kill the British prime minister in the 1984 Brighton bombing, their communiqué summed up the stark reality that in the long run luck is not on the side of targets of terrorism: 'Today we were unlucky. But remember: we only have to be lucky once. You will have to be lucky always'.[1]

Good fortune played a part in the discovery of some of these plots. Another reason why it turned out differently has been the counter-terrorism efforts of the leading Western states, and the fact that ordinary citizens – terror targets – have dutifully waited in long queues, removed items of clothing, unpacked laptops, and complied with restrictive conditions for the greater good.

Some counter-terrorism measures have come in for a great deal of criticism. One such is the allegation of 'profiling', where behaviour is automatically but erroneously inferred from racial and ethnic characteristics, or displays of religious identity. On this and in other things, there has been a great deal to question, and we do not hesitate to do so in the chapters that follow, but at the outset we want to acknowledge the weighty responsibility and the intense pressure faced by governments and their agencies when faced by an international threat of the sort posed by al-Qaeda.

Moments after the 9/11 attacks, those responsible for counter-terrorism in Western countries were under the most intense pressure from their leaders and publics to come up with speedy answers to urgent and vexing questions. What other spectacular incidents were being planned, where, and when? (Note that the 'when?' meant that intelligence services were under pressure to provide knowledge immediately, not after leisurely research, as the next attack might be days away.) What might the next attacks be like – was there no limit to the casualties today's terrorists would inflict? What extra resources could be committed to counter-terrorism, to save civilian lives (and political careers)?

As you consider the possibility that a number of terror incidents in the recent past might have exceeded 9/11 in their lethality, and might yet in the future, bear in mind that respected RAND senior advisor Brian Jenkins has characterised al-Qaeda as the world's first terrorist nuclear power without having the capability. There can be little doubt that al-Qaeda would acquire a nuclear capability if it could (and chemical and biological weapons too). Even if it fails in its quest for them, it nevertheless provokes fearful respect for its ambitions, and its potential targets can never be completely sure that it has failed; and they know that if its quest is successful its agents have to be lucky once (more).

Ten years that shook the world

9/11 + 10 could have been catastrophically worse than it has been, but it has been bad enough. The publicly available data throws up some interesting questions. Did you know that since 9/11 the number of world-wide fatalities from non-state terrorism in an eight-year period is comparable with the deaths of US soldiers in Vietnam (over a longer duration)? Why are state terror deaths declining sharply year-on-year when non-state terror deaths have risen sharply in the aftermath of 9/11, peaking in 2007? How is it that the magnitude of 9/11 is frequently normalised (especially by the 'left') by comparing the risk of death-by-traffic incidents as opposed to death by terror attack? Such comparisons badly overlook the fact that the 2,949 who died on 9/11 were victims of politics not poor driving skills or mechanical error. In other words, they were deaths resulting not from 'accidents' but from the violent struggle over meaning between jihadist extremists and their enemies in the West.

Key information about terrorist attacks since 9/11 is included as an Appendix. The information there supplements facts about 9/11 with data on subsequent mass atrocity terrorist incidents (to the end of 2008). The Appendix highlights every attack in which more than 50 people lost their lives: by this measure, there were 110 mass-casualty attacks, killing 13,557 and injuring 140,351. The fatality figure for all terrorist incidents (without the 50 threshold) in the eight years following 2001 is 54,569; this figure is still likely to understate the lethality of terrorism since what has come to be called microterrorism incidents have probably been under-reported. But fatalities and injuries are only the start; grief and dread cascade throughout societies as trust networks come under stress and strain.

Our conception of terrorism in this book is broad, and includes states among the potential perpetrators. We will argue that it is illogical and unjustifiable to exclude states and their agents from the language of terror, terrorism, and terrorist – words relating to patterns of violence that seek to leverage fear beyond those that are directly targeted. Yet this book is not about states as terrorists. This is partly because state terror – while certainly in evidence in the past decade – has declined markedly (see Table A.2 and Figure A.1 in the Appendix) though not necessarily permanently; also, where there have been examples of state terror (in Burma, the Congo, and Sri Lanka, for example) these have not had systemic effects, as has been the case with al-Qaeda and its enemies.

Even when they are not the focus of attention, state power and purpose remain prominent. While our focus in Terror in Our Time is centrally about al-Qaeda's challenge, it is necessarily about the mobilisation of massive military power and state resources against them. Once organised violence becomes a significant tool of choice to fight terrorists there is an ever-present possibility of mirroring behaviour, as people get caught up in a cycle of terrorism and counter-terrorism.

We show in the book that 9/11 has had consequences that have radiated far beyond the target of the original attack. International alliances have been refashioned, with new strategic allies coming together in South Asia and the Arab Middle East. The Libyan leadership quickly realised the opportunity 9/11 presented for gaining some international respectability, by attempting to reconstitute its international identity from Western pariah to ally. Counter-terrorism policies in scores of countries beyond the central players in this book – notably Russia, China, Indonesia, and Malaysia – were used to rebalance political power in favour of state authorities and away from individual citizens and their activities in civil society. And Israeli authorities saw the enhanced political opportunity to use the label 'terrorists' against Palestinian groups it opposed. Although the term War on Terror[2] is always identified with the US president, George W. Bush, it was the prime minister of Israel, Ariel Sharon, who is credited with the first use of the phrase. In a televised speech on September 11 he said, in ways that immediately opened up political possibilities for his own country,

The war on terror is an international war waged by a coalition of the free world against the forces of terror and all those who think they can threaten freedom. It is a war between good and evil, between the human and the bloodthirsty.[3]

Similarly, the phrase 'global war on terror' did not emerge from the White House, but was first used by UK prime minister Tony Blair on 17 September 2001, in an attempt to build an anti-terror coalition and cement his special relationship with Washington.[4]

In more profound ways than such impacts on individual state policies, these ten years shook world order. Ideas about the conduct of war were altered, untested strategies of counter-terrorism were implemented, and legal questions about how to deal with countries that have radical jihadist extremists on their soil remain unanswered. Sovereign states generally saw a hardening of their boundaries – through tighter border controls – rather than the loosening that advocates of globalisation anticipated. Executive authority was invoked by prime ministers and presidents in the name of securing the state. The most egregious example of this was the challenge mounted by the United States to the international Convention against Torture. Leaked government documents give evidence that US decision-makers no longer deemed themselves to be accountable to the 'court of world opinion', the phrase John F. Kennedy's ambassador to the United Nations used at the time of the Cuban Missile Crisis. Advocates of universal human rights in the West had become used to defending themselves against the charge of 'Eurocentrism' thrown at them by former colonised countries; they probably never imagined, in the early years of the new millennium, that the land of Eleanor Roosevelt and Martin Luther King would be leading other liberal states down the path of torture, rendition, and detention without trial.

Other dimensions of world order were reconfigured. The decade saw the further articulation of the neoconservative vision of America's destiny to lead the world through the active and forceful promotion of democracy. At the same time, there was a weakening of American hegemony as the War on Terror generated enemies abroad, sceptics at home, and growing doubters among traditional allies. After spending something like three trillion dollars, and failing to win the peace following two wars, the United States looks a diminished world power as the tenth anniversary of 9/11 approaches. Going abroad 'in search of monsters to destroy', as John Adams warned against in 1821, has tarnished America's reputation. He went on to say, in one of the great speeches on foreign policy, 'Her glory is not dominion, but liberty. Her march is the march of the mind.'

There have been several surprises, too, regarding the fortunes of al-Qaeda since 9/11. The prolonged failure of the United States to kill or capture Usama bin Laden was one of the biggest: how could the world's major terrorist escape for so long? Al-Qaeda also failed to carry out another spectacular exceeding 9/11 in lethality – something many expected and feared as images of the Twin Towers buckling and collapsing were replayed time and again in the days and weeks following the attack. Al-Qaeda also failed to enhance its legitimacy in the Muslim world, and indeed it went into marked decline in the second half of the decade, paralleling the decline in US hegemonial authority, but more so. This was manifest in its increasing dependence on local microterrorist activity, where it is hoped that small amounts of resource (in money and lives) will bring high returns in terror.

This has been a decade of intensive change in world order, and terror and counter-terror have been a significant part of the story. The decade opened with the attacks on 9/11 and closed with the killing of Usama Bin Laden and whatever revenge and other symbolic terrorist actions follow in its wake. The momentum and meaning of this distinctive decade will continue for many years to come. 'A decade without a name' is how the public intellectual Timothy Garton Ash described these years, but where was he? This was the age of al-Qaeda and a time of terror for the tens of thousands of victims of its violence, the hundreds of thousands more who were killed by counter-terrorism, and the countless millions across the world caught up in one way or another by the changes resulting from terror in our time. This was 9/11 + 10.

Moral choices and doing better

We do not promise readers an answer to questions such as 'Where will it all end?' – though we do offer some pointers. We also offer pointers to thinking about what should have been done, and what should be done. In so doing, we emphasise that social behaviour – what defines the limits and possibilities of human existence – cannot be understood if politics and ethics are separated.

We consider 9/11 + 10 with hindsight, but we hope not with the 20:20 hindsight which is easily ridiculed. The pathologies of world order that we point to – outlined below – were evident to some immediately after 9/11. Numerous critics of how leading Western states responded to international terrorism were convinced from the outset that there were alternative paths to those chosen by world leaders: lawyers emphasised the rule of law, citizens protested against the rush to war with Iraq, realists complained about the absence of cool, strategic logic in White House grand strategy, historians warned of imperial blowback, and journalists pointed to the propaganda own-goals Western states were scoring with every corroborated story or photograph of torture committed by coalition troops or military police. We believe, therefore, that it is possible to do better in the future, not only because we can learn from the mistakes of the recent past, but because we can also recover its good ideas. If we went back to the future we could do it all again with the political, social, and strategic intuitions that many had in their minds at the time.

While individual chapters below focus on specific facets of 9/11 + 10 ('Wars' and 'Democracy' for example) the notion of world order is a persistent theme. By world order we mean the interplay of dominant ideas, patterns of violence, disparities of local and global power, and institutional adaptation. The book explores certain pathologies of contemporary world order (such as hypocrisy and cultural insensitivity) while pointing to values (less militarised, more democratic), leading to a world order in which terrorism will be less likely to be a choice for groups and individuals. This would still not be a risk-free world, however, for the possibility of new forms of oppression might provoke new forms of violence.

The book is divided into two parts. This part ('Terror and danger') begins by showing terrorism to be a strategy deployed by different actors as a brutal form of communication. When a terrorist act takes place, the reaction of the targeted group can be more destructive than the original attack – an impact the terrorist group concerned is likely to consider a success. The 'inhumanity' often associated with terrorism, we believe, is inherently human, and as such is open to rational analysis; and it is the task of scholarship in these hardest of cases to try to reach the human person behind the mask labelled 'terrorist'. From here, subsequent chapters examine the dangers of terrorism and the meaning of concepts such as 'fundamentalism' and 'religious terrorism'; the growth and characteristics of al-Qaeda and its establishment of a base in Afghanistan from where it could engage the 'Far Enemy'; and finally we look at how the Far Enemy reacted, in particular through two major US-led invasions, of Afghanistan and Iraq.

Part II ('Security and world order') uses the world order framing of the book to make the general argument that countering terrorism is not ultimately the challenge of perfecting counter-terrorism measures, conceived narrowly, but reconfiguring the way human society is organised globally. In developing this argument we show that Islam is not the problem and democracy is not the answer, though both play a part, and that more sophisticated understandings of both are required. In this regard, the external policies of America have been, and will be, critical. Military responses to terrorism are sometimes necessary but they must be kept limited, operationally and politically; this is the opposite of the unlimited long war that US Department of Defense planners started to conduct after 9/11. Ends and means must be in accord, and so the rule of law is critical to international governance against terrorism; by weakening law we strengthen the opportunities for terrorism. Equally, it is no longer sensible to separate different levels of security policy; in a globalised world, attention must be paid to both geopolitics and human security, for they are more

interdependent than ever. The final chapter argues that terrorism can never be disinvented. It will always be a choice, because
terror is primordial. But a world order is conceivable, step by step,
in which the threat of al-Qaeda will be contained and dissolved,
thereby consigning to history the most lethal period yet of international terrorism.

Further reading

The best general books on international terrorism written in the post-
9/11 decade are: Audrey Kurth Cronin, *How Terrorism Ends: Understanding
the Decline and Demise of Terrorist Campaigns* (Princeton: Princeton University
Press, 2009); Adrian Guelke, *The New Age of Terrorism and the International
Political System* (London: I.B. Tauris, 2009); Walter Lacquer, *No End To War:
Terrorism in the Twenty-First Century* (New York: Continuum, 2003); and
Louise Richardson, *What Terrorists Want: Understanding the Enemy, Containing
the Threat* (New York: Random House, 2006).

2 Terror

Nobel Peace Prize winners can be terrorists too. We are not the first to note this, but it is worth repeating because it is a historical quirk that helps to reveal the human face of terrorism – a persistent theme in this book. Look for a start at that most human of political giants, Nelson Mandela. In 2000, the then former president of South Africa said on the TV programme *Larry King Live*:

> I was called a terrorist yesterday, but when I came out of jail, many people embraced me, including my enemies, and that is what I normally tell other people who say those who are struggling for liberation in their country are terrorists. I tell them that I was also a terrorist yesterday, but, today, I am admired by the very people who said I was one.[1]

The occupation of 'Lives and Minds'[2]

Terrorism begins in the minds of humans. It lives there because of a fact of human experience: the emotion of terror. Terror is primordial. Numerous studies show how the activity we call terrorism is historically conditioned, in the sense that its tactics, its normative connotations, and its aims alter over time; but terrorism, we will argue, is not merely a word that has symbolic meaning. It is an activity, a practice, whose instrumentality is rooted in a transhistorical human reality.

Terror is commonly understood as the most intense of fears, a feeling of alarm caused by an expectation of pain and disaster that is *terrifying* and *overpowering*. One way of conceiving terror, suggested by the incomparable novelist Don DeLillo, is to see it as the *occupation* of minds and lives, an idea that links the power of terror to the idea of the occupation of one's homeland by an alien power. Terror becomes an occupying force in the mind, bringing about panic, hysteria, and trauma – all of which can have decisive political consequences. Fear in a lower register than terror affects behaviour, and can produce unwelcome consequences. It can stoke suspicion, the desire for revenge, and ruthlessness; and can lead to the most primitive feelings towards those one blames for the fear. In terror, such feelings are greatly intensified; this is why we call terror *fear beyond fear*.

Through history, terror has had many sources: a sabre-tooth tiger appearing at the entrance of an early human's cave; the holy terror of the Inquisition; genocidal acts against an ethnic group; strategic bombing on residential areas, night after night in total war; the imminence of being tortured; systematic rape-gangs organised by foreign forces; the belief that somebody sitting opposite you on a subway may have a bomb in his or her backpack; the sound of a tsunami warning in a coastal town . . . and on and on. Experiencing terror is as human – though thankfully not as common – as sociality, the ability of humans to form complex social groups. Although fear beyond fear is an intimate part of the human story, it is only in recent years that a beginning has been made in the study of politics and international politics showing that the basic emotion of fear has a history, a culture, and a politics.[3] Even works on terrorism spend little time considering the emotion whose affect gives it meaning.

As an emotion, terror can be felt bodily and read on faces. Experience of terror, in individuals and groups, is mediated by culture, but it would be a rare and dysfunctional person (from any culture) unable to read the terror on another human face, regardless of the latter's culture. The face of terror in this book derives from the ways in which it can be manipulated instrumentally in order to further political plans. Fear itself, we must stress, is not a dysfunctional emotion. There is a rationality to fear that has been of inestimable evolutionary importance for the human animal. Without it, our ancestors would have made themselves prey to other dangerous animals, would have built settlements on unsafe ground, and would have been forever tempted to indulge in pleasurable short-term practices with potentially disastrous long-term consequences. Fear can provoke both rational and irrational behaviour, and the challenge is to understand its appropriate place in our political lives, as individuals, societies, states, and species. Rising to this challenge was the point of Franklin D. Roosevelt's remarks about fear in his inaugural address in Washington in March 1933: 'The only thing we have to fear is fear itself', the new president intoned. Not only was this the most famous political speech about fear, it has also been the most misunderstood. Roosevelt was saying that the only thing that it is 'mandatory' to fear is 'fear itself'; fear of anything else can be overcome.[4] This distinction, we will argue in the next chapter, is very pertinent to how we think about terrorism.

Terror is what does the work in terrorism, but it is impossible to write effectively about it, for the emotion of terror does not translate well onto the page. If Virginia Woolf was correct in observing that it is impossible to describe a headache, how are we to describe fear beyond fear, the occupation of minds by overpowering terror? Film is perhaps a more effective way of representing terror, with its ability to build up tension through sound and picture, and its power to shock us into wanting to hide behind our seats gripped by unbearable tension (even if our rational minds tell us we are safe). The written word – generally the most effective means of transmitting complex knowledge – happens to be weak in representing terror: what it feels like, and what it can do through raising fears about dying or dying horribly, or from living horribly or having those one cherishes living horribly. Fear beyond fear exercises its hold by exceeding all 'everyday fears' such as becoming ill or losing a dear friend.[5]

That said, the power of terror today has almost become part of the 'everyday fears' of people in many parts of the world. The dread of terror has become normalised; it is in people's faces as a result of daily newspaper headlines and TV/radio news bulletins. Living in this time of terror means that routine aspects of twenty-first-century life have become occupied by terror's routines: anxiety in taking the subway, doubts about boarding an aircraft, concerns about sitting in a café in certain cities, or a decision to watch the World Cup on TV in a crowded bar. These have all become potentially life-threatening if one is in the wrong place at the wrong time. Putting oneself in such situations is a choice, just as it is the choice of somebody else to kill you and others, indiscriminately and without remorse, as you go about your life.

Central to this book is the view that political choices are grounded in ethics, and that 'the grounding of a moral argument is ultimately in facts about human life', and what it is rational for humans to want. This approach to the choices we make is based on the idea that arguments about behaviour have to be rooted in things that are fundamental in human society. Philippa Foot, a philosopher identified with this view, writes that the evaluation of human action depends on 'essential features of specifically human life', such as being able 'to bind each other to action through institutions like promising'; and to teach and follow morality ('We can't get on without it'). A great deal 'hangs' on what she calls these 'facts of human existence' deriving from the evolutionary crucible of human biology and sociality.[6]

Geoffrey Warnock, a moral philosopher of similar views, put it like this:

> That it is a bad thing to be tortured and starved, humiliated or hurt is not an opinion: it is a fact. That it is better for people to be loved and attended to, rather than hated or neglected, is again a plain fact, not a matter of opinion.[7]

While the expression of what it is 'to be loved and attended to' will vary across cultures and time, the anthropological evidence supports this underlying understanding of human social reality.

Our view is that inflicting terror on the defenceless – whether driven by sheer political ambition or, paradoxically, by idealism – represents the very opposite of loving and attending to the human in another group of people. The infliction of terror, therefore, gets its meaning, its political shock (communication) value, from being the sort of conduct that is beyond the norms of human social behaviour; this is why almost nobody wants to be labelled a terrorist.

'People running for their lives'

Although terror is primordial, and has been manipulated for centuries for political purposes, there is a widespread view, which we will argue is unsustainable, that 'terrorism' cannot be satisfactorily defined. Let us begin this refutation by going back to the 'essential features of specifically human life', and the fact that when minds are under occupation by terror, the power of terror can be seen, heard, or otherwise sensed. On 9/11, at the southern end of Manhattan, it was palpable. Don DeLillo described it like this:

> Stories generating others and people running north out of the rumbling smoke and ash. Men running in suits and ties, women who'd lost their shoes, cops running from the skydive of all that towering steel. People running for their lives are part of the story that is left to us.

That day, DeLillo reports, there were 'stories of heroism and encounters with dread'. Such accounts of people running for their lives (or others petrified into fatal and fatalistic immobility, or tales of great heroism like that of so many of the NY Fire Department on 9/11) can be replicated from other places and other times when terror takes over. Terror is real, it is causal, and it does political work.

Words matter in relation to terror, terrorists, and terrorism, just as they do through the whole of politics: word problems can be world problems. Yet reaching a common view on what terrorism is and who perpetrates it has proven to be elusive. In particular, if state authorities who make international legal rules cannot agree on a definition, then the 'governance' of terrorism will be much harder to achieve.

Research on terrorism, conducted over two decades ago, found that there were then 109 separate definitions. A similarly large number of usages can be found in UN documentation. Surprisingly, the UN resolutions in September 2001 condemning the terror attacks on the United States, avoided an explicit statement about what kinds of action constituted 'terrorism'. Surely this is persuasive evidence of the impossibility of defining terrorism?

It is not: all this shows is an absence of a settled meaning, not its impossibility. The reasons for the lack of settled meaning are straightforward. First, the meaning of 'terrorism' has changed historically. In the 1940s and 1950s terrorism was commonly used to describe the violent struggles by nationalist or anti-colonial movements in Africa, Asia, and the Middle East. With the completion of decolonisation, the term became attached to the actions of dissatisfied national and ethnic groups within states such as the United Kingdom (by the Irish Republican Army), Spain (by ETA, the front for the Freedom of the Basque Homeland), and Canada (by the FLQ or Front de Libération du Québec).

A second impediment to an agreed definition has been the fact that the term has been applied to a diverse set of organisations pursuing different (often multiple) goals: Chechens seeking independence from Russia as well as religious goals; supporters of militant Islamic groups seeking revenge against the Infidel West and wanting to overthrow the leadership of 'apostates' who have compromised their strict interpretation of the Islamic faith; and others still seeking the narrower political goal of liberation, as in the case of Hamas in Gaza and the Liberation Tigers of Tamil Eelam in Sri Lanka. Such diverse groups and networks favour different tactics: some target infrastructure with the aim of raising the costs to the 'enemy' of continuing the struggle; others target civilians. Suicide terrorists ('martyrs') in a growing number of countries have wrapped themselves in plastic explosives and sacrificed their own lives in the hope of killing and maiming as many enemy civilians as possible.

A third reason for the relative lack of clarity stems from divergent political interests and expediency. This is the vexed issue of whether states can be terrorists too, a debate we address in the next chapter. For the moment we simply note that we will be using a broad definition of terrorism, which will include states.

Despite the difficulties in defining terrorism, describing terror, and labelling terrorists, we do not think the task is completely insurmountable. In any case, it is vital it is attempted, for as the philosopher John Locke argued in the seventeenth century, it is a duty that befalls scholars to labour to provide definitional and analytical clarity. Putting it briefly, if we cannot define terrorism, terror, and terrorists, how do we know what we are confronting, and how can we hope to achieve satisfactory levels of security from them? It is not difficult to illustrate that there are boundaries to the deployment of some of these terms. In 2001 Robert Mugabe referred to EU journalists as 'terrorists' because they had written about political violence in Zimbabwe; nobody other than those on his payroll gave this meaning any significance. The terms terrorism and terrorist are highly politicised, and this makes dispassionate analysis of the associated practices hard to achieve.

Despite the different formulations of the definition of terrorism, we believe there is a stable core to the activity we are discussing. The great French sociologist Raymond Aron came close to this when he argued that 'an action of violence is labelled "terrorist" when its psychological effects are out of proportion to its purely physical result'.[8] This puts in different words our earlier points about terror being like an occupation force of the mind, and of it being politically causal. Terror is inflicted to elicit a response: *it is a type of brutal communication*. As such, while we recognise that inflicting terror for political purposes has taken different forms in different contexts through history, the essential strategy it describes – terrorism – is intelligible in a time-transcending sense. Think of the Zealots 20 centuries ago, attempting through violence to strike fear into the Roman occupiers of Judea.

Some definitions of terrorism are inordinately long, others are rather short. We favour the following:

> Terrorism is a strategic doctrine involving the threat and use of violence against a target public, with a view to advancing the political aims of the attackers. The objective is to instil and spread *fear beyond fear* in the audience, in the hope that their lives and minds will be so occupied that changes in attitudes and behaviours on the part of relevant groups or authorities will result.[9]

Several elements of this definition need unpacking. First, we do not follow the tendency of many to define terrorism as a 'tactic'. Terrorism is not a tactic, if this term is used in its proper military sense, namely what is planned in face-to-face engagements with a target. Suicide bombings and hijacking are different types of tactics that terrorists employ in contact with their targets, but terrorism itself is the strategic doctrine guiding such acts. A strategic doctrine is a coherent body of ideas about the use of violent means to further political ends. Terrorism, like other strategic doctrines (blitzkrieg, for example), can employ different tactics and combinations of weapons.

Second, we use the general phrase 'target public' in order to avoid more loaded terms such as 'innocent civilians'. We are concerned with a social status (that of being a member of the public) not a moral category (that of being innocent). Moreover, we do not endorse the conventional assumption that terrorist acts are necessarily committed only against civilian targets.[10] This distinction cannot be maintained for the following reasons. First, it obscures a category of terrorist violence against political and economic institutions. When the IRA bombed the City of London in 1993 they gave a short period of warning so evacuations could take place; the aim was to damage the city of London rather than maximise civilian fatalities. Second, when terrorists target military bases where soldiers are off-duty, or naval vessels that are not engaging an enemy (such as the USS *Cole* attacked by al-Qaeda in 2000), to our minds this is consistent with the definition of terrorism set out above. Third, in conflict zones on many continents, a clear distinction between soldier and non-combatants is increasingly hard to sustain. Fourth, terror attacks frequently cause harm to a mixed group of victims (the 125 victims of the Pentagon attack on 9/11 included civilian accountants and budget analysts, as well as serving officers and defence planners). Finally in this grey zone, a distinction can be made on the basis of purpose. There might be attacks (which we would not label terrorism) against representatives of a government to bring about a coup, or against military forces to degrade their capability as a fighting force in a campaign. If the attacks were for neither of these purposes, but were symbolic or communicative, to undermine whatever level of public peace or trust existed in the minds of the population as a whole, then we make a judgement call and define them as 'terrorism'.

Although in definitional terms we are on the broadening side of the debate, this is not a book about state terror. While acknowledging this practice, our focus is on terrorism as practised by substate groups and networks. There has been little that is new about state terrorism during 9/11 + 10 – governments have wielded terror and committed egregious human wrongs against their citizens (or a defined group within them) for several centuries, and have continued to do so. Mass-casualty terrorism carried out by non-state groups, on the other hand, became a more prominent feature of world politics, and since 9/11 has accounted for higher 'terror deaths' than terror practices performed by governments. We believe the data support our choice of focus: terror deaths from non-state groups were five times greater than state-terror deaths in the eight-year period between 2001 and 2008 (see Table A.3 in the Appendix).

The other situation where state institutions come into consideration is with respect to the purpose of terrorist violence. The phrase 'groups or authorities' in our definition denotes the political target sought through the actual terrorising of a target public. Terror might be employed by a non-state group to change a government's policy, or it could be employed by a government to cause groups that oppose it to desist from particular actions. Frequently these dynamics co-exist in a terror cycle, an example being the second Intifada in which rock-throwing by Palestinian youths, and suicide bombing missions, were met by a massive military response by Israeli armed forces.

A further reason why there have been such extensive debates about the meaning of terrorism – who does it, why, where, and how? – is that terrorism is frequently considered to be 'an essentially contested concept' (to use the phrase coined by the philosopher W.B. Gallie). In other words, it is seen as a concept that is forever doomed to disagreement, like 'justice'. Our view is that terrorism is *contingently* (that is, non-essentially) contested.[11] Following the lead of the political theorist Terence Ball, we argue that just because a particular concept happens to be contested does not mean in itself that there must always be disagreement about it.

If we admit that terrorism is contingently contested, then there is the possibility of bridging the different meanings and usages. It is noteworthy, in this respect, that all usages seem to include the following: the threat or use of force (this distinguishes it from other instruments of political change such as demonstrations or passive resistance); the goal of having impact beyond those immediately affected by the violence (assassinations are terrorist acts only if they are intended to communicate a message to others as opposed to simply removing one leader so that a rival can take over); and a political aim (even if it is vague and even if some individuals might be motivated primarily by other drivers).[12]

Fashioning a 'morality of destruction'

Terrorism is all-too human in its inhumanity, and recognising this (in)human face is critical if it is to be successfully countered. While the choices individuals make with respect to joining terrorist groups are sometimes driven by psychotic impulses, religious extremism, nihilist anarchism, and other facets of extreme personality types, our basic contention is that for the most part those who become terrorists look remarkably like most of the rest

of us. This, paradoxically, is particularly the case with suicide terrorism, a type of behaviour that most readers will find particularly
horrific. Nonetheless, the substantial research done on suicide
terrorism suggests that those individuals who take, or who are
persuaded to take, such a course are far from being 'crazies', but
instead are overwhelmingly rational, idealistic, and even altruistic,
and are motivated less by hate than by sacrificing for a cause.[13]

Does this mean that we are all terrorists, or potential terrorists?
So far, we have been confident in using the terms terror and terrorism, but we are more cautious about the label 'terrorist'. This
might seem contradictory, but it is not difficult to explain.

The label 'terrorist' is almost wholly negative these days. Terrorists themselves do not like it, and so they invariably attempt
to bellicise the violence they commit, by calling themselves
freedom-fighters, soldiers of Allah, insurgents, 'sons of the
nation', and so on, and if captured they demand to be treated not
as criminals but as prisoners-of-war. The negative connotations of
the term are now so powerful that virtually all those who engage
in acts of terrorism try to euphemise the terror their actions bring
about, and certainly shy away from being labelled terrorists. It
was not always such a pariah activity, however. In the early days of
the Soviet Union, V.I. Lenin, after leading the Bolsheviks to power,
did not apologise for the use of terror. He said: 'We have to state
explicitly that terror is in principle and politically correct, and
that what underpins it and makes it legitimate is necessity.'[14] An
equally forthright leader, Winston Churchill, embraced terror as a
strategy both in the Second World War, in the bombing of German
cities in order to destroy the morale of the civilian population,
and in advocating an international order in the Cold War based
on a 'balance of [nuclear] terror'.[15] These days, few would say,
like Usama bin Laden, that terrorism and the killing of civilians
is 'a legitimate and morally demanded duty'.[16] Such a forthright
defence of killing civilians is rare, because of its connotation with
the pejorative terms 'terrorism' and 'terrorist'.

For the most part, the label 'terrorist' today serves a propaganda function; it is virtually unusable as a dispassionate analytical

concept. This is evident in the old (and misleading) line: 'One man's terrorist is another man's freedom-fighter.' From the earlier discussion, it should be clear that when one is employing a strategic doctrine conforming to the criteria of terrorism, one can be acting as both a freedom-fighter and a terrorist. There is no necessary contradiction: to put it simply, being a terrorist is a temporary role one adopts in a struggle, a struggle one might well conceive as that of a freedom-fighter. As a role, the term does not capture the whole of a person's selfhood, hence the possibility of former 'terrorists' becoming Nobel Peace Prize winners.[17]

The contemporary sensibility, as mentioned, usually shies away from self-labelling as a terrorist, though there is little hesitancy about so labelling one's opponents. As the term is one of propaganda rather than analysis, it should be used with care, and very sparingly. One reason for this is to defend against the temptation to believe that to label is to explain; when this happens, and a group is described as 'terrorist', it leads seamlessly to the imposition of the familiar repertoire of 'counter-terrorism' tactics and techniques. Another reason for advocating its sparing use is that the label hides the human behind the terrorist mask, and one must always hope (as the list of Nobel Peace Prize winners suggests) that there is a different human to engage with behind the terrorist mask from the one seemingly defined by the mask. 'Terrorist' is, therefore, a label that should be employed rarely, even in books about terrorism, because there is hardly a person conceivable whose settled and single identity is that of *terrorist*.

We caution, therefore, against any scatter-gun approach to using the term 'terrorist' but we certainly would not want to abolish it. Indeed, it would be futile to attempt to, for acts of terror would not go away by the abolition of a word. More fundamental changes have to take place in human society before we could contemplate terrorism becoming irrelevant. In the meantime, scholars must be sensitive to the 'politics of naming' while at the same time avoiding having the meaning sucked out of highly charged but necessary words. How can we hope to see the marginalising and delegitimising of terrorism and terrorists if we cannot agree about naming the strategic doctrine and category of people to be opposed?

So who can, and should, be labelled a terrorist? Logically, and for analytical purposes, the term can be applied to all those engaging in acts of terror for instrumental purposes. To become an agent of terrorism is a choice, for individuals and groups (including governments). It is to choose to play a role, and with the very rare exceptions of those who become terrorists purely for psychotic reasons, to be a terrorist is a sometime thing. This is the point Mandela was making in the quotation at the opening of this chapter.

One of the major themes in this book, therefore, is to try to look at the human face behind the terrorist mask, or, to put it more boldly still, to make the argument that the difference between them ('terrorists') and us (who think of ourselves as different) is not a chasm: it is a slippery slope. The only people who are in a position to assert that it is a chasm (for them) are those who are absolute pacifists (though even here it is possible to point to complicities in strategies of terror, if they pay taxes to governments that employ terror strategies or governments whose economies triumph in a global economy in which millions are terrified about the prospects of survival of themselves and their children). Most of us stand on a slope that is slippery, not at the edge of a chasm.

In the study of strategy the point is often made that history shows that people (especially military planners) have often found it easier and more congenial to think about what they might do to the enemy, while ignoring somewhat what the enemy might do to them. The reverse seems to be the case with terrorism. Paul Lacey, a Quaker, has written about the tendency of people in the years after 9/11 to fantasise about being victims of terror – experiencing 'a flash of that extreme vulnerability'.[18] He adds that fantacising ourselves as victims is 'a safe, morally comfortable position, for there we get to be the unambiguous, innocent heroes of a sympathetic story'. He goes on to describe a tougher imaginative leap: 'It is far harder to conceive of ourselves in the role of victimizers, those whose actions are predicated on breaking down an enemy in the humiliation and dehumanising fear that is the essential experience of terror.'

If one accepts the images of terrorist masks and slippery slopes, then one begins to confront complex political, strategic, and ethical questions. For this reason we believe that when we try to think analytically about terrorism the best metaphor is not the familiar image of scientists looking at something through a microscope, but rather that we are looking at this aspect of the world in a 'cracked looking-glass', in which we see glimpses of ourselves reflected, as well as the subject-matter.[19]

In suggesting that *we see glimpses of ourselves* we are not saying that 'we are all terrorists'. Instead, we are saying that we could imagine ourselves, in the future as in the past, giving support to campaigns of terrorism, or defending the acts of terrorists, and conniving in strategies of terror. The authors of this book, as British citizens, would have had little compunction in welcoming the thousand bomber terror raids over Nazi Germany, to unload bombs on civilians, as a 'no choice' strategy to strike back at Hitler's regime, then terrorising most of Europe. Likewise, imagining ourselves in a land occupied by alien oppressors – engaging in institutionalised racism or acts of ethnic genocide – we would have had sympathy towards those on our side who decided they had 'no choice', that enough was enough, and that violent actions would speak louder than words. As it is, as UK taxpayers for many years we have connived in (while democratically objecting to) a defence policy based on the procurement, deployment, and targeting of nuclear weapons – weapons we regard as the most frightening and indiscriminate of all terror devices in the spectrum of possibilities of political violence.

Terror, Mark Twain brilliantly observed in his remarks on the French Revolution, came in two forms: 'swift death' (the Reign of Terror associated with 'murder in hot passion') and 'lifelong death' (the suffering resulting from poverty and cruelty).[20] Recalling this distinction, we must remember that as inhabitants of the rich world, our daily lives are complicit in a global economic system that consigns countless millions to an existence which so many of us, to use Twain's words, have never learnt to see in 'its vastness or pity as it deserves'. Perhaps there is a difference between killing and letting die: but perhaps not. In any case, there are degrees of complicity. It is another step, of course, and a big one, from accepting any degree of complicity, and imagining justifying the unjustifiable (acts of terror against defenceless people), but it is strategically foolish and analytically dishonest to refuse to see glimpses of ourselves, as well as those labelled terrorists, in the cracked looking-glass of world politics.

The difference between us and them –those who reject terrorism and those who directly carry it out, those who seek to delegitimise the acts of terrorists and those who incite them, and those who abjure terror and those who glorify it – is not as great as is implied or asserted by orthodox terrorism experts, the discourse of governments, or the popular press. It is important as observers to remember the old adage that where one stands on an issue importantly depends upon where one sits. Don DeLillo's description of 9/11 is again relevant:

> For all those who may want what we've got, there are all those who do not. These are the men who have fashioned a morality of destruction. They want what they used to have before the waves of western influence. They surely see themselves as the elect of God whether or not they follow the central precepts of Islam. It is the presumptive right of those who choose violence and death to speak directly to God. They will kill and then die. Or they will die first, in the cockpit, in clean shoes, according to instructions in the letter.

Those who want what others do not, through recorded history, have been willing in some circumstances to use violence to further their aims. The modalities of that violence, and the targets, have differed according to power differentials and other circumstantial factors. But fashioning a 'morality of destruction' is as old as politics: terrorism is merely one brutal dimension of the way humans have learned to live and to communicate and to die.

Further reading

On the politics and international politics of fear, see Corey Robin, *Fear: The History of a Political Idea* (Oxford: Oxford University Press, 2004); Ken Booth and Nicholas Wheeler, *The Security Dilemma: Fear, Cooperation and Trust in World Politics* (Houndmills: Palgrave Macmillan, 2008); and Frank Furedi, *Invitation to Terror: The Expanding Empire of the Unknown* (London: Continuum Books, 2008). On the ethical perspective outlined in this chapter see Philippa Foot, *Natural Goodness* (Oxford: Oxford University Press, 2001); and for the best book on terrorism by a political theorist, Robert Goodin, *What's Wrong with Terrorism* (Cambridge: Polity Press, 2006).

3   Dangers

We are often told that there is a greater risk of being killed in a traffic-accident driving to an airport than being blown up by a terrorist action once in the air: but should this accurate risk-assessment mean that we can travel without worry, or stop taking terrorism as other than a high priority threat? We think not. The death toll of 9/11 continues to rise. On that day it was 2,981,[1] but it has subsequently risen to hundreds of thousands and counting. Many were killed that day; many many more have later been killed in its name, and will continue to be.

'Everything changed!'

When one's homeland, especially if it is that of the world's only superpower, is attacked in a novel and terrifying fashion, it is not surprising if those called upon to speak for the dead and fearful are tempted into hyperbole. 'Everything changed', President Bush said, and other leading figures in the administration echoed his conviction that a historic turning-point had been reached; they also endorsed his determination to respond decisively to the atrocity. In his address to the joint session of Congress on 20 September 2001, President Bush declared that the response would not stop with the perpetrators of 9/11: 'Our war on terror begins with al-Qaeda, but it does not end there. It will not end until every terrorist group of global reach has been found, stopped and defeated.'[2] If the government of a superpower believes everything has changed, then its risk-world is redefined, altering its estimates of probabilities of danger, and also impelling it into actions that reorder the dangers not only for itself, but also everyone around.

But did *everything* change after 9/11? Some, at once, were sure that such language was an exaggeration. Kenneth N. Waltz, the leading academic theorist of International Relations over the past 50 years, argued that terrorism can be 'terribly bothersome' but that it does not change the basic facts and basic continuity of international politics. He has not changed his mind over the decade, commenting in 2010 that 'terrorists are not able to mount sustained attacks, to rend the fabric of societies, and to occupy state territories. They can frighten and annoy states without the slightest ability to undermine them'.[3] This latter verdict might appear complacent in relation to weak or 'failed' states, such as Palestine or Somalia, or even the prize of nuclear-armed Pakistan, but his general point about the basic continuity of international politics is surely valid. 9/11 did not reverse the dynamics shaping the contemporary international system: the rise of China, the growth of India and Brazil, the imbalances of military and other sources of power and so on. In these terms, 9/11 was no more than a ripple on the surface.

If the big picture remains unaffected, at the level of state units and their interactions a great deal was changed by 9/11; how permanently is another matter. The headline changes arose from the intense insecurity felt by the American people after being attacked so outrageously. In a public-opinion poll immediately afterwards, 74 per cent of Americans agreed that the events of 9/11 would 'fundamentally change things forever'.[4] There was a shrivelled sense of security. By 2011, however, though the fear of terrorism remains high in the United States,[5] the pre-occupations of most Americans have shifted to the economy and other familiar 'pocket-book' issues.

In Europe the shrivelled sense of security immediately following 9/11 fed already-existing anxieties about the porosity of borders, the rapid expansion of Muslim populations, and the implications of multiculturalism. Was 'the enemy' being harboured within? The terrorist attacks on Madrid and London, and the uncovering of multiple plots, showed that this was indeed the case to a degree; this sense of danger persists, and is kept in people's minds, especially in Britain, by governmental warnings that the threat is still very much alive. Meanwhile, insecurity grew throughout Muslim countries as a result of the reactions of Western states to 9/11 and the spread of al-Qaeda's influence. The US declaration of the War on Terror, and its global dimensions, confirmed in the minds of many Muslims their traditional long-held fears about Western hostility to Islam. Immediate human sympathy towards the US people for what happened on 9/11 was soon blown away by the shock and awe of US military force, and perceptions of US political arrogance. For a time outsiders felt America's pain, but America seemed unable to feel anybody else's, whatever the administration's rhetoric. Western military actions – notably in Afghanistan and Iraq, but to a degree also in Libya in 2011 – confirmed for Muslims their view of who had the most military might, and who ruled the world: this was global business as usual rather than 'everything changed'.

9/11 did mark a change in the foreign and defence policies of several states, but for how long remains to be seen. Here US policy was decisive. When the world's most powerful state argues that everything has changed, and readjusts its policies, the effects are global; others, to a greater or lesser extent, have to readjust. For many governments, this involved accommodating to the global counter-terrorist narrative developed and imposed by Washington. Such a turn was not unwelcome to all, by any means, for it helped them legitimise what they were attempting against certain opponents at home. Some states were able to be closer to the United States in the same fight against 'international terrorism'. Russia was one such beneficiary. States with less than impressive human rights credentials were able to offer military bases needed by the United States, or secret facilities (for 'extraordinary rendition'), or diplomatic support; and in return they hoped that the US government would back those who supported it.

A counterfactual can make our point more effectively than a real but familiar illustration of the bad company Washington has kept in the global War on Terror. Imagine if Slobodan Milosevic had held back for a short time in 1999 from escalating his brutal imposition of Serbian authority on its sovereign territory of Kosovo. Had he done so, Milosevic would have been able to incorporate his campaign against the KLA (Kosovo Liberation Army) into the US War on Terror; the KLA, after all, was an internationally defined terrorist organisation. This solidarity would have been strengthened by the shared opposition of both Milosevic and Bush to the International Criminal Court. In such a scenario, there would have been no NATO war against Serbia, no interventionist hubris (low-casualty wars, easy victories) on the part of Blair and Bush, no new (and only partially recognised) sovereign state carved out in the Balkans, and perhaps no Iraq war. Timing is all: 9/11 came too late for Milosevic, too early for Bush.

In public perceptions, especially in the West, terrorism obviously had heightened visibility through the media after 9/11. Terror sells. 9/11 also stimulated a new academic research industry. There were three times more articles on terrorism in the main academic journals in 2002 than the previous year, and the number has continued rising. A new book on the subject was published approximately every six hours.[6] The momentum continues. That said, the spotlight of academic attention, like that of the media, moves on when the story does, though more sedately.

Our argument is that a spectacular act of terrorism is bad enough without exaggerating its historical significance, and thus inflating the dangers one is facing and raising the stakes one is prepared to risk. But *everything* did not change after 9/11: some things changed radically, but not necessarily permanently, while other things changed hardly at all. Our guess is that the internal changes in states – especially the rise of surveillance and new legal restrictions (to be discussed in Part II) – will be the longest lasting effects of 9/11, rather than transformational changes in international politics. The declaration that 'Everything changed!' must be challenged, even if we grant it was an understandable piece of rhetoric in the aftermath of an outrage. Words matter, especially if they are spoken by a president of the United States and relate to a major security challenge. For governments, 'security' is sometimes conceived as a 'speech act', meaning that to call something 'security' has a performative significance that goes beyond mere words; it is designed to produce an effect on listeners, to do with threats and how to deal with them.[7] In other words, to speak security is to act politically, and this is never so globally consequential as when a US president continues to insist that everything has changed.

Bathtubs versus bombs

Risk analysis and management is central to the business of government. There is no escape from risk – what the former US secretary of defense Donald Rumsfeld famously called the 'known unknowns'.[8] In this book the particular risk conundrum being addressed is that of terrorist actions which are relatively low in probability, but whose consequences can be catastrophic.

There are many reasons why risk analysis and management is difficult when the subject is terrorism. For one thing, one of the main aims of terrorists is to surprise their enemies. Here we offer three guidelines for clear thinking about the 'risks of terrorism':

First: do not confuse the low probability of any individual being involved in a terrorist attack with the danger represented by terrorism to a society as a whole.

Readers of works on terrorism will be familiar with lists produced by researchers intended to calm our fears about involvement in a terrorist incident. They show, for example, that the risk of being killed by terrorists in the United States or the UK is vanishingly small compared with life's everyday dangers. Statistics show, for example, that the *global* annual figure for deaths caused by international terrorism outside of warzones from 1968 to the present is approximately 300–700, while the approximate annual fatalities from 'bath drowning' in the *United States alone* is approximately 320. The estimated probability of death from international terrorism in the United States is 1:80,000, whereas the estimated probability of death from 'falling down' is 1 : 236.[9] How reassured should we feel about this?

Our view is that such actuarial calculations do not get us very far. Low probabilities of individual involvements should not be allowed to lull us, as a society, into sleepwalking about terrorism (though the figures are undoubtedly a warning about taking more care in the bath). Such calculations focus on the low probability of *individual* risk rather than the potentially catastrophic political threat to *society*. When contemplating the latter it is necessary not only to think about the risk of attack, but to the consequential political dangers resulting from the nature of the reaction of one's own and other governments. There is much more to the risks than comparing death-rates from bathtubs and bombs.

One has heard it said that 'only 3,000 died' on 9/11, while nearly 4 million die annually across the world from influenza. Here again, the comparison is of no political meaning in the sense the comparison is made. When a state is attacked by a terrorist organisation, it has to stand up for itself in some way: statistics on relative mortality rates are of very limited significance unless at the same time one factors in the probable dangers (including losses) that will ensue as a result of the retaliation that a terrorist attack will provoke. Such calculations are beyond sensible statistical calculation. This is easily illustrated. To say that 'only 3,000' were killed on 9/11 is as unhelpful from the perspective of international politics as saying that only two people were assassinated in Sarajevo on 28 June 1914. What matters politically is the meaning of deaths, not their precise numbers. In 1914 the terrorist assassination of Archduke Ferdinand and his wife radically altered the political atmosphere and group dynamics in the major European capitals.[10] What followed was the Schlieffen Plan, the Western Front, a world war, the collapse of empires, a cultural earthquake, the US rise to world powerdom, the October Revolution, the Treaty of Versailles, Hitler, another world war in a generation, and on and on. In international politics, numbers don't always add up.

Similarly with 9/11. The fact is that the death toll continues to grow. It has been magnified into hundreds of thousands, in

Afghanistan, in Iraq, in Bali, in Madrid, in London and other cities, and in all the dirty wars on terror around the world. Put like this, sleepwalking becomes even more dangerous if the perils of the relevant risk-world are increased by the exaggerated reactions of the most powerful. It is sometimes said that terrorism has never been a major cause of human deaths; this conclusion cannot be drawn if we resist the habit of de-linking terrorist acts from consequential state-retaliation.

Second: being killed by terrorism has a different meaning from death by natural causes or accident.

There are not only problems in comparing the numbers of terrorist-caused and natural/accidental death-rates; the question also arises as to whether it is appropriate to compare the two kinds of death.[11] There are good reasons for thinking that terror deaths induce a different type of fear than everyday deaths (nobody – hardly – fears death-by-car, even knowing that the risks are significant). Terror deaths are simultaneous rather than sequential (and so have more shock impact). Terror deaths are visually shocking (and are communicated by the media to the world, whereas we are not shown the sequential deaths in bathtubs). And terror deaths are more psychologically damaging than everyday deaths because of the realisation that somebody (even a fellow-citizen) has actually willed the harm done: and this undermines one's existential sense of safety and trust. Jeffrie Murphy has called such 'intentional wrongdoing' a 'moral injury'. These important points overlap with the first guideline in the sense that everyday deaths produce grief and sadness that is friends-and-family sized, whereas terror deaths provoke widespread grief and intensified fear; terror deaths are society-sized.

The undermining of trust, just mentioned, is not only felt among the public: it can have very serious consequences at the diplomatic level. Acts of terror, fear of more, and 'national narratives' about terrorism have caused repeated and serious 'missed opportunities' for the positive development of US–Iranian relations since 1989. John Tirman of MIT has persuasively shown this, out of numerous examples, in three big cases: hostages in Lebanon, the bombing of the Khobar Towers, and the overture occasioned by cooperation in Afghanistan after 9/11.[12] The Middle East today would look very different if Washington and Tehran had developed and cemented constructive relations. This is not to say that such an outcome would necessarily have come about in the absence of being blown off course by terrorist acts, but there would have been a chance. Over the years, similar negative diplomatic dynamics have been in play in relations between Israel and the Arab world, and in Northern Ireland.

Third: however low one assesses a risk, if the consequences are catastrophic, then the precautionary principle is vital.

The worst-case scenario is, by definition, of very low probability, but low probabilities/terrible consequences are far from uncommon: in public policy (the 2008 banking collapse); in natural disasters (the 2011 tsunami in Japan); and in family life (the 2007 abduction from a holiday apartment in Portugal of little Madeleine McCann while her parents were nearby). With regard to worst-case thinking in relation to terrorism, the risk of 'nuclear terrorism' has attracted considerable and continuous attention since 9/11.

Officials in the West have not been slow to tell publics of the dangers. Ever since 9/11 the former UK prime minister Tony Blair expressed his conviction that terrorists would have no qualms about using any sort of violence or inflicting any number of casualties. In 2004 the chief of the International Atomic Energy Agency, Mohammed al Baredei, warned that the threat of a terrorist attack using nuclear weapons was 'real and imminent': it was 'a race against time', he said. His words repeated Blair's warnings about an alliance between al-Qaeda and 'rogue states'.[13] In 2006 the Director of MI5 in the UK, Dame Eliza Manningham-Buller, revealing that '30 UK terror plots' were being tracked and 1,600 people were under surveillance, warned that the terror threat was 'serious' and 'growing' and could be chemical or nuclear.[14] Such warnings gave weight to the predictions of some politicians and academics before 9/11 that 'it was only a matter of time' before terrorists employed what were always unhelpfully categorised as 'WMD' – chemical, biological, and nuclear weapons – as if the lethality of each was similar. In addition, the risk of a 'dirty bomb' was often mentioned – a weapon whose terror-inducing name is greater than its destructive potential. The sarin gas attack on the Tokyo subway in 1995 by the Japanese religious cult, Aum Shinri-kyo, strengthened these fears.

Since 9/11, on the whole, academic specialists on 'nuclear terrorism' have sought to calm such fears, with John Mueller, in particular, emphasising the considerable obstacles a terrorist group would have in constructing or obtaining a nuclear weapon in the first place, and then in successfully deploying and exploding it.[15] Whether or not he is correct, and some disagree, there is more to it, politically, than risk assessment. As Brian Michael Jenkins, a long-standing RAND specialist has argued, al-Qaeda may be the world's first terrorist nuclear power without having the actual capability.[16]

While those who seek to calm nerves about the risk of nuclear terrorism reject what they consider the alarmist language of politicians, on the whole they do not question what is actually done in relation to lessening the threat of it. Mueller, for example, states that his case is not 'to argue that policies designed to inconvenience the atomic terrorist are necessarily unneeded or unwise'. After arguing that the atomic terrorists' task is already 'monumental', he nonetheless adds that efforts 'to further enhance this monumentality, if cost-effective and accompanied with tolerable side effects, are generally desirable'. When it comes to security measures, he concedes that: 'Some policy projects do seem to be worth the effort.'[17] In other words, it is good not to be panicked about low-probability events, as long as the precautionary principle is employed in relation to the danger of the catastrophic consequences. However sure we are that there will not be a terrorist on the aircraft we are boarding, few if any of us would ask the airport authority to abandon all security checks.

So, estimates of probabilities have to be considered in relation to the counter-measures taken and, in particular, their quality. Here it is important to remember the danger of self-fulfilling prophecies. The Star Wars debate in the 1980s (the idea of creating a 'missile shield' over America against the threat of incoming Soviet nuclear missiles in the highly improbable event of a first-strike attack) threw up the analogy of somebody so obsessed by having their house destroyed by asteroids that they put thicker and thicker layers of concrete on the roof – only for the roof eventually to fall in on itself by the weight of its own 'defences'. This is a useful warning about the dangers of over-reacting against terrorism – and bringing about the outcome one wanted to avoid. The British terrorism specialist Andrew Silke has warned against this. In a study of retaliation against terrorists, he referred to the view of the deputy speaker of the Knesset, Naomi Chazon. In criticising the Israeli policy of retaliation and pre-emptive assassination, she said it is 'an ineffective policy. It breeds more hatred and more terrorism instead of eliminating or even reducing it'. According to Silke, 'Too few, it seems, are willing to heed such a message'.[18]

States of terror

When we consider potential agents of terror, states of course have greater violent potential than sub-state groups. Historically, they have been the biggest political killers ever invented: one estimate for the whole of the twentieth century is of 170–200 million deaths by governments against their own citizens.[19] It is worth remembering here that violence was the midwife in the birth of the state (Nietzsche's 'coldest of all cold monsters'); and in the case of the United States, in Susan Sontag's controversial formulation, that midwife was called 'genocide'. So, surely states can be terrorists too?

Many terrorism specialists think not, and reject the very notion of 'state terrorism'. Three main arguments are employed – arguments that are buttressed by a view, made concrete in the US State Department's definition of 'terrorism', which limits the capacity to employ terror to 'subnational' groups only.[20] First, they argue there already are international laws against illegitimate state behaviour (such as 'war crimes') and so adding charges relating to terrorism would be redundant. Second, they argue that 'analytical clarity' demands that states be excluded from the category of agents of terrorism or otherwise the term would be weakened, and with it the ability to frame counter-strategies. Finally, they argue that states 'by definition' cannot engage in terrorism. This is rooted in the Weberian idea that the state has a monopoly on the *legitimate* means of violence: by implication, violence committed by non-state actors is illegitimate and falls outside the framework of the laws of armed conflict. If terrorism is illegitimate force, so this argument goes, state terrorism must be a contradiction in terms. States, of course, can inflict terror, but a prominent defender of this view, Colin Wight, asserts that this must not be conflated with terrorism: 'to terrorise is not to engage in terrorism', he writes, 'or else the meaning of the term loses any political specificity'.[21]

Robert E. Goodin calls such arguments a 'definitional ploy', precluding 'the possibility of "state terrorism" purely by definition'.[22] When it comes to politicians making this argument, he says, there is something 'morally suspicious . . . about people making laws that apply to everyone except themselves. The sheer fact that politicians have entered into a mutual-protection pact not to prosecute one another as "terrorists" cannot change any logical or deontological facts of the matter.' Terrorism is terrorism, in the view of this distinguished social and political theorist, regardless of the agent; and 'If that wrong is not technically termed "terrorism", under conventions that politicians succeed in establishing as international law, that fact is simply of no *moral* consequence.' We agree. In logic one must ask why *to terrorise is not to engage in terrorism* if the act of terror has a political end, the target is the public, and the aim is to communicate a brutal message?

States obviously have employed, and do employ, terror when it is thought to be necessary. The three primary modalities are: state sponsorship of terrorism as part of one's foreign policy; the use of direct terror against internal opponents (mass killings, torture of prisoners, disappearances, mass arrests, and ultimately geno-cide – terrorism's absolute); and as part of military campaigns in war (notably strategic bombing against civilians). Looking back at the twentieth century, as noted earlier, the greatest acts of terror against civilian populations were committed by agents acting on behalf of governments. These included the terror inflicted by the internal security services of totalitarian states (Nazi Germany, the Soviet Union, Maoist China) to deter internal dissent. More directly, governments have commissioned death squads to kill and spread terror (as in many Latin American states). And governments can also be complicit in using terror to eliminate or disperse a target ethnic group, as with the use of chemical weapons by Saddam Hussein's regime against the Kurds in 1998.

Western states have been no strangers to wielding the weapons of terror. In Latin America, for example, Washington engaged in covert terror operations, utilising local proxies, in the 1980s. Since 9/11 it has been the state sponsorship of terrorism by 'rogue states' (a pejorative term for states regarded by the leading Western powers as unpredictable and lawless) or by the 'axis of evil' (Bush's label for Iran, Iraq, and North Korea), which has attracted most attention. Such state sponsorship of terrorism is generally conceded even by those who otherwise reject the idea of 'state terrorism'. Louise Richardson, for example, writes:

> So in some ways they [weaker state sponsors of terrorism] have a better case than the US did for using terrorism as an instrument of their foreign policy. I make this point not to indict American foreign policy but only to underscore that not only the bad guys use terrorism as an instrument of their foreign policy. Sometimes the good guys do too.[23]

When states employ terror in these ways, even the good guys, it throws into question the old adage that terror is a 'weapon of the weak'. Normally, this phrase is used to separate states (possessing air forces and armies) and non-states (possessing only explosives and willing bodies). But it is worth thinking about the phrase 'terrorism is the weapon of the weak' from another angle. To employ terror as a political weapon, even for an ostensibly powerful state, is always in some sense an admission of political weakness; it shows that the perpetrator lacks authority, lacks 'soft power', lacks convincing arguments. The use of terror is an expression of weakness, even by the 'strong'.

The argument that states cannot be terrorists, therefore, fails on every count, though we accept that in actual situations there will be grey areas. To conclude otherwise would be to let states off the hook. State authorities often exceed what is morally and legally acceptable in terms of using violence and the threat of violence to crush opposition groups. Table A.2 in our Appendix lists the examples where governments have been engaged in 'one-sided violence' which we equate with state terrorism. Russia appears because of its brutal response to Chechen separatism, Burma appears because of its crushing of Aung San Suu Kyi's pro-democracy movement, Nepal appears because of its crackdown on Maoist insurgents.

Accepting that states can 'do' terror is not the same as 'attaching the label terrorism to all forms of state practice we find objectionable'.[24] In our view, there are clear limits on what kinds of activity can be included in the 'state terrorism' category. Inter-state war, however terrifying and possibly unjust, is not sensibly categorised as state terrorism as it is better understood as 'war' in accordance with the laws of armed conflict (though certain strategic doctrines within war can be categorised as equivalent to terrorism).

'The thing I fear most is fear'

Bernard Brodie, perhaps the wisest of US academic strategic thinkers in the Cold War, now sadly forgotten, used to like to warn that 'men get mad in war'. It was a reminder that policy-makers and publics are not rational computers, but are animals with emotions. Men, and women, also get mad when targeted by terrorists.

As we have emphasised throughout this chapter, when calculating the risks and dangers of terrorism, we must always pay at least as much attention to possible responses of the targets as the possible nature of the attack. Terror is not guaranteed to produce a rational, considered response from its target. Emotion has its say, and, in the words of the American writer Mary McCarthy, 'in violence we forget who we are'.[25] At the start of her book How Terrorism Ends, Audrey Kurth Cronin quotes Alexis de Tocqueville's claim in 1840 that 'a democratic people will always find [it] very difficult, to begin a war'.[26] If it was true then, it was not in 2001 and 2002–03 when the White House led the charge to invade Afghanistan and Iraq. People in democracies can be quickly riled to violent fury when terrorised; likewise, they can excuse terrible behaviour if they feel badly wronged.

Emotions and feelings are key variables when studying terrorism, but their very uncertainty means that we must beware of fuzzy thinking about them. A few years ago, Dominique Moïsi, founder of the French Institute of International Affairs, wrote a book intriguingly entitled The Geopolitics of Emotion following a successful article in the journal Foreign Affairs and appearances in the US media. Unfortunately the book did not live up to the expectations generated by the title: it contained breathtaking generalisations, lacked rigour about concepts, and failed to engage the complexities of historical causation. The book structured the world into three: the West, Muslims and Arabs, and Asia. Europe and the United States are said to be dominated by 'a culture of fear'; they fear 'the other' and the loss of national identity and purpose. Muslims and Arabs are dominated by a culture of humiliation (which has produced a culture of hatred), resulting from historical grievances, civil and religious warfare, and their exclusion from the economic benefits of globalisation. And while the West and the Muslim world confront each other, much of Asia embraces a culture of hope, made up of the confidence and empowerment coming from 'the material progress they can see, feel, hear, taste, and experience in the rapidly changing world around them'.[27]

Is Moïsi correct? Can emotions be distinguished so easily? Is a suicide terrorist seeking to make a political gesture out of a family tragedy driven by humiliation or hope? How valid is it to homogenise the emotions of whole continents? Do we even know how to think sensibly about 'emotions' in a political context? Take the emotion of fear, for example, which Moïsi claims grips 'the West'. Is our 'perception of our vulnerability and of our relative loss of centrality . . . at the very centre of our identity crisis'?[28] Are we (all?) in the West gripped by fear? Do we have an identity crisis? Do we know how to think about fear in the first place?

Fear, as we pointed out in the previous chapter, is not a dysfunctional emotion. Fear is not the problem: how one handles it might be. We referred in the previous chapter to Roosevelt's famous line, 'The only thing we have to fear is fear itself'. His speech, a morale booster in the Depression, has been understood as meaning that if his audience (the people of the US) could cease to be afraid of fear itself, they should not be afraid of anything, and so could achieve whatever they set out to do. There is reason to think that this was not Roosevelt's intention. According to Stuart Walton, Roosevelt was saying that people should not fear anything – because the problems they faced could be met – but that fear itself should be respected.[29] For Roosevelt, fear itself was the only thing that it was mandatory to fear.

Roosevelt's words should echo down to the present, to every society that might be a target of terrorism; he spoke directly to the predicaments, dilemmas, and challenges of our time. Roosevelt understood that fear can make people act irrationally; and he knew it could be immobilising (he himself had internalised his ideas about fear from Henry David Thoreau, who in turn had internalised them from Michel de Montaigne, who wrote in the sixteenth century that 'the thing I fear most is fear').[30] The fear of fear, Roosevelt believed, had to be resisted. He believed that the predicaments, dilemmas, and challenges faced by the American people as a result of the Great Depression could be overcome, but not if they were gripped by 'fear itself – nameless, unreasoning, unjustified terror which paralyzes'. In fear and violence we can forget not only who we are, but how we should behave. We should not fear terrorism, we can hear Roosevelt saying, despite its great dangers, because it can be overcome; the only thing it is mandatory to fear is 'fear itself' because fear can paralyze, cause unreason, and make us mad.

Further reading

Chapter 4 'States Can Be Terrorists, Too' in Robert Goodin, *What's Wrong with Terrorism* (Cambridge: Polity Press, 2006) is probably the best discussion of this debate. Richard Jackson *et al.*, *Terrorism: A Critical Introduction* (Houndmills: Palgrave Macmillan, 2011) gives a critical terrorist studies perspective on states as terrorists. Alexander George (ed.), *Western State Terrorism* (Cambridge: Polity Press, 1991) is the leading early book on the subject. For a discussion of the risks of nuclear terrorism see John Mueller, *Atomic Obsession: Nuclear Alarmism from Hiroshima to Al Qaeda* (Oxford: Oxford University Press, 2010) and Brian Jenkins, *Will Terrorists Go Nuclear?* (New York: Prometheus Books, 2008). A readable source for understanding risk in general is Dan Gardner, *Risk: The Science and Politics of Fear* (London: Virgin, 2008).

4 Base

Behind the *fear beyond fear* discussed in previous chapters is al-Qaeda, the most bloodthirsty, resourceful, and global (non-state) terrorist force ever. In August 1996 its leader Usama bin Laden declared war against the United States and its allies: 'Terrorising you', he wrote, 'is a legitimate and morally demanding duty'. To be able to terrorise the 'Far Enemy', as the West became known, bin Laden needed a 'secure base' to educate and train jihadist warriors. This Base – al-Qaeda – was established first in Pakistan, then in Afghanistan. The term 'al-Qaeda' is the Arabic word, usefully inclusive, referring to a base (in the sense of a secure place), or a rule, principle, or method (in the sense of the fundamentals of a way of thinking). This term was employed by Islamic fighters who joined the Afghan resistance against the Soviets in the mid-1980s, but soon was appropriated by the most ambitious jihadists. Al-Qaeda was the 'vanguard' base in Afghanistan after 1988 for the training and coordination of jihadists in their continuing struggles once victory had been achieved over the Soviets.[1] It quickly became the name, above all, that is now synonymous with terror in our time.

The globalisation of terror

Numerous groups are committed to the 'global jihad' – the term the terrorists use themselves. Traditionally these groups were state-based in their organisation and operations, and were located primarily in Islamic and particularly Arab countries. They include: the Armed Islamic Group (Algeria), the Egyptian Islamic Jihad, the Moroccan Islamic Fighting Group, Hamas (Palestine and Lebanon), the Libyan Islamic Fighting Group, al-Qaeda in the Islamic Maghreb (Algeria based), al-Qaeda in the Arabian Peninsula (Yemen based); Harakat-ul-Jihad-Islami and Laskhar-e-Taiba operating in Kashmir; the Abu Sayyaf group (Philippines) in south-east Asia, and various Central Asian groups operating out of Tajikistan and the Taliban-controlled areas of Afghanistan. Such groups broadly share doctrinal beliefs about Islam (jihadists are exclusively Sunni) and about the historic struggle against 'unbelievers' – infidels and apostates. They have also followed a similar development pathway. Initially, their followers made enemies of their home countries; some then went to the Base in Afghanistan where they received military training and operational guidance; they then returned home to wreak havoc on the Near Enemy – those Islamic regimes and Muslim-majority countries that did not live in accordance with God's law (shari'a). At the same time they demonised those ideas seen as 'Western', particularly democracy, secularism, and modernity.

Al-Qaeda became the pre-eminent jihadist network after developing a strategy for attacking the Far Enemy. An authoritative source describes how, in the late 1990s, the movement underwent not just an evolutionary change but a 'monstrous mutation'.[2] To grasp the complex interplay of personalities and opportunities that brought this mutation about, it is necessary to reflect on the emergence of al-Qaeda in the late 1980s, and 'the empire of circumstance' that allowed the organisation's leadership to be forged. Central to this was the emergence of a charismatic figure President Bush called 'the Evil One'.

Usama bin Laden was the seventeenth son of Mohammed bin Laden, a wealthy businessman and owner of a construction company that facilitated Saudi Arabia's rise in the 1950s and 60s. Throughout his education he devoted a great deal of time to reading the Qur'an. One of his closest friends recalled: 'We were trying to understand what Islam has to say about how we eat, who we marry, how we talk. We read Sayyid Qutb. He was the one that most affected our generation.'[3]

Qutb was an Egyptian writer, literary critic, and civil servant who spent time in the United States from 1948 to 1950. In that period, his devotion to Islam became co-mingled with an unwavering disenchantment with civilisation in the West. He came to understand 'true Islam', in the words of the political theorist Susan Buck-Morss, as 'the inverted other of Western modernity'. What this meant, in her words, was that Islam is 'spiritual where the West is materialistic; communal where the West is egoistically individual, socially just where the West is greedy and competitive, [and] morally disciplined where the West is negligently libertine'. True Islam, for Qutb, meant a return to the literal meaning of the Qur'an which in turn propelled him to declare Egyptian society of his day as 'un-Islamic'.[4] He believed that, unless resisted, Western ways would corrupt Islam through controls asserted by colonial and neocolonial structures of power.[5] Qutb spent the last years of his life in prison for plotting to overthrow the state. While in prison his political writings were published as *Milestones* in 1962. This work reiterates the theme of the West's moral atrophy allied with a Leninist argument for a 'vanguard' to lead an Islamic revival.[6] Qutb was executed in 1966 by the secularist-nationalist Egyptian president, Gamal Abdul Nasser, for calling for the armed overthrow of the state.

In addition to influencing bin Laden, Qutb's thinking exerted a powerful attraction on Ayman al-Zawahiri, who became the second in command of al-Qaeda and – in the minds of many – its leading intellectual and theologian. Like bin Laden, al-Zawahiri was from an educated and successful family, though in his case his birthplace was Egypt. Al-Zawahiri's uncle, a protégé of Qutb, told stories to al-Zawahiri about his mentor's purity of mind and the cruelty Qutb had experienced in Egyptian prisons. All this impressed al-Zawahiri, who wrote: 'The Nasserite regime thought that the Islamic movement received a deadly blow with the execution of Sayyid Qutb and his comrades' but Qutb's ideas had instead become 'the nucleus of the modern Islamic jihad move-ment in Egypt'.[7]

Initially, both bin Laden and al-Zawahiri focused on the enemy 'who is near'. Bin Laden spent his university years debating Islamic resistance to the corrupt Saudi state, and building coalitions with other jihadists, comprising a 'hybridisation' of Salafism and Wah-habism.[8] ('Salafism' was a reform movement, dating from the start of the twentieth century, calling for a restoration of a pure form of Islam, unmediated by the clerical establishment and deriving from the *salaf* or 'pious ancestors' – the early companions and interpret-ers of the Prophet. 'Wahhabism' is an older and more conservative strain of Islam.) Defeating the Near Enemy was also al-Zawahiri's priority for jihadi Salafists, in his case Egypt's secular regime. Tack-ling the Far Enemy – the United States and its allies – would wait until shari'a law had been imposed at home.

Following the Soviet invasion of Afghanistan in 1979, al-Zawahiri was quickly drawn to the Afghan–Pakistan border to attend to refugees fleeing the invasion. Bin Laden was drawn to the mujahidin – the 'warriors of God' – in their struggle against the 'infidel' invaders, and he used his wealth and Saudi connec-tions to bring 'Afghan Arabs' through Pakistan into the war-zone. It was there, towards the end of the decade, that the two men became associated. Lawrence Wright sums up their convergent skills and interests:

> The dynamic of the two men's relationship made Zawahiri and bin Laden into people they would never have been individu-ally; moreover, the organisation they would create, al-Qaeda, would be a vector of these two forces, one Egyptian and one Saudi. Each would have to compromise in order to accommo-date the goals of the other; as a result, al-Qaeda would take a unique path, that of the global jihad.[9]

The decade-long resistance to the Soviet invasion was a vital crucible in the development of jihadist terrorist strategy and tactics.

War makes strange bedfellows, and the mujahidin were not only supported by bin Laden's wealth (plus the Saudi and Pakistani governments and mainstream Islamists), but also by Ronald Reagan's government in Washington. The United States funded and armed the mujahidin, including supplying them with the Stinger surface-to-air missiles that inflicted decisive losses on Soviet air capabilities. Strategists in Washington sensed that Afghanistan could become the Soviet Union's Vietnam, and were keen to share their experience of asymmetric defeat with their superpower rival. Today, the political elite in the United States does not like to be reminded of how it contributed to the establishment by jihadist extremists of a secure base in Afghanistan, and especially one on which they consolidated their power and ultimately set forth to damage Western interests. Some of the players at the time have been less apologetic. Zbigniew Brzezinski, former US national security adviser, has said that bringing about the end of the Cold War mattered more than the harm that could be done by 'some stirred-up Muslims'.[10] He was wrong about both the ending and the stirring. 'Stirred-up' Muslims eventually shook US society to its foundations.

One part of the jihadist network in Afghanistan, funded by Saudi Arabia, was run by Abdullah Azzam, a one-time professor of Islamic jurisprudence who was an influential figure for both bin Laden and al-Zawahiri. He ultimately became a rival with the latter for bin Laden's support, and soon after the Soviet withdrawal was killed in mysterious circumstances. His lasting significance is that he is seen to have been pivotal in persuading local jihadist groups to shift focus from the Near Enemy (un-Islamic Arab regimes) to the Far Enemy (the West, including Israel). He wrote: 'Jihad is an obligation upon the whole earth from East to West'.[11] Bin Laden himself, by the mid-1990s, was holed-up in the cave complex of the Tora Bora mountains on the Afghanistan–Pakistan border, having been exiled from Saudi Arabia and Sudan. Among his coterie of followers were 'the ragtag leftovers of the Muslim foreign legion of Afghanistan' for whom 'the fire of the armed jihad still burned'.[12] Opportunities to seize upon local Islamist wars of resistance were limited, as insurgencies had been defeated or contained in a number of key countries, notably Algeria, Egypt, and the Philippines. This gave further impetus to the idea of projecting al-Qaeda's 'jihadist zeal' onto the Far Enemy. With this 'monstrous mutation', terror became globalised.

Towards a 'dialogue of bullets'

Though the Base had been operating since 1988, out of Peshwar in Pakistan, it was not inaugurated until 23 February 1998 when it became known to its followers as the 'World Islamic Front to fight Jews and Christians'. Through the 1990s, as the Taliban movement gradually took control of postwar Afghanistan, bin Laden and his followers gathered – uninvited – at the scene of their wartime victory over a superpower. This Base became the training ground where recruits were mobilised for a global struggle; they comprised disillusioned young Muslim men living in the West, and militants from across the Islamic world keen to help advance a cause which political Islamism had so far failed.

Al-Qaeda relies on the use of internet and mobile phone technologies to ensure that it reaches an audience vastly bigger than the territorial spaces it is able to occupy. Skilful use of the global media, including satellite channels such as Al Jazeera enabled al-Qaeda to enrage and inspire ordinary Muslims to join the struggle. These new recruits in dozens of countries have been mobilised by a message that can be summed up by the phrase: 'sacrifice yourself for a pure new world Islamic order'. The relationship between martyrdom and the media is one of interdependence. Martyrdom has no meaning as an existential act, rather, it becomes real when it is witnessed by the media and transmitted onto a TV/PC screen. In what can be thought of as a postmodern twist to the traditional and fundamentalist self-understanding of Salafi jihadists, suicide bombing becomes a form of advertising.[13] It is difficult to exaggerate the significance of the internet for al-Qaeda in helping turn a virtual community of potentially militant Muslims in different countries into a real community of jihadists.

The recruits that have found their way to the Base have been given a 180-page manual entitled *Military Studies in the Jihad against the Tyrants*. Field manuals set out the standard operating procedures of an armed force, and tell us something important about the identity of the institution; likewise with al-Qaeda. The *Jihad* manual begins with the following:

> The confrontation we are calling for with the apostate regimes does not know Socratic debates . . . Platonic ideals . . . nor Aristotlean Diplomacy . . . But it does know the dialogue of bullets, the ideals of assassination, bombing and destruction, and the diplomacy of the cannon and the machine gun.[14]

This dark discourse – which Qutb expressed in the 1950s and al-Zawahiri in more recent decades – points to al-Qaeda being in the business of destruction; but it is destruction as a form of communication, the 'dialogue of bullets'.

The Base is more than a training camp for fighters, however. It is the hub for the movement's 'vanguard' – the kind that Qutb had called for in his prison notebooks. In this respect, the Base generates political messages that resonate with the marginalised, the alienated, and the angry. The detail of the messages constantly shifts, but the themes are constant: the apostate regimes, the injustices perpetrated against the Palestinians by the 'Zionist crusaders', and the on-going presence of US forces in the holy lands.

There is a command structure and a set of rules governing al-Qaeda's leadership succession in the event of the possibility of individuals being killed or captured. This will be severely tested in the months and years following the killing of bin Laden in May 2011: with the charismatic leader gone, will there now be factionalism? Its middle and senior leadership ranks are thought to number just a few hundred (sometimes known as 'AQ Central'). Around this inner core are alliances with other jihadist groups and cells (known as the AQ 'network' or 'affiliates'). There is then an outer circle of local factions with no direct communication with the leadership but who claim membership and share in the organisation's worldview.[15]

The most talked-about doctrinal element of al-Qaeda is the jihad. It is context dependent, and no single definition commands a full consensus. The term can refer to a struggle against one's own negative inclinations, or to exerting moral force for the betterment of one's Islamic community. However, jihad is most associated, these days, with the idea of fighting in the name of God. For conservatives, this covers the need to take up arms when Islam is under threat, but for the global jihadist extremists constituting al-Qaeda's leadership this defensive ethos is rejected; to them, jihad is an obligation to wage war 'against the enemy in their heartlands whenever possible'.[16] It is the global scale of its activities – some see it as a 'Cosmic War' – that sets al-Qaeda apart from all the other groups of jihadist extremists.

The goals of this war have been much discussed since 9/11, and it is an issue we will develop later. For the moment it is important to point out that amid all the apocalyptic language and imagery one should beware of concluding that al-Qaeda has *not* been interested in the classical goal of statecraft, namely, the seizure and control of territory. In his autobiography, *Knights Under the Prophet's Banner*, al-Zawahiri wrote: 'Confronting the enemies of Islam, and launching jihad against them require a Muslim authority . . . Without achieving this goal our actions will mean nothing.'[17] Since its beginning, the Muslim land of choice for al-Qaeda has been the Afghanistan/Pakistan frontier (or AfPak as it is know in Western intelligence agencies). This is where tens of thousands of jihadist foot soldiers have received basic training in combat, in the use of firearms, and in the making of explosives – in short, in learning the methods of the terrorist.[18]

Terror in the name of God

While the strategic shift in jihadist activity at the start of the 1990s was becoming known to Western intelligence experts, what put al-Qaeda on the map was the explosion at the World Trade Center on 26 February 1993. Ramzi Yousef, who had been trained at the Base, ignited a truck full of explosives under the Twin Towers. Six people were killed, and 1,042 were injured.[19] With the exception of this attack, al-Qaeda had to that point been less successful than Hamas or Hezbollah when measured against the kind of body-count benchmarks that are understood by jihadist extremists and counter-terrorist officers. This changed dramatically on 7 August 1998. For the first time the world witnessed the al-Qaeda signature attack: simultaneous suicide bombings on high-value Western targets, and with mass casualties. On this occasion the targets were the US embassies in Nairobi and Dar es Salaam: 224 people were killed, and 4,585 wounded. In retaliation, President Clinton ordered Tomahawk cruise missile strikes on al-Qaeda targets in Khartoum and Khost (an al-Qaeda camp in Afghanistan, near the Pakistan border).

The first significant al-Qaeda action of the new millennium was the audacious attack on the USS *Cole* on 12 October 2000, as it docked in Aden; it resulted in 17 dead and 39 injured. The mastermind of this operation, Abd al Rahim al Nashiri, was one of those involved in the planning and execution of the 9/11 attacks on the United States. Various individuals within al-Qaeda have been identified as being the 'architect' or 'mastermind' of 9/11. Two others deserve a brief mention. The first is Mohammed Atta, from the Hamburg cell of al-Qaeda, who years before the attack had spoken to bin Laden about a 'planes operation' against US targets. Atta and his fellow operatives had discussed targeting with bin Laden, though in characteristic al-Qaeda style the execution of the operation was left to those with the responsibility to carry it out. Like the rest of us, bin Laden watched the attacks on his TV; the interval between the two collisions with the World Trade Center towers being ideally planned for live news programming. The other key figure to mention is Khalid Sheik Mohammed, who was revealed as the mysterious 'Mukhtar' ('the chosen') of 9/11. Pakistani born and with a degree from North Carolina Agricultural and Technical State University, 'KMS' was given delegated authority by bin Laden for the 9/11 attacks.[20] He later claimed to have been the person who beheaded the *Wall Street Journal*'s reporter, Daniel Pearl, in the ghastliest-ever exhibition of terrorist internet propaganda. Captured in Pakistan on 1 March 2003, Khalid Sheik Mohammed's interrogation (he was 'waterboarded' 183 times) drew the world's attention to the Bush administration's redefining of the definition of torture.

US retaliation for 9/11 began within a month ('Operation Enduring Freedom'), in the form of air-strikes at suspected al-Qaeda bases in Taliban-controlled Afghanistan. The fighters of al-Qaeda, footloose, were more confident of survival than the Taliban authorities, with their fixed sites of power. Having read military strategy, studied the history of modern war, and experienced the victory over the Soviets, senior al-Qaeda commanders believed that they had cause to hope that the superiority of US weaponry could be countered by following Sun Tzu's dictum that 'if your enemy is superior . . . make good use of the terrain by spreading out on rugged mountains and lanes'. And they knew that by dragging the enemy into a 'long war' (the US invasion of Iraq helped this) they could deploy their limited forces in ways that might exert maximum damage to their enemy's morale, leading to an ignominious withdrawal. The leaders of al-Qaeda saw war as a form of brutal negotiation, in which it was not necessary to win great set-piece battles; and in this regard the recent memory of the mujahidin success against the mighty Red Army was a great morale booster.

Al-Qaeda was helped by the flawed strategy of its opponents. The US-led invasion of Iraq in 2003 presented the al-Qaeda leadership, in bin Laden's own words, with 'a golden and unique opportunity'. In destroying the country's authority structures, in addition to toppling Saddam Hussein's personal power, the Western 'coalition of the willing' destabilised the country in a way that enabled al-Qaeda to become a significant force in Iraq. Though not the only radicalised Islamist group operating there, al-Qaeda was 'the deadliest'.[21] What had been called 'Operation Restore Hope' created the circumstances for this powerful jihadist enemy – the source of the suicide terrorists of 9/11 – to become established on a territory where it had not taken root previously. What is more, the invasion of Iraq supplied al-Qaeda with a legitimating narrative about the West being an enemy of Muslim people. In so doing, it radicalised mainstream Arab and Muslim public opinion and deepened anti-American sentiment throughout the world, and not just in lands dominated by Muslim communities. As one al-Qaeda operative put it, by invading Iraq the United States 'fell into our trap'.[22] A CIA document suggested that Iraq could turn out to have been a more effective training ground for a new generation of jihadists than Afghanistan was in the 1980s.[23]

Similar concerns were felt among the British intelligence community. The then Director of MI5, Eliza Manningham-Buller, interviewed on television in March 2011 said that her organisation had become increasingly worried about radicalisation resulting from the invasion of Iraq, and had warned Blair's government of the growing risks.[24] But the prime minister was not to be diverted from his chosen course. Manningham-Buller's frank verdict, in hindsight, was that the radicalisation had been expected, but not the actual extent of it. Although (as we will show later) al-Qaeda was suffering setbacks elsewhere, the bombings that took place in London on 7 July 2005 were a reminder of the threat posed by local al-Qaeda affiliate groups. In quick succession on the morning of that day, three bombs exploded on the underground and a fourth on the top-deck of a bus; 52 people were killed and hundreds injured. The atrocities were committed by three British citizens of Pakistani origin, and a fourth of Caribbean origin who had lived in the UK for over 20 years. Two of them, the ring-leader Muhammad Siddique Khan and Shehzad Taneer, had gone to Pakistan in February 2005 for training. In addition to the radicalisation caused by US and UK policy in Iraq and Afghanistan, in the case of Siddique Khan a trip to Israel in which he witnessed at first hand the plight of Palestinians was also critical.[25] Later that year, a video message by Khan was broadcast on Al Jazeera television, in which he denounced atrocities 'against my people' by 'democratically elected governments'. To which he added 'We are at war and I am a soldier.'[26]

While the US-led invasion and occupation of Iraq was a trigger for violent radicalisation, al-Qaeda was also suffering a 'blowback' of its own. The self-appointed leader of al-Qaeda in Iraq, Abu Musab al-Zarqawi, caused mayhem in his campaign to force the Americans out of the country; his model was Hezbollah's success in October 1983, when the US army barracks (Khobar Towers) in Beirut was blown up, killing 241 servicemen and women. In Iraq, al-Zarqawi and his followers carried out numerous indiscriminate acts of terror following the post-invasion collapse of order; these included the public beheading of hostages and massive atrocities against fellow Muslims. So bloody was the reign of terror that it prompted a rebuke from leaders in the Base. Ayman al-Zawahiri made it clear to al-Zarqawi that his strategy and tactics were wrong. A letter in 2005 shows the rift that had developed. Al-Zawahiri cautioned al-Zarqawi against being deceived by the praise of 'the zealous young men'. 'They do not', he warned, 'express the general view'.[27] This division lasted until al-Zarqawi was killed by a US air-strike north of Baghdad in June 2006. During these years, in addition to al-Qaeda's legitimacy crisis among Muslims, US military and intelligence services were having a good deal of success in finding, killing, or imprisoning a large number of al-Qaeda fighters and commanders, such that the old core of the organisation was seriously disrupted.

By now it was time for AQ Central to examine its own mistakes, and those of its followers. The leadership knew that the organisation's popularity was in decline, with the global jihad having killed thousands of Muslims in Iraq, in Afghanistan, and in Pakistan. For a group that claimed to be defending the Islamic community of the faithful, these murders had significantly damaged its credibility. Muslims might have been divided about whether to take up arms against US-led coalition forces in Iraq, but the vast majority were united in believing that 'Shi'as' and 'Iraqi Kurds' were not the enemy. As a tactic to win back support, al-Zawahiri began an internet conversation with his supporters. A typical question in the online 'Q and A' came from geography teacher Mudarris Jughrafiya, who asked: 'Excuse me, Mr Zawahiri, but who is it who is killing with your excellency's blessing the innocents in Baghdad, Morocco, and Algeria? Do you consider the killing of women and children to be jihad?' The point behind this teacher's question is supported by the data on the victims of al-Qaeda attacks which suggests 'at least 40%' of their victims have been Muslims.[28]

Where and what next?

As we approach the tenth anniversary of 9/11 — al-Qaeda's one truly universal moment — how are we to assess its current potential? One immediate answer is to suggest that the absence of further successful 'spectaculars' (and not a few failures) means that America is winning this particular 'long war'. This view, as we will show in later chapters, raises far more questions than it answers. It is more justifiable in our view to conclude that al-Qaeda is losing it, rather than US preventive measures are winning it.

Unlike Hamas and other organisations which are seen to be resisting the Near Enemy — oppressive regimes 'at home' — al-Qaeda has come to be seen 'by most Arabs and Muslims' as a purely terrorist organisation.[29] Its popularity since around 2003 has been fading in the Middle East and in South Asia. Key Sunni clerics have criticised al-Qaeda's reliance on the 'dialogue of bullets' and have sought to redefine jihad in ways that do not involve the slaughter of innocent Muslims. Without legitimacy power ebbs away, if not the ability to lash out in violence. This, in 2011, is as true for terrorist organisations like al-Qaeda as it can be for dictators hanging on for their political life like Colonel Qaddafi.

Despite its violent acts in the name of God and of defending Islam, al-Qaeda has found it increasingly difficult to mobilise support among ordinary Muslims. One method of doing this has been by emphasising or widening the list of just causes; in bin Laden's 2006 statement for example, broadcast by Al Jazeera, he talked about the Palestinian victims of the 'Christian-Jewish conspiracy' and urged his followers to join the Sudanese struggle against United Nations peacekeepers. This reinforced al-Zawahiri's attempt, from 2005, to mould al-Qaeda into an organisation that could use its strategic power to support grassroots Islamist resistance movements. The challenge for al-Qaeda was becoming the same as faces all radical movements when the limelight shifts: in the words of Bruce Hoffman, the RAND terrorism specialist, 'how to remain relevant over time'.[30]

The ability to carry out spectacular strikes against key targets is one way of trying to demonstrate relevance and regain legitimacy. Against this benchmark, al-Qaeda's capability seems to have diminished markedly. In contrast to earlier successes, more noticeable has been the string of failures of potentially horrific missions. These include the thwarted attempt to blow up seven transatlantic planes (August 2006), the New York City Subway Plot (2008/9), and the attempted attack on Northwest Airlines Flight 253 on Christmas Day 2009. Comprehensive research covering a five-year period (from 2004 to the 2009) suggests that of the 21 serious terrorist attacks planned (and known about), three alone were successful (the Madrid bombings, the assassination of the Dutch filmmaker Theo van Gogh, and the London bombings).[31]

As a result of these developments, there has been a steadily cohering view since the middle of the decade that while the threat of spectacular terrorism remains, the risks are declining. According to a secret FBI report obtained by ABC News in 2005, the reason why 'networks' of al-Qaeda operatives had not been uncovered in the United States was because there might have been nothing to uncover; and, while not entirely ruling out another 9/11, RAND terrorism specialist Brian Michael Jenkins judged that 'there is a growing consensus among analysts that such an attack on the United States is not likely'.[32]

But there is another view. This argument emphasises that setbacks suffered by AQ Central in Afghanistan and elsewhere – notably the killing of bin Laden in Pakistan – does not mean that the appeal of jihadism has weakened irrevocably. The distinguished ex-CIA terrorist specialist Bruce Riedel, who is a Brookings senior fellow and senior adviser to four US presidents, is instructive here. He picks out five components to consider in assessing the future global Islamic jihad: al-Qaeda's 'old core senior leadership in Pakistan', its allies in Pakistan and Afghanistan, its franchises, its 'cells and sympathizers' in the Islamic diaspora in Europe, North

America, Australia, and elsewhere, and the idea of global jihad itself.[33]

At this point we want to explore the franchises and diaspora, as they seem not only to represent a particular danger, but they are a warning against assuming that al-Qaeda's time has passed, as was sometimes imagined in the period following the Soviet withdrawal from Afghanistan. These al-Qaeda outliers – showing that jihad is truly global – have the potential to re-energise jihadi hopes, while those making up the old Base lick their wounds. Each local franchise gets its broad strategic direction from AQ Central, but then has considerable operational independence. They also have their own propaganda arms. Not surprisingly, depending on local conditions and the nature of radicalisation, the local franchises are of very different strength and potential. If we go back to the start, and think of the Base as a set of fundamentals rather than a location, there is no reason why the focus should forever remain on the traditional borderlands between Afghanistan and Pakistan. Like a plague bacillus – an analogy to which we will return in the Epilogue – a terrorist project need not be active to be in existence. Nor, indeed, need it be active to be communicating its message to fearful targets.

While what happens in Pakistan still could be what Riedel calls 'a nightmare', of particular significance in recent years have been the activities of al-Qaeda in Yemen, especially after the suppression and dispersal of the franchise in Saudi Arabia.[34] Not only have several attacks on aircraft been masterminded from Yemen (including the planned attacks on cargo planes referred to on p. 4), but Yemen has also attracted attention because of the very influential internet jihadist, the Yemeni-American Anwar al-Awlaki. As a result of various terrorist scares emanating from Yemen, Secretary of State Hillary Clinton, in January 2010, declared Yemen 'an urgent national security priority' for the United States, and in August it was reported that for the first time since 9/11 CIA analysts regarded Yemen 'rather than the core group now based in Pakistan – as the most urgent threat to U.S. security'. In 2010, out of Yemen, al-Awlaki and also another US citizen, Samir-Khan, launched the first online global jihadist propaganda magazine in English, *Inspire* (also with a women's version) hoping to recruit in the United States and Europe.[35] In May 2010 the US Department of Homeland Security reported that attempted attacks against the US over the previous nine months 'surpassed the number of attempts during any other previous one-year period'. (Russia also reported the increased frequency of attacks.) The prominent US commentator Fareed Zakaria related this to 'the rise of a new kind of warfare: microterrorism' – small-scale operations, organised locally, and where successful completion outweighed spectacular results. He noted that the rationale behind microterrorism had been explained by the editors in the first issue of *Inspire*: the 'strategy of a thousand cuts', they said, was the way ahead. Zakaria's view was that the threat is presently small, but 'the democratisation of technology, access, information and all those good things is also leading inexorably to the democratisation of violence. Welcome to 2011.'[36]

The internet is vital for inspiring what Riedel considers the essentially 'self-radicalised' youth in the diaspora, people who are 'angry and extreme'; once identified, though, he believes that al-Qaeda is 'quick to respond to nascent recruits'. He also offers a worrying statistic to the authorities, lest they feel complacent about al-Qaeda's loss of legitimacy among Muslim populations as a whole; he points out that if only 1 per cent of the overwhelmingly non-violent Muslim communities in the UK and France become sympathisers and potential terrorists, 'this amounts to a massive counter-terrorism challenge'. The issue of 'homegrown terrorists', usually seen in the West as a distinctively Western European problem, had by the start of 2011 become an issue of some publicity in the United States; this was as a result of Senate Hearings (the Committee on Homeland Security and Government Affairs) into 'Violent Islamist Extremism and the Homegrown Terrorist Threat', marked by the issuing of a report entitled 'A Ticking Time Bomb'.[37]

Terror in our time remains global. In the March 2011 interview we quoted from earlier, former MI5 Director Manningham-Buller

– speaking for all governments – said that the state cannot guarantee security, whatever its resources and however clever its intelligence services. She said that there are still hundreds of terrorist suspects 'out there' in the UK, and that while they are there, we face a threat. In the short term the expectation of increased levels of terrorism was heightened as a result of the prospect of revenge actions by radicalised individuals and franchise groups seeking to avenge the killing of bin Laden by American forces. But for some the stakes will continue to be far higher than this. The struggle 'out there' for the most radical jihadists is for the very highest stakes of all. One of the 9/11 suicide terrorists described the enemy as 'the allies of Satan' and 'brothers of the Devil'. In al-Qaeda's constitution its aim is to 'establish the truth and get rid of evil'.[38] Such pre-occupation with fighting devils and ridding the world of evil presages a battle without end and the legitimation of extreme measures.

Further reading

The 9/11 Commission carefully tracks the emergence of al-Qaeda through the struggle against Soviet forces in Afghanistan. Other key sources on al-Qaeda include Fawaz Gerges, *The Far Enemy: Why the Jihad Went Global* (Cambridge: Cambridge University Press, 2005); Lawrence Wright, *The Looming Tower* (London: Vintage, 2007); Faisal Devji, *Landscape of the Jihad: Militancy, Morality and Modernity* (Ithaca: Cornell University Press, 2005); Jason Burke, *Al-Qaeda: The True Story of Radical Islam* (London: Penguin Books, 2004); Peter Bergen, *The Longest War: The Enduring Conflict between America and Al-Qaeda* (New York: The Free Press, 2010); and Audrey Kurth Cronin (2007) 'Ending Terrorism: Lessons for Defeating Al-Qaeda', *Adelphi Paper*, 47: 394. On the use of language, both neoconservative and jihadist Arabic terms, see Fred Halliday, *Shocked and Awed: How the War On Terror and Jihad Have Changed the English Language* (London: I.B. Tauris, 2010).

5 Evil

'Terrorists are evil folk.' 'Terrorism is evil.' 'These are evil acts performed by evil people.' Since 9/11 the air has been full of evil talk, and the persistent question: what drives people to inflict terror on the general public? We need to think about this question by confronting one ever-popular answer: 'Evil'.

Evil talk

We saw at the end of the previous chapter how evil is central to the worldview of al-Qaeda and its supporters. In this chapter we want to focus on the way images of Evil, sometimes capitalised for demonic emphasis, have flourished in the West since 9/11. They were especially prominent during the headiest days of the War on Terror. According to President Bush, the fight was against 'the Monster of Terrorism', and it involved engaging with a 'demonic enemy' which was 'defined by hate', driven by 'mad intent', and drew on 'monstrous evil'. For many people, evil talk has been difficult to resist: for what words do we have to describe the unspeakable? While President Obama's use of language has been far more nuanced than his predecessor (he phased out talk of the 'War on Terror' in order, he said, to avoid offending Muslims[1]), he nonetheless was drawn to Manichaean accounts of what 9/11 meant. On its eighth anniversary he contrasted 'the human capacity for evil' with 'the human capacity for good', the former being about destruction, the latter being about serving and building. His opponent in the presidential race a year earlier, Senator John McCain, was very explicit about the nature of America's enemy: 'This is a transcendent evil', he said, 'that wants to destroy everything we stand for and believe in.' Evangelical thinking has been the mirror image of al-Qaeda's: Lieutenant General William G. Boyd, who as Undersecretary of Defense for Intelligence had been central in the search for Usama bin Laden, told an audience: 'Our enemy is a spiritual enemy because we are a nation of believers . . . His name is Satan . . . Satan wants to destroy us as a nation and he wants to destroy us as a Christian Army.'[2]

The invocation of evil as an explanation of certain types of extreme behaviour is the norm in societies where religiosity is high. If you believe that God is blessing you, then those who attack you must be evil; but what is this 'evil' we must confront? Is it 'real'? Or is it a 'myth'? The answers we individually come to have profound consequences.

For many people 'evil' is simply the word of last resort for describing morally repugnant behaviour; it expresses what the philosopher A.C. Grayling calls 'the furthest condemnatory reaches of our calibration of moral quality'. It is the word (and implicitly the explanation) for what is virtually unspeakable. But that does not mean that it is not 'real'; for many, the notion of evil goes beyond words; it is metaphysical. The distinguished philosopher Leszek Kołakowski, for example, in questioning Marx's assumption that human shortcomings are rooted in social circumstances, argued that some sources of conflict and aggression are inherent in the human species: 'The Devil is part of our experience.' Evil, he maintained, 'is not contingent', but a 'stubborn and unredeemable fact'.[3] The literary theorist Terry Eagleton also insists on the reality of evil, setting himself against those liberals and leftists (with whom he is usually associated) who want to dismiss it; he considers evil a 'condition of being', 'what ought not to exist'.[4]

Eagleton, who asserts that evil is 'a real phenomenon with palpable force' attacks those who think otherwise in part because he believes it makes them 'impotent' to deal with it. Our book is based on the opposite view. Our argument is that 'Evil' is best understood as a 'myth', and that to reify it – to treat it as if it has a real, concrete, existence – only makes matters worse. This is as true in dealing with terrorism as any other area attracting the label. The mythology of evil (which includes the Devil and metaphysical superstition) is no way to counter a strategic doctrine. For example, Eagleton asserts that those who inflict evil are not amenable to argument. To many observers of terrorism, groups with a religious dimension are particularly intransigent. But it is clear that some terrorist organisations do at some point become amenable to argument (the IRA in the 1990s, for example). If this is so, they presumably cease to be evil. To accept this, one must think that the particular evil of terrorism resides in a group's non-negotiable aims rather than their murderous actions. This is not a view likely to find favour even among fellow-believers in evil.

The understanding of evil as myth has been argued in considerable detail by the philosopher Philip Cole.[5] He writes: 'To describe someone as evil is not to say anything about them, but it is to place them as victims of a narrative force, as characters in a story in which they play a specific and prescribed role.' This understanding of evil perfectly matches Reza Aslan's depiction of the 9/11 hijackers, who saw themselves as participants in the ritual drama of cosmic war: 'The conflict may be real and the carnage material, but the war itself is being waged on a spiritual plane; we humans are merely actors in a divine script written by God.'[6]

To locate explanations of human conflicts in an agent like the Devil, or something 'beyond human comprehension', is something we will show is dangerous and counter-productive. The images of 9/11 – as mesmerising today as they were ten years ago – seem almost beyond imagination and, therefore, beyond rational explanation. But the plain fact is that they are neither. Fantastical scenarios have never been beyond the imaginations of the makers of horror films, and obviously the actual 9/11 scenario was not beyond the imagination of its perpetrators. We will not get to grips with terrorists until we understand that what drives them is all-too-human, and is amenable to rational analysis. This does not mean that analysis is easy.

Humanising the unspeakable

The challenge for us is to try to accumulate reliable knowledge, and develop plausible theories about those rare but heinous acts that seem beyond ordinary comprehension – those very acts that touch 'the furthest condemnatory reaches of our calibration of moral quality'. Such acts are uncommon, but not unfamiliar: sex abuse by priests, children murdering other children, the slaughter of neighbours in civil wars, genocide, and so on. The ultimate heinous act, for many, is the Holocaust – the Nazi attempt to exterminate the Jewish population of Europe. If this was not the face of evil (or 'radical evil' to use Hannah Arendt's term) what was?

The well-known historian of the Holocaust, Yehuda Bauer, argues that to explain the Holocaust in terms of a mysterious force like evil removes it to an 'ahistoric sphere' where it cannot be touched by rational thinking – 'not even by rational explanations of the irrational'.[7] Moreover, to argue that the Holocaust was the result of the Nazis being gripped by a monstrous evil is to argue that 'the criminals would become tragic victims of forces beyond human control. To say that the Holocaust is inexplicable, in the last resort, is to justify it.' Bauer refuses to consider the behaviour of the Nazis as anything other than 'human': we consider the same to be equally the case with terrorism.

Crucial to this understanding is recognition that evil begets evil. Bauer explains that it was the discourse of evil – the Nazi belief that the Jews represented a cosmic evil destroying German civilisation – that helped put the German state on the road to the Holocaust in the first place. Similarly, but without implying any moral equivalence, one can see how those inclined to categorise the perpetrators of 9/11 as a 'demonic enemy' placed the American state on the slippery slope to losing its moral authority (and international regard) through reinterpretations of 'the rules of the game'.[8] Once one identifies another people or religion as being driven by evil, extreme counters are sanctioned; and extreme counters are made easier if the enemy is dehumanised.[9]

It is possible to account for extreme behaviour without invoking the force of evil, though of course such understanding might not come easily. In the case of the Holocaust, Bauer writes: 'That something is in principle explicable does not mean that it has been explained or that it can readily be explained.'[10] Part of the difficulty is the way mythology can obscure the human face of the perpetrator; 'our moral problem' with the Holocaust, Bauer writes, 'is not that the perpetrators were inhuman but that they were human, just like ourselves, and that we human beings are prone to the kind of murderousness they evinced'. This insight is missed by evil talk. It is bad social science, bad history, and bad politics to reject systematic analysis of human behaviour and, instead, seek comfort in a dash of religious or cosmic eschatology. The parallels between trying to understand the Holocaust and trying to understand terrorism should be clear. We need to look for a reasoning (if perverted or malevolent) human behind the label, whether that label is 'Nazi murderer' or 'terrorist'. Understanding will be gained in exploring circumstances and choices, not in invoking Satan. History helps.[11]

We are dealing with people, not Monsters. Terrorists, like Primo Levi's camp guards, have 'our faces'.[12] The humanising of terrorists, attempting to understand what drives them in human terms – to normalise them – is profoundly worrying to some. The worry is about the implications of the old adage 'to understand all is to forgive all', when the political consequences could be disastrous. It is a familiar anxiety. During the Cold War, those attempting to interpret Soviet policy empathetically were sometimes under suspicion for being the 'useful idiots' of the Kremlin. And more recently there were critics of the film *Downfall*, on the last days of Hitler, who complained that it turned the Nazi leader into a human being. We believe this is exactly what researchers, film-makers, and others should try to do, rather than resorting to narratives of cosmic collisions, which forever place rational understanding beyond our grasp.

Fundamentalism

Any discussion of evil in the context of politics and, more specifically, terrorism, leads seamlessly to the phenomenon of fundamentalism; this is another favoured explanation for the deterioration of relations between the Islamic world and the West.

'Fundamentalism' in popular usage is a 'boo word': to attach it to somebody is invariably meant to be pejorative. Fundamentalists, whether they are the Christian right, Jewish zealots, or Muslim extremists, are generally regarded with suspicion outside their own communities. But we should be wary of crude syllogisms: fundamentalism (whether religious or atheistic) is not synonymous with terrorism, though terrorists are sometimes fundamentalists.

As the American Quaker Paul Lacey has explained, the concept 'fundamentalist' is complex as well as controversial. Even among the religious, the conservative traditions embodied in fundamentalism cause people to feel 'estranged and even alienated'.[13] This has two major dimensions: one scriptural and the other countercultural.

The scriptural theme refers to a dogmatic commitment to a literal interpretation of whatever is considered to be the holy book. Consequently, the relevant sacred text is believed to be the guide to history, to everyday life, and to personal destiny; it is an explanation of the past and a road-map to the future; it binds its true believers into a close community.[14] The 'counterculture' theme, as explained by the theologian Karen Armstrong, is 'militant piety'. In *The Battle for God* she describes how, in the first half of the twentieth century, a counterculture developed in all three of the major monotheistic faiths. Fundamentalists began to retreat from mainstream society, often 'impelled' by horror and fear, anxiety and passionate rage, and a 'conviction of ever-encroaching evil'. As such, she interpreted fundamentalism as an attempt to fill the spiritual void that Jean Paul Sartre called 'the God-shaped hole in human consciousness'; fundamentalism offered 'adamant opposition' to the secular, relativistic, and scientific values of modernism.[15]

The two themes are brought together in the definition of fundamentalism by anthropologist Richard Antoun:

> Fundamentalism . . . is an orientation to the modern world, both cognitive and emotional, that focuses on protest and change and on certain consuming themes: the quest for purity; the struggle between good and evil; the search for authenticity; totalism and activism; the necessity of certainty (scripturalism); selective modernization and controlled acculturation, millennialism and the centering of the mythic past on the present (traditioning).[16]

Fundamentalists, as Antoun explains, struggle against many things.[17] Christian fundamentalists, for example, oppose the science of Darwin. And fundamentalists often regard themselves as losers in life's 'struggle for power and recognition'. This is a familiar theme among Muslim fundamentalists. Modernity in all its forms – secularism, individualism, consumerism, science, and materialism – represents a challenge to traditionalist commitments, and it is Antoun's view that the evidence shows that these fundamentalists are losing the struggle.

The strategies fundamentalists of various religious persuasions have adopted 'in the Quest for Purity' have included 'flight, separation, or militant struggle'.[18] Violence is but one of the possible strategies and it is one that is opposed by some fundamentalists. In short, fundamentalist views can lead to lives devoted to pacifism and self-sacrifice in the service of others, as well as lives committed to a cosmic fight, full of dogmatic self-righteousness and a disregard of the feelings and lives of others.

Seen in this light, there is no necessary connection between fundamentalism and violence, never mind terrorism. Antoun is, therefore, justified in concluding that the great majority of 'confrontational acts' carried out by fundamentalists across the world are non-violent, involving demonstrations, boycotts, propaganda, and pressure group activities. The 'overwhelming majority of fundamentalists are law-abiding people, like the general population of all nations'; only 'a tiny minority of fundamentalists resort to violence, not to speak of terrorism'.[19]

Even if this is accepted, the label 'fundamentalist' is not one that attracts positive regard. The implications for the lives of women, for example, in fundamentalist societies is an affront to those holding liberal notions of female equality. The greatest concern, however, continues to come from those who associate fundamentalism and terrorism. The two phenomena are 'connected', Lacey says, but they are not the same.[20] For one thing, terrorists need not be religious fundamentalists: he points out that in the Palestine–Israel conflict bombs and rockets have been fired by both left-leaning socialist and right-leaning governments. Nonetheless, Lacey accepts that 'we must acknowledge that some fundamentalist adherents in the major world religions are also violent extremists who rest their political views and justify their terrorist actions on theological grounds'. Religion, in other words, does some, or indeed all, of the 'political' work.

Religious terrorism?

But precisely how much and what work is religion doing? This is one of the knottiest issues in studying terrorism. When faced by a conundrum of this sort, the ancient Greeks often have an answer; but in this case the ancients would not understand the question. This in itself is revealing. People in ancient Greece were plagued by lots of questions, but not this one. Their concern was rather: 'What do the gods want from us?'[21] In the polytheistic landscape of Athens, people were expected to pay their dues to a range of gods; and this involved regular worship, collective devotions, and the ultimate belief in 'something invisible' in the 'building blocks of everything'. For the people of Athens, religion and being were indistinguishable: 'Life itself was thought to be a religious experience' is how the classical scholar Bettany Hughes sums it up.

To separate 'religion' and 'non-religion' – the idea that we can go about our day operating in quite distinct bubbles of being – is a particularly Western and modern worldview. Up to the Reformation, there was no understanding of 'religion' as being a separate dimension to the rest of life; thereafter in Europe, religion and politics became divorced, each with its own distinct concerns. Religion, in this sense, is a relatively recent invention, and the construction above all of secularisation. Once one grasps this, the earlier question about the relationship between religion and politics takes on a radically different complexion. How can they have a 'relationship' if they are not separate: if *politics itself is a religious experience?*

For those who do not distinguish the worlds of politics and religion, questions about the *role* of religion in politics are of little relevance. For the fighters of al-Qaeda, as we saw, terrorism is a religious experience. Jihad embraces their lives; their interpretation of Islam offers a comprehensive explanation of, and road-map for, life. For those believing that matters of religion and matters of the world cannot be divorced, the idea that religion is employed as a 'veil' for political ambitions completely misses the point. For example, to the Salafis, it is a Western conceit to distinguish between human and superhuman sites of sovereignty; sovereignty rests with God. The modern view of sovereignty, as a construct of human politics, is tenable only if the place of religion is understood from a secular viewpoint.[22]

There are, therefore, those believers for whom life is a religious experience: life is religion, and religion is life. For such believers, the phrase 'religious terrorism' is redundant. The whole of life is religious. But such believers cannot have it both ways. If life is religion, and religion life, then their terrorism is also religion. The phrase 'Islamic terrorism' is appropriate for a type of terrorism conceived through particular Muslim lenses – those of the global jihadist. They can no more deny terrorism as a religious experience as some well-meaning outsiders (certain political leaders in the West) can claim, to the contrary, that Islam is 'essentially' peaceful. Religion is what believers do. In Chapter 8 we show that this means multiple things, beautiful as well as bad.

For terrorists with a more 'modern' secularist outlook, where religion and politics are separable, the phrase 'religious terrorism' does have relevance. Religion is added to politics and stirred, to whatever flavour appeals. Whatever a fighter's conception of religion – atheist terrorists are not our concern here – many observers consider that 'religious terrorism' is the most intractable. It is a type of 'new terrorism' which is particularly dangerous because its adherents are seen to be beyond the reach of reason, and the most willing to inflict the heaviest casualties.[23]

This discussion of religion and politics underlines the dangers of making sweeping generalisations about religion and terrorism, because we have shown that 'religion' is at least as problematic a term as 'terrorism' itself. What we can say for sure is that however one conceives the drivers of the practice of terrorism – religious, non-religious, or anti-religious – the context for acting is the realm of politics. Echoing Clausewitz's famous conceptualisation of war, Lacey writes: 'terror becomes politics by other means'.[24]

Terror framed in politics

Despite our concerns about the meanings of the concepts of politics and religion, we nonetheless consider that politics, broadly understood, is the most useful frame in which to understand terrorism; we borrow our understanding from Harold Lasswell who defined politics as 'Who gets What, When, How?'[25] This definition invites world order responses and, long before 9/11, the international lawyer Richard Falk gave one such response to the roots of terrorism:

> given the way the world is organized – repressive governments, aggressive foreign policies – it is unrealistic and arrogant to insist that victims acquiesce in injustice. We may be exceedingly sceptical about violent strategies, and yet there does not seem to be either an ethical basis or a political structure that could sustain an invariable practice of nonviolence.[26]

We are not here endorsing – any more than Falk was – what particular terrorist groups have sought to achieve, or the violent methods by which they have sought to achieve them. However, like Falk, we want to argue that terror campaigns carried out by non-state groups exhibit a sense of reacting against some injustice, repression, or aggression, while at the same time claiming that those they speak for are victims. Likewise, in the case of state terror, there is also both a sense of rationality (the government of Peru thinking it 'must' respond to Shining Path) and victimhood (the UK government in 1984 believing it 'must' respond to the Brighton bombing).

We are not claiming that whenever terrorism takes place the campaign is, in some objective sense, reacting against injustice, repression, or aggression; our point is that those who resort to terror *believe* that there is injustice, repression, and aggression; and that, to some degree, those they claim to represent are victims. What matters in human behaviour is not what some Omniscient Being knows to be true, but what less than omniscient human minds believe or are persuaded to believe is true. Once people are convinced they are victims, and are fighting against injustice, repression, and aggression, history shows that it is a short step to believing that the ends justify the means. This philosophy, articulated in different ways, has guided people across space and time.

The attempt to understand the drivers, aims, and rationalisations of terrorists has occupied a good deal of academic and other effort since 9/11. There is a rich academic literature,[27] but this is of necessarily limited use to decision-makers, who face the strategic challenge of having to act on partial knowledge in real time. In more relaxed settings, when thinking about the perennial question 'What do terrorists want?' it is helpful to distinguish between the *motives* of individuals and the *aims* of groups. Motives are those *drivers* of attitudes and behaviour of which the actor concerned may or may not be conscious; they include emotions, desires, needs, ambitions, perceived interests, and so on. *Aims* are something proposed (clearly or vaguely) on the part of the group, and terrorist groups come in a variety of types, wanting different things (e.g. nationalist, state, religious, etc.).

The motives shaping individuals include: individual psychological variables (e.g. desire for status, attraction to violence, idealism); historical and geographical context (time and location are important); social situation (e.g. one's class) and attitudes (racist/tolerant, disposed to violence/disposed to pacifism); the ideological environment (what are the contemporary issues?); one's political disposition (e.g. idealist/realist, pessimist/optimist); religious views (fundamentalist/modernist/secular); circumstantial factors (personal experiences such as a close relative or friend having been killed by a repressive government); identity issues (joining a group engaged in a historic struggle might provide a role in an otherwise meaningless life); social dynamics (some people are swayed by hate propaganda, some are brought into groups step-by-step – as in a cult they are manipulated, indoctrinated, socialised, brainwashed, and radicalised by others who are totally committed ideologically). Here, clearly, is multicausality: we eschew psychological reductionism on these matters, such as the idea that one can get 'inside the mind' of terrorists[28] and draw conclusions that are generally applicable. It is not much easier at the macro-level; there can be no crude equations such as 'poverty = terrorism'.

Individuals can, in principle, be quite conscious of their reasons for their actions, but we also know that other things might be going on as well – things, as Freud taught us, that lie below the surface of our conscious and rational minds. As a result, even with the accumulation of generally reliable information about terrorist groups, it remains difficult to predict with accuracy whether a particular individual in a given context will choose the role of terrorist, sympathiser, or opponent of violence. This is because of the difficulty of identifying individual motives, with multiple personal variables coming into play.

So, for example, an individual terrorist could be a troubled and immature youth. He might desire to join a group of tough men whose lives seem to have real purpose. Some of his motives will be little understood by himself or his family. Such a young man, were he to become a suicide terrorist, would not reveal – perhaps would be incapable even of understanding – the deep drivers of his behaviour in his martyr video. What would instead be displayed would be the rationalisations and justifications as spoken by his superiors. His expressed reasons (group aims) for his act of martyrdom can be separated from the drivers (individual motives). The leading figures of any movement are more likely to be motivated by more purely ideological or political motives; but the key point is that reasons and causes are not the same, nor necessarily are individual motives and group aims. All, importantly, can be framed in politics.

An individual's life is partly shaped by biology; it is partly the result of the structures he/she inhabits (economic and social); it is partly a matter of luck (the roll of the genetic dice has a role in one's health and when one's parents met affects where and when one is born); and it is partly a matter of individual choice (free will). All these interact in a dynamic historical context. In listing these variables, we are not saying that people who become terrorists do so simply as playthings of structures and circumstances. Note above, at the end, 'free will'. There is always an element of choice. Ultimately terrorism is choice, not destiny, though for some it might seem a choice among very limited options.

Individuals, other than the psychotic, are unlikely to choose to act against the 'facts of human existence' by choosing to inflict terror on others without very powerful reasons. The suicide terrorist is an iconic example. There are now many substantial pieces of research which show that suicide terrorists are neither crazy people nor in the grip of evil inexplicable forces. One of the most influential works, by Robert Pape, holds that there is a common pattern underpinning the phenomena of suicide bombings – the strategic aim of compelling 'modern democracies to withdraw military forces from territory that the terrorists consider to be their homeland'.[29] Invariably, they are educated people moved by rational, if extreme, responses to what they regard as utterly desperate circumstances.

This chapter has shown the complexities of the relationships between politics/religion/terrorism as a way of revealing a multiplicity of answers to questions such as 'What do terrorists want?' and 'What drives people to inflict terror on non-combatants?'. Nonetheless, the chapter suggests that politics provides a masterframe for thinking about answers; in addition, we insist on the academic commitment to the idea that what might appear inexplicable at one moment will, in time, be amenable to rational analysis. Whether the challenge is to try to understand the motives of individual terrorists or the aims of groups embracing terrorism, all involved 'have our faces'. Terrorists are made in society, not born in evil.

Further reading

Bryan S. Turner (ed.), *The New Blackwell Companion to the Sociology of Religion* (Chichester: Wiley-Blackwell, 2010) is a superb set of essays helping readers to think about religion from sociological, anthropological, historical, and comparative perspectives. The best introductions to fundamentalism are: Karen Armstrong, *The Battle for God: Fundamentalism in Judaism, Christianity and Islam* (London: Harper Collins, 2001) and Richard T. Antoun, *Understanding Fundamentalism: Christian, Islamic and Jewish Movements* (Lanham, MD: Rowman & Littlefield, 2008). Among the key works on suicide terrorists are Walter Laqueur, *No End to War: Terrorism in the Twenty-First Century* (New York: Continuum, 2003) and Robert Pape, *Dying To Win: The Strategic Logic of Suicide Terrorism* (New York: Random House, 2005).

6   Wars

Plain-talking General Tommy Franks, who led the US invasion of
Iraq in 2003, described it as a 'catastrophic success'.[1] We agree.
His words also ring true for the conventional military phase of the
first US-led invasion in the name of the War on Terror – Afghanistan. Decisive battlefield success was not followed by the securing
of long-term political goals. 'So it goes' is likely to be the weary
response of students of military history.

An unwinnable war?

Operation Infinite Justice – quickly renamed Operation Enduring
Freedom to avoid religious offence – began within a month of
9/11. On 7 October 2001, US and UK air-strikes took place in
Afghanistan, and operations followed on the ground against the
Taliban using local allies (the Northern Alliance). At home and
abroad political support for the invasion was high. In Resolutions
1368 and 1373 the UN implicitly affirmed the US claim of the
right of self-defence in attacking the Afghanistan base of the 9/11
terrorists. Domestically, even longstanding opponents of President
Bush and of US military interventionism considered the decision
to go into Afghanistan to destroy the threat posed by al-Qaeda to
be a Just War: it was self-defence, al-Qaeda's aims appeared absolute, its willingness to inflict violence were extreme, and dialogue
seemed impossible.

Within nine weeks of 9/11, the US-backed Northern Alliance forces had 'liberated' the capital Kabul from the rule of the Taliban. Hope was in the air. It even seemed likely that bin Laden and the other leaders of al-Qaeda would be rounded up or killed. Ten years on, it all *feels* so different. As the endgame approaches in Afghanistan, the dominant feelings are disappointment and anxiety, not hope. The death of bin Laden does not change that, except for the hopelessly naive. The basics of the situation will remain in place for some time to come.

As the months of occupation and pacification of the historically impregnable land of Afghanistan turned into years, some of the oldest lessons of war had to be relearned, and at great and growing cost. Perhaps the most obvious, and most deadly, was the lesson the International Security Assistance Force (ISAF)[2] learned, namely that there are no last moves in military tactics, and that counters (sometimes cheap ones such as improvised explosive devices) can be devised by clever opponents against those with far more advanced military technology. This tactical lesson went alongside the growing strategic appreciation that to successfully occupy territory won in battle is sometimes both more difficult and more costly than winning it in the first place. The former liberators were soon transformed into an occupying foreign force not only in the minds of remnant Taliban fighters, but also the non-Taliban Afghans who wanted to join in resisting the invaders.

As the nasty, brutish, and long struggle against the Afghan insurgents dragged on, and as the original mission of ousting al-Qaeda crept into building a post-Taliban political reality, the Just War banner became tattered. Evidence mounted that NATO forces – and private military contractors associated with the challenge of postwar reconstruction – mistakenly ('collaterally') but routinely killed civilians and not their intended military targets. Documents disclosed in 2010 on the WikiLeaks website give numerous examples of such errors. In June 2007, for one, US Navy Seals fired rockets at a suspected al-Qaeda commander, but a classified document reports: 'They did not find the commander. But they did find that seven children had been killed in the strike.'[3] From whatever causes, 2,800 civilians were reported to have been killed in the conflict in 2010.[4] Concerns about the conduct of the war, as well as doubts about its achievements and costs have contributed to undermining the war's legitimacy in the minds of many ISAF members.

On top of the growing casualty lists of occupying (especially US and British) troops, the mounting toll of Afghan civilians killed and injured, and the war-weariness in America and Britain, there is the stark fact of the strategic failure to defeat the Taliban after nearly ten years. The liberation of Kabul proved not to be the pivotal moment of victory, like the raising of the flag above the Reichstag in 1945; it was merely the end of the beginning. The next major phase in the war, the pursuit and elimination of al-Qaeda, soon became fatally undermined by the shift of US focus to the planning and execution of the war in Iraq. As a result of opening this unnecessary second front, special operations forces in Afghanistan became depleted, while the number of troops generally available was radically reduced below the level deemed sufficient by senior US generals. Usama escaped, nation-building proved fragile, and there was no direct exit-plan. Afghanistan became a classic 'couldn't win/couldn't leave' situation, bringing back haunting memories of the Vietnam War in the late 1960s. This was the legacy the largely discredited president George W. Bush left his successor, Barack Obama, at the start of 2009.

Not for the first time, an incoming US president promised to put an end to a war; and again, not for the first time, he escalated it. Echoes of the old rallying-cry, 'One last push!' could be heard across the mountains of Afghanistan, except now it was an exhortation to back 'the Surge'. The final results of this strategy are not yet in, and military experts on the ground or in TV studios or in armchairs, are divided. One astute observer, Joe Klein, wrote in *Time* magazine at the start of 2011 that important tactical successes had been achieved against the Taliban. He listed: an area 'successfully cleared'; 'significant weapons caches and bomb-making factories' found; 'markets . . . reopening'; 'hundreds of Afghan civilians' being willing to work for the Americans where in the past they had been too frightened of the Taliban; successful Afghan National Army (ANA) patrols; 'the first stirrings of local governance'; 'elders' looking for more practical support from the United States, and more.[5] So far, so good for the Surge. But remember Vietnam.

An important lesson of modern war, bitterly learned in Vietnam between 1965 and 1975, is the need to interrogate all real-time reporting. Yes, territory might have been gained, but are the gains only temporary? Yes, weapons might have been found, but what about new sources? Yes, markets are opening, but is the enemy standing back playing a waiting game? Yes, many Taliban have been killed, at all levels, but estimates of enemy casualties always contain a mix of hope and guesswork. Yes, the Afghanisation of security patrols is growing, but can the ANA continue in the absence of US backup? Real-time war reporting always demands a respectful, inquisitive, 'but'.

On the political side, there is less disagreement about the lack of progress. Of central significance have been the growing strains between the regime of President Hamid Karzi and his Western backers, and its limited legitimacy and authority in many parts of Afghanistan. The war is unwinnable in the sense of turning the country into a model liberal democracy in any foreseeable time-frame, given the relative lack of economic resources and social capital. Again, the memories of the corrupt and fragile puppet-regimes in Saigon 40 years ago have faded when we need them to be clear. Also reminiscent of that era is the decline of support for continuing the war on the part of US opinion (not to mention that of its allies). The commitment of NATO countries to supply forces to ISAF continues to shrink: casualties, costs, disappointments, and strains are the drumbeat, and departure is the goal.

While the resilience of the Taliban continues, alongside the fragility of external efforts at nation-building, the situation in neighbouring Pakistan deteriorates. Suicide bombers, terrorist threats, and assassinations pile pressure on a political system that struggles also to cope with the aftermath of natural hardships, such as the disastrous floods of 2010. Nobody is forecasting a speedy return to stability in Pakistan. The Taliban is a significant nuisance in the north of the country (Waziristan), where there are also elements of al-Qaeda following their escape from Afghanistan; this region has threatened to become a major front in the War on Terror for a long time, and not only for the government in Islamabad. We will return to Pakistan again; for the moment we simply endorse Joe Klein's view of the need to assess the struggle in Afghanistan in relation to the wider South Asian security problem, and recognise that instability in Pakistan is 'potentially the world's greatest security threat'.

One matter in the Afghanistan situation seems certain as the tenth anniversary of 9/11 approaches, and that is the withdrawal of increasing numbers of US and other NATO troops. President Obama's original declaratory policy when the Surge began was to start withdrawing US troops from July 2011. Given the nature of this promise, and with a presidential election in the following year, something would have been done, even if the first withdrawals had been largely symbolic. With the situation on the ground still being difficult, however, senior US military officers indicated their preference for a slow withdrawal, to consolidate gains. With this in mind, and the old rule that a Democrat president should never appear weak on national defence (and especially when the right-wing of the Republican Party is resurgent), Obama retreated from his original statement and said that US combat forces would now remain until the end of 2014. There is a much more radical move on the president's part possible, even if it seems highly unlikely. With an election looming, Obama could go for broke, minimise the time of transition to the Afghanisation of security matters, and withdraw US forces rapidly and almost completely. The president could declare that Afghanistan is free of al-Qaeda, that security will henceforth be the responsibility of the ANA, that the country is on the road to peace and democracy and that, from here on, the journey is, properly, almost entirely the Afghan people's responsibility. In other words, declare 'victory' and leave.

2012 is election year after all, and a good time for a president to bring troops home.

As this war begins to outlast even the failed Soviet invasion, Obama has somewhat more wriggle room than Mikhail Gorbachev had in the late 1980s. While the Taliban has recorded operational successes, it has also made political mistakes. Many Afghans prefer the opportunities opened up by modern democratic society, and there has been no mass mobilisation behind the Taliban's flirtation with al-Qaeda and the agenda of the global jihadists. Furthermore, the one certain appeal of the Taliban, as a focus of resistance to foreign interference, will decline as the foreign forces fade into the background and drift home. Many Afghans want neither foreign invaders nor a corrupt proxy government; they want national sovereignty, law and order, and uncorrupt governance (without too much government). There are grounds here for negotiations, even with elements of the Taliban and their supporters. All is not lost for Afghanistan politically,[6] but the future remains full of anxiety.

It should have been so different. It looked so promising at the end of 2001. What went wrong?

Hubris

In the planning of the invasion, and in the early years, there was altogether too much overconfidence based on heavy military power and technological superiority. The world's then hyper-power opposed a 'backward' country. The leaders in Washington and London were driven by hubris, not informed by history. We need not rehearse the story of Afghanistan as the graveyard of foreign invaders over the centuries, but we do need to emphasise, following the teaching of the greatest theorist of war, Carl von Clausewitz, that war is 'movement in a resistant medium' and 'friction' plays havoc with early plans and the grandest hopes. The White House was not open to tough questions about the unpredictability of war in the emotion-drenched weeks after 9/11.

The absence of an exit-strategy

The history of war is full of generals whose focus on what they will do to the enemy pushes out all serious consideration of what the enemy might do to them. Military interventions/invasions require not only a plan of attack, but also an exit-strategy in case things go wrong. In Afghanistan, there was no exit-strategy beyond having the troops return in triumph following a classic military victory; in the event, without a carefully considered set of goals, the invading forces and their political leaders became inexorably drawn into broader nation-building objectives. In August 2009, Imran Khan, the former Pakistani cricket captain and founder of the political party Movement for Justice, was asked about his solution to the war in Afghanistan. He answered: 'There has to be an exit-strategy; NATO has to leave Afghanistan. Otherwise more and more people will be dying, most of them innocent.' (His interviewer correctly reminded him that they were also 'dying at the hands of the Taliban'.) Khan's point was that Afghanistan had to be an Afghan matter. Such an option was essentially available from the start. The initial invasion could have been carried out alongside a timetabled withdrawal plan; this could have identified a limit of six months after the fall of Kabul. There could have been a commitment to put in place some preliminary infrastructure for development and political reconstruction, but making it clear that governance was to be an Afghan responsibility, that further aid depended on progress, and that any return of al-Qaeda would result in airborne 'shock and awe'. In other words: limited war, limited aims, limited occupation.

Putting boots on the ground

If one is not to seek an early exit from an intervention or invasion, then one must be prepared to occupy the relevant territory for the long haul; this needs the deployment of enough soldiers in all key tactical and strategic locations. There is much talk these days about networks, globalisation, de-territorialisation, and so on, but the hearts and minds one has to win over exist in specific sites, and boots have to be firmly planted on the ground in those specific sites to influence those hearts and minds. This, in turn, means that there is a high human cost to be borne if things do not turn out well. Even if they do turn out well, a different sort of price might have to be paid; this is the sort paid by the victors over Naziism, who had to deploy continental-sized armies in central Europe for several generations. If these prices cannot be contemplated at the outset, it is best not to become involved in the first place. The 30,000 troops of the Surge in December 2009 were too few, too late.

Avoiding ethnocentrism

The history of war is full of military mistakes, political failures, and unsuccessful strategies because of ethnocentrism. This refers to the inability of leaders, planners, and publics to understand the political and other realities inside the heads of their opponents – and friends – because of cultural biases, limited knowledge, and various psychological predispositions. When this is the case, the interpretive ability and predictive potential on which successful planning and policy depends is seriously degraded.[7] In the war in Afghanistan, lack of knowledge and understanding imperilled postwar political reconstruction, led to the underestimation of nationalist feelings, and produced ill-judged nation-building ideas and counter-insurgency operations. In addition, miscalculations were made on wider regional matters, notably in relation to Pakistan, India, and Iran.

By the time major foreign troop withdrawals will have taken place at the end of 2014, Afghanistan will not have had time to become radically different from today. It might not have any, or many, al-Qaeda, but it will not be Taliban-free, democratic, and predictably stable. The war was not winnable as conceived because the peace that was envisaged was not achievable. It is now a matter of salvaging scraps. There are periodic rumours of Western contacts with the Taliban and the possibility of talks. A political process might be fashioned to cover the exit, but the stronger NATO determination becomes to pull out its troops by a certain date, and the more urgent the talks with locals, the clearer will be the endgame for the Taliban. Their strategy will be to wait and see, fairly confident that in the time-frame envisaged they need have little fear of the Karzai regime or its successors hunkering down, constructing a modern state, and winning hearts and minds. There is an obvious disjunction between the need for foreign troops to occupy territory effectively for security-building, and the desire of their political leaders to withdraw them. It is the historic predicament of interveners. US forces are there for the short term, however extended that might be, while the Taliban will remain, in some form, for the foreseeable future. As the British journalist Mehidi Hasan put it in August 2010, 'All the Taliban have to do to win is not to lose – and they're not losing'.[8]

An unwon peace

The second invasion of the War on Terror also began with considerable military success. The invasion of Iraq was launched on 20 March 2003 and the capital, Baghdad, was occupied by early April (the symbolic toppling of Saddam's statue took place on 9 April). This outcome of the campaign was not a surprise given the disparity of forces, but again a resounding military victory failed to deliver an equally resounding political success.

The Iraq War was always controversial, and it remains so. Before it began, there were protests against it across the world; but there was also plenty of support, especially in America and the UK.[9] Many believed what their governments told them about the threat represented by Saddam Hussein, once the West's dictator-of-choice in the region. As the postwar situation in Iraq erupted into massive violence between internal factions, as well as between 'insurgents' and Western forces, there was a steady decline in support for the war.[10] Even prominent supporters of Bush's neo-conservative project had defected by 2006. As the years went on, the original motives and goals of the war were increasingly questioned, as well as current strategies and tactics. But in America many remained loyal to the president, tied by the emotions of 9/11 and in the tragic grip of the old feeling that 'sacrifice creates value' – the compulsion to believe that because the sacrifice in life was so great, the cause must also be valued.

The Iraq War and its aftermath are a study in tragedy, calling for a latter-day Shakespeare to dramatise the failings of the two leading characters, Bush and Blair. As it unfolded, the plot of the war exposed three such failings, as detailed below.

Leadership

The Iraq War was a mistake waiting to happen for the Bush administration and its neoconservative base.[11] The neoconservatives, in and out of the administration, had long favoured an invasion of Iraq as part of establishing a stronger US military presence across the Middle East; this would serve US geopolitical interests in securing oil and stability, and in defending Israel. The president also had personal motives, relating to his father's conflict with Saddam. 9/11, therefore, offered the opportunity to act against Iraq, pushed along by drivers that long predated it. The nearly 3,000 deaths that day added emotional as well as strategic imperatives; the latter were the (false) beliefs about Saddam's support for al-Qaeda and (false) beliefs about his possession of weapons of mass destruction (WMD). Donald Rumsfeld, the defense secretary, has recently written that despite the Department of Defense being fully occupied in the days after 9/11, the president started asking him within 15 *days* to look at US military plans on Iraq, and come up with 'creative' options.[12] Even before the first invasion of the War on Terror had begun, therefore, the White House was planning to open up a second front against another Muslim country.

The invasion of Iraq has often been described as a 'war of choice' for the United States; but was it? Arguably, it *would have been* a war of choice for an administration comprising open-minded and wise strategic thinkers and political analysts. But for the actually-existing White House it was an ideological and psychological reflex action. Bush and his most influential advisers were driven on by neoconservative convictions about the utility of force, US superiority, their convictions that they could reorder reality in the Middle East, individual and collective psychological predispositions going back to the first Gulf War, 'groupthink' dynamics, and emotions still raw from the 9/11 outrages.

In the UK, Prime Minister Blair and his select advisers had more choice, but once it had been decided that being Washington's best ally was the priority, British options were limited to *how* rather than *whether* to act against Iraq.[13] In order for this to be possible, strategic facts had to fit (or be psychologically compatible) with Blair's political preferences rather than vice versa. Blair's self-confidence as a leader (a trait that is often synonymous with self-delusion) was boosted by his evident pride in his championing of liberal internationalism in the conflicts in Sierra Leone and Kosovo in particular. Blair, like his friend Bush, had some anxieties about winning the war despite the technological disparities between the adversaries – though they should not have; but neither seems to have worried about winning the peace – though they should have. Like other leaders in the past, they erroneously equated military victory with political success. Wise leaders know that military campaigns are not won until the peace that follows is a success. War is chancy, but the real challenge begins, not ends, with the flowers and cheers and victory parades.

Key decisions about Iraq were taken without awkward questions being satisfactorily addressed by leaders impatient to go to war. What is more, having set their course in this way, their subsequent conduct led to an undermining of trust in government and institutions. In the United States, there was an unacceptable assertion of executive power.[14] Two examples suffice. First, the president secretly authorised the National Security Agency to conduct 'warrantless wiretapping' of phone calls in direct contravention of a criminal law; and second, the Pentagon's spooky Total Information Awareness (TIA) plan to mine computer data threatened effectively to destroy all privacy. In the UK there was an equally troubling assertion of prime ministerial power, as Blair rode roughshod over established procedures. The country's most senior civil servant, Sir Gus O'Donnell, told the Chilcot inquiry in 2011 (set up to investigate the war) that the cabinet should have been told by Blair (the 'ministerial code is very clear' on such matters) of the doubts of the attorney general (the leading law officer) about the legality of invading Iraq. The cabinet was not shown the written advice as Blair apparently did not believe the cabinet was 'a safe space' in which to debate going to war. 'That was one of the reasons why the former prime minister preferred informal meetings with no record taken', said O'Donnell.[15] When democratic leaders cannot trust their closest colleagues, how can they expect their citizens to trust them?

Strategic judgement

The disregard of their own area specialists by those responsible for strategic policy in the relevant areas is an old and paradoxical story in the history of 'foreign' affairs.[16] This was the case yet again in the Iraq War. Relevant State Department specialists felt shunned, while Arab experts associated with the UK Foreign Office were dismissed as the 'camel corps' by Blairites. State Department concerns emerged, for example, after it was reported in 2003 that a year-long study by the State Department had predicted many of the problems that bedevilled the US-led occupation of Iraq following the fall of Baghdad.[17] The Foreign Office concerns emerged following a 'searing letter' signed by 52 former diplomats, specialists on the Arab world, critical of Blair's policies in the Middle East; they complained that Middle East expertise available in the government was ignored.[18] In both cases, a culture of disdain for independent analysis and expertise took hold and specialists in the diplomacy of the region were sidelined.

Specialists in intelligence were not. The full story remains to be told about the 'known unknowns' of the military threat represented by Saddam's regime. The evidence so far suggests that the main intelligence services in the West did have at least some evidence that could be deployed to confirm the picture of the threat that had already been constructed in the minds of key decision-makers in Washington and London. But the claims that Iraq had WMD, and that there was a positive link between Saddam's regime and al-Qaeda have both been exposed as false.

The first claim, about WMD (see p. 85), was challenged at the time by reliable evidence, and, after the war, by the evidence of everybody's eyes. Before the war, UN inspection teams under Hans Blix were able to do their job largely unhindered, though without being able to satisfy everyone of their suspicions. But for leaders rushing to war, the very absence of evidence was yet more proof of the duplicity of the Iraqi regime. Interestingly, the ability to disregard discrepant information continued after the war, on the part of those who continued to support its goals. Philip Bobbitt, for example, adviser to the White House, the Senate, and the State Department, mentions the United Nations Special Commission (UNSCOM) only once in a nearly 700-page tome, and then to record that a former head, Rolf Ekeus, said it 'trivializes' the US-led invasion to 'say that it was about finding and seizing Saddam Hussein's *existing* stocks of WMD'.[19]

No policy was without risk or moral consequence, of course, but Saddam could have been contained without the need for war. At the beginning of 2011, regime change was brought about in Tunisia and Egypt; it was achieved 'from below', and at vastly lower human cost. Only time will tell how permanent these changes in a democratic direction have been, but this remains also the case in devastated Iraq.

The second claim, a relationship between Saddam and al-Qaeda, looked implausible at the time, and it has subsequently become known how over-cooked it was by the Bush administration. Richard Clarke, a leading adviser to several US administrations on al-Qaeda, was asked to advise Bush, in the days immediately following 9/11, whether there was a link between al-Qaeda and Iraq. This is how the 9/11 Commission described what happened next:

> Clarke's office sent a memo to Rice on September 18, titled 'Survey of Intelligence Information on Any Iraq Involvement in the September 11 Attacks.' Rice's chief staffer on

Afghanistan, Zalmay Khalilzad, concurred in its conclusion that only some anecdotal evidence linked Iraq to al Qaeda. The memo found no 'compelling case' that Iraq had either planned or perpetrated the attacks.[20]

In his book *Against all Enemies*, Clarke also notes how the advice of Charles Duelfer, the leading American expert on Iraqi WMD, was ignored before the invasion and afterwards.[21]

Not only was the rush to war facilitated by a flawed political reading of the available intelligence, the very idea of a war in Iraq represented a major strategic distraction from what was then the 'centre of gravity' (to use a Clausewitzian term) in the War on Terror, namely Afghanistan. The invasion and occupation of Iraq took troops away from clearing al-Qaeda from Afghanistan, and possibly fatally weakening the Taliban; it distracted special operations forces from seeking bin Laden following his escape to Tora Bora; it drew terrorists into Iraq, where there had previously been none other than Saddam and his henchmen; and, in a much-used term, it turned Iraq into a 'recruiting sergeant' for jihadists everywhere.

How different the situation might be today had the pacification of Afghanistan continued in the absence of the massive distraction of a disastrous war next door. To make matters worse, this distraction affected wider geopolitical developments. We will return to this in Part II.

Finally in our assessment of strategic misjudgements, we point to the grave issue of 'preventive war'.[22] Such a doctrine is contrary to the UN Charter and international law. The UN, as a result of the collapse of international order leading to the Second World War, made preventive war illegal. Only wars of self-defence (where an attack has occurred or is imminent) or wars authorised by the Security Council, were deemed to be legal. The latter was not achieved in 2003, despite Blair's efforts. He took a massive diplomatic gamble (promising the Europeans he would deliver the US to the UN, and promising the Americans he would get Europe on side) but by early March 2003 it was clear that the 'coalition of the willing' would not be going into battle with legal authority and the consent of the UN Security Council.

As part of the 'everything changed' agenda after 9/11, it was the view of Bush and Blair that international politics had entered a new era of threat, demanding new thinking. In particular, new threats from international terrorists (willing to inflict mass casualties), rogue states (especially Bush's 'axis of evil'), and the spread of WMD (including the possibility of their possession by terrorists) led the Bush administration (with their unilateralist poster-boy, John Bolton, leading from the front at the UN) to consider the old rules of international politics to be anachronistic. As the president put it in his State of the Union speech on 29 January 2002:

> I will not wait on events while dangers gather. I will not stand by as peril draws closer and closer. The United States of America will not permit the world's most dangerous regimes to threaten us with the world's most destructive weapons.

For the Bush administration and its supporters, preventive actions were legitimate to stop the dangerous threats of the present century becoming a reality. Vice-President Cheney went as far as to suggest that preventive war is reasonable even when the possibility of an attack on the US is as low as 1 per cent.[23]

Ends and means

All the main players in Washington and London responsible for the invasion of Iraq continue to assert that what they decided was 'right', even if some information on which the decision was made was flawed, and the costs proved to be much higher than expected. The mantra 'the world is better without Saddam Hussein' was repeated ad nauseam in self-justification. Had a stable peace followed the successful military campaign in 2003 these decision-makers would have naturally soaked up all the attendant glory; it follows, therefore, that they should accept the responsibility for what went wrong: the costs in lives (including Iraqis')[24] and treasure, the declining trust in government, the rents in the fabric of international law, the dented reputations internationally of both countries, and the bloody chaos of postwar Iraq.

Following the brief moment of victory over Saddam, the situation in Iraq deteriorated. It became the furthest imaginable from the image of a flower-strewn peace, with victory parades and honour, dreamed of by armchair warriors in the months before the fighting began. Looting rather than order dominated TV news, and the Coalition Provincial Authority (CPA) proved largely helpless. Chaos, insurgency, expanding casualty lists, and civil war among religious and other factions followed. The peace was unwon, and remains so. Iraq today is deemed to be a fledgling democracy, but 4,000 civilians were reported killed in factional conflict in 2010.[25] And around this fragile state is a near-nuclear Iran, a warring Afghanistan, a fractious Pakistan, and a Middle East in flux.

The peace was not won for many reasons, some of which have been suggested above, but one critical matter was the failure of the victorious powers to have consistently had ends and means in concert. If political goals are pursued by means that represent their opposite then the very objective being sought will be prejudiced.[26] A few illustrations will suffice: aggression in international politics cannot be delegitimised if the principle of 'preventive war' is legitimised; claims cannot be made on behalf of something called 'the international community' if its institutions (notably the UN) are disregarded; the rule of law will not become universally embedded if the most powerful state does not scrupulously follow it; and advocates of human rights should not engage in human wrongs (such as prisoner abuse).

Old democracies expect the best from their leaders and, in this regard, the Iraq War was a tragedy in many acts. In the most high-publicity excesses of the war, notably the photographs of prisoner abuse, those in power tend to blame the 'bad apples' far down the chain of command. Of course, participation in excesses of one sort or another involves some choice, and those involved should pay some price. But even more so those responsible for putting people in terrible situations should also pay a price. 'War is hell', General Sherman said. War coarsens humane sensibility (when it does not break it entirely). War is to blame for bad things happening, and our leaders were to blame for this one.

Further reading

On the lessons of strategic history, there is no better starting point than Bernard Brodie, *War and Politics* (Basingstoke: Macmillan, 1973), and Edward M. Earle ed., *Makers of Modern Strategy: Military Thought from Machiavelli to Hitler* (Princeton, NJ: Princeton University Press, 1943). The strongest pre-invasion case for the Iraq War was Kenneth M. Pollock, *The Case for Invading Iraq* (New York: Random House, 2002); for a strong case against, see Andrew Bacevich, *The New American Militarism: How Americans are Seduced by War* (New York: Oxford University Press, 2005). There have been several excellent articles on the manipulation of intelligence, including Lawrence Freedman (2005) 'War in Iraq: Selling the Threat', *Survival*, 46(2): 7–49, and Robert Jervis (2006) 'Reports, Politics and Intelligence Failures: The Case of Iraq', *The Journal of Strategic Studies*, 29(1): 3–52. For an account of the 9/11 wars against the backdrop of the continuities in US foreign policy, see Timothy Lynch and Robert Singh, *After Bush: The Case for Continuity in American Foreign Policy* (Cambridge: Cambridge University Press, 2008).

Part II

Security and world order

7 America

'We are all Americans now!' was a common refrain at the end of the last century. It was not that in the beginning all the world was America, as Thomas Paine expressed it, but there was a sense in which all the world had *become or was becoming* America. Literature, film, social commentary, internet technology, iMacs and iBooks, Microsoft, and Starbucks, were all produced in America and consumed by the world. And US leadership went beyond economic and cultural globalisation. After 1945 a large part of the world – and more after 1989 – became joined to America through bilateral and multilateral security arrangements. In this chapter we will see how far the post-9/11 world order represents a break from the US-led order of the previous half-century.

From both sides

In the course of reading this book, the reader will encounter many criticisms of the choices US leaders made during 9/11 + 10. We make these while recognising that America continues to be an *idea* as well as a polity to which countless victims flock, seeking refuge from tyranny and hunger. The United States' capacity for economic regeneration is such that it is one of the few countries to treat immigration as a resource rather than a burden. One wonders how many self-proclaimed 'anti-Americans' in places like Iran, Pakistan, and Iraq, would pass up the opportunity to join generations of Poles, Italians, Cubans, and others who have been drawn to 'the land of the free'. The US academic Reza Aslan amusingly recalls that he has watched Muslims chant 'Death to America!' on the streets of Tehran, and then 'privately beg' him to help them get a visa to the United States.[1] Many Muslim asylum seekers have chosen the United States as the destination for their hopes for themselves and their families, rather than countries at the heart of the Islamic world. And despite the catastrophic failings of earlier military interventions – in the name of human rights or disarmament – it was to America that the Arab world turned when Libyan citizens were exposed to state terror by the Qaddafi regime in 2011.

In the immediate aftermath of 9/11 many countries declared their solidarity with America, and no leader did it with more earnestness than the UK prime minister Tony Blair. Sixty-seven Britons died that day, and for this and historic reasons Blair declared that Britain stood 'shoulder to shoulder' with America. Even *Le Monde*, on its 12 September front page, repeated the cry heard elsewhere in earlier years, but not in Paris: 'We are all Americans now'.[2] Beyond Europe, a similar sentiment was expressed, as groups of ordinary citizens in far off places held vigils for the people killed in New York, Washington, and Pennsylvania.

By March 2004, *Le Monde* ran a different kind of story. The title posed the question, 'Are we still "all American"?'. The paper's editor, who had also written the earlier article, argued that we 'must remain "American"', while acknowledging that the ties that bound Europe and America together had come under strain. For this condition he blamed two major aspects of US foreign policy, pre-emption in the security sphere and protectionism in the trade sphere. Together these constituted 'a threat to the very foundation of the historical alliance between the U.S. and Europe'.[3]

When considering such judgements about America and the world after 9/11, three general considerations need to be borne in mind. First, media headlines exalting turning-points in the global view of American leadership – from injured ally to irresponsible hyperpower back to global protector (again) – significantly exaggerate the changes in US policy while obscuring the continuities. Second, commentaries on America often overlook the crucial distinction between America as a nation and a society, and the conduct of the institutions of the US *state*. Putting it plainly: Washington is not America (we might add that the presidency is not the government, and Fox is not public opinion). At the same time, the executive and political and legal institutions of the state retain a degree of popular legitimacy, which is the reason why it is impossible to decouple the policies and preferences of the 'administration' in question and the concerns of 'ordinary' Americans. Third, when probing the United States and its purposes, it is important to consider both sides of the moral register: America as a progressive ideal where liberties are valued and protected at home, and America the militarist superpower that sometimes adopts a brutal foreign policy. It is a society that refers to its political representatives as 'lawmakers', and a superpower that has shown disdain for international legal rules.

'Why do they hate us?'

9/11 revealed just how contested American-led globalisation had become. Not everyone wept for the victims of 9/11. A few celebrated openly, responding to Usama bin Laden's call to dance on the grave of every dead American (ignoring the inconvenient fact that individuals from around 60 nationalities had been massacred). Others were cautiously critical. The *London Review of Books* published reactions to 9/11 shortly afterwards, and the highly regarded classicist, Professor Mary Beard, wrote that 'however you dress it up, the United States had it coming'. Bullies in world politics, she added, 'will in the end pay the price'. The following issue contained a riposte from Marjorie Perloff, Professor of English at Stanford University; Perloff admitted that the United States had committed atrocities but asked, 'Does it therefore follow that "the United States had it coming?" And which one of us in the United States are included?'[4] For every Mary Beard (or Tariq Ali) who regarded the terrorist attacks as a kind of 'blowback', there were others such as Christopher Hitchens and Samuel Huntingdon who were equally misguided in regarding Islamism as the 'new fascism'.

Other intellectuals refused such a polarised choice. The French deconstructionist Jacques Derrida suggested a way of traversing the boundary between *being* and *hating* America. After such an assault, he argued that people had a duty to show unconditional compassion toward America and Americans; at the same time, he said it must be recognised that the attack was 'a response to the state terrorism of the United States and its allies'.[5] State terrorism is not something the US government has ever admitted to. As we pointed out in Chapter 3 the State Department defines terrorism as politically motivated violence committed by sub-national groups.

Many Americans, convinced of their society's essential goodness, find the criticism to which their country is regularly subjected by foreigners, even ostensible friends, to be incomprehensible. Brought up with assumptions about the land of the free, the home of the brave, and the shining city on the hill, the national ideology insists that America is a force for good in the world. Against such powerful socialisation, Americans find it truly shocking when told by one of their own leading intellectuals, Susan Sontag, to confront their own history of terror, namely that inflicted upon the indigenous peoples of America by waves of 'settlers'.[6] Far more congenial is the self-image projected by Madeleine Albright, former secretary of state. She spoke for most of her fellow citizens when she said: 'If we have to use force, it is because we are America. We are the indispensable nation. We stand tall. We see further into the future.'[7] Self-righteousness allied to a flawed self-image are always dangerous foundations from which to engage the world.

Prior to 9/11 President George W. Bush was widely thought to be an 'accidental president' (to quote the title of a book that made *Newsweek*'s front cover). He was also, initially, expected to be very much a president who would concentrate on domestic rather than foreign affairs. There were jibes in the liberal media about the 'gone fishing' sign over the Oval Office. All this was brought to an abrupt end with the terror attacks of 9/11. Having appeared to be hesitant and ineffective in the early days of his first administration, George W. Bush grew in stature as he took on the persona of a war president. His approval ratings soared to a high of 90 per cent at the end of October 2001 (with only 7 per cent disapproving) and the ratings remained positive during the rest of his first term.[8] Al-Qaeda's actions were potentially the making of the 43rd president of the United States, but by the end of his second term much of America's international reputation had been squandered, and the president's own domestic support badly dented. Republican candidates in the 2008 election did not seek him out for photo-opportunities.

Given the national self-image discussed above, many bewildered Americans asked, 'Why do they hate us?' as they stared at the images of 9/11. This question formed the centrepiece of President Bush's address to the joint session of Congress on 20 September. It was, he said, because 'they hate what they see right here in this chamber, a democratically elected government'; 'they hate our freedoms'; and 'they hope that America grows fearful'. Underpinning the president's response was a clear – but flawed – understanding of both 'America' and the world from which 'they' had emerged.

In presenting 9/11 as a struggle between good and evil, democracy and totalitarianism, and civility and barbarism, it was logical for the US administration, as the next step, to declare war on 'the enemies of freedom' who had 'declared war on our country'. The limits of our language are the limits of our world, Wittgenstein taught us. In this regard, a society in trauma, like America after 9/11, contrasted the loss of 'our' innocent lives with 'their' nihilistic disregard; in so doing, all the qualifications that Bush and other leaders made about not being at war with Islam tended to be swept away. The distinction made by Bush and Blair in their declaratory policies between 'moderates' and 'jihadists' became marginalised by the politics of the War on Terror.

One answer to the question 'Why do they hate us?' was the one highlighted in Chapter 5: 'they' are 'evil'. *They-ing is always* a dangerous way of engaging with a complex world,[9] and this construction of the Islamic world relied on distortions and simplifications which will be addressed in the next chapter. Despite the fact that CNN's strap line for foreign news stories is 'beyond borders', the paucity of analysis of terrorist atrocities – from the Oklahoma bombings to 9/11 – was a contributing factor in the construction of the 'War on Terror'. As media specialists argue, the framing of 'Islamic terror' was sufficiently strong that it enabled different threats to be connected in their meaning and countered by the same narrative and strategy.

Following his 2002 State of the Union address, the president's militarised response to 9/11 became elevated to the status of a 'doctrine'. George W. Bush sought to widen 'the enemies of freedom' to include not just al-Qaeda but the states who offered terrorists protection. States like North Korea, Iran, and Iraq, the president said 'constitute an axis of evil, arming to threaten the peace of the world . . . these regimes pose a grave and growing danger'.[10] The acquisition of so-called WMD by failed states, or even the intent to develop any element of these weapons, now constituted a legitimate *casus belli* in the minds of leading neoconservatives in the Bush administration. Leading liberal academics and intellectuals joined in, claiming that the United States and its allies had a 'duty to prevent' unstable authoritarian regimes from weaponising research into nuclear, chemical, or biological weapons. Many of the same 'B52 liberals' who, in the 1990s, advocated armed humanitarian intervention, were now adapting the rationale for how and why the West had to impose order upon the so-called 'arc of crisis' across Africa, the Middle East, and South-East Asia.

Uncritical and ill-informed answers to the question 'Why do they hate us?' – not least who *they* are? – paved the way for a redefinition of America's role in the world. For neoconservatives, September 11 was a wake-up call in that it showed in a dramatic fashion that the world was a very dangerous place and that it could get more dangerous if no firm action was taken promptly. As President Bush put it: 'We understand history has called us into action and we are not going to miss that opportunity to make the world more peaceful and more free.'[11]

The ideology of neoconservatism relies heavily on an imperial logic. Rooted in exceptionalism – the belief that America is qualitatively different from other developed nations due to its unique origins and historical evolution – and a vision of America as a redeeming force in international politics, this doctrine endorses the projection of United States power as the primary instrument of change. In so doing, the Bush doctrine was an explicit challenge to what had previously been thought of as the settled norms of the UN order in relation to the prohibitions on the use of force and the idea that all countries are equal in so far as they share the same prerogatives as sovereign states.

The imperial ambition of the neoconservatives was exacerbated by the absence of balancing behaviour on the part of other states in the international system. Was this because America was regarded by others as a benign hegemon? Or was it that they feared the consequences of not being seen to be on-side? The United States, after all, held a massive advantage over all others. Its GDP roughly equalled that of China, Japan, Germany, Russia, France, and Britain combined; that is, one quarter of the global GDP. Moreover, US expenditure on defence was and remains the highest in the world – amounting to close to half of global military spending.[12] Thanks to this material preponderance, the United States possesses the capability of projecting massive military power virtually anywhere in the world. This encourages US leaders to think of their country as a 'system-shaper'; the earlier words of Albright spoke directly to that belief. 'Being number one', observes US foreign policy specialist Michael Cox, 'generates its own kind of imperial outlook'. Most members of the Washington foreign policy establishment, he adds, 'tend to see themselves as masters of a universe in which the United States has a very special part to play by virtue of its unique history, its huge capabilities and its accumulated experience of running the world for the last 50 years'.[13]

Why do they hate us? Other than the 19 young Arabs who hijacked the airliners, and the hard core membership of al-Qaeda, few actually *hated* the United States prior to 9/11. And immediately afterwards, as the quotation from *Le Monde* suggested, America attracted a good deal of sympathy. But by the end of the second Bush administration, it was all rather different. As a result of the convergence of brute state power with the neoconservatives' plan for a new world order, most of America's allies were, at best, begrudging associates, while new enemies and even more critics had been created. America's legitimacy as a global hegemon, like that of al-Qaeda as the leader of the global jihad, took a sharp nose-dive in the second half of the post-9/11 decade.

'What are we fighting for?'

The call to arms in the United States after 9/11 met little domestic opposition. For neoconservative ideologues in Washington DC it was an opportunity as well as a threat, and polls showed that millions of ordinary Americans concurred with the decision to respond forcefully to the attack on the United States by initiating a war against the Taliban: well over 80 per cent of those polled supported the administration.[14] Among public intellectuals in the country, the view of Jean Bethke Elshtain, an ethicist, political theorist, and student of democracy, was particularly interesting in itself and also as a barometer of the time. She argued that 'it would have been a flight from the serious business of politics – to fail to respond'.[15] In a moving passage, she argued that the experience of witnessing horrific violence prevents people from being good neighbours, devoted mothers, and concerned citizens. 'We cannot', in her words, 'reveal the fullness of our being, including our deep sociality, if airplanes are flying into buildings and cities become piles of rubble composed in part of the mangled bodies of victims'.[16] This, by the way, is an excellent expression of fear beyond fear, and of the ideas of minds being occupied by an alien force.

'What are we fighting for?' was the question posed by Elshtain in a document she drafted which was signed by other public intellectuals sympathetic to the Just War tradition, including Francis

Fukuyama and Michael Walzer. Their answer was 'to protect the innocent from certain harm'. If conducted responsibly, war can be a 'force for good' in the world, advancing the goals of peace and security. Such sentiments have propelled, in the same decade as the War on Terror, the development of the Responsibility to Protect doctrine; 'R2P' as it is colloquially known, recognises that states have the primary responsibility for protecting their own citizens, but that if this is not done, and atrocities occur, then that responsibility for protection is transferred to the 'international community' as a whole.

Liberal interventions for human rights, and neoconservative interventions *against* failed states or 'evil' regimes, are more convergent in practice than either care to admit. But whether governments are engaging in humanitarian wars or the War on Terror, the justification given for their conduct is always framed in a moral language. While it is claimed that it is morally justifiable to forcibly disarm terrorists, caution must be exercised by those who take up arms to ensure that their behaviour is right and just: in other words, echoing the point made on pp. 11 and 90 that means must be compatible with ends.

To prevent the slide into unlawful violence, and to preserve the distinction between a Just War and one fought unjustly, a number of conditions must be met. In terms of the decision to wage war, the Just War tradition sets out clear criteria. Drawing on material considered earlier in the book (especially Chapter 6), we indicate below that these *jus ad bellum* principles have not guided the War on Terror.

The most significant Just War principle is that all wars must be fought for a just cause (such as self-defence, protection of the right to life, 'resistance to aggression'): there are few who have dissented from the view that the United States, and other countries, cities, and peoples, have had just cause in responding to al-Qaeda aggression. But this was patently not the case with Iraq in 2003, where the moral argument for pre-emptive war was unpersuasive because it could not establish the imminence of the threat.

The second principle is 'right intention', by which Just War scholars mean that leaders and 'warriors' must be pursuing the goal of the just cause and no other motives. Right intention remains the most plausible justification for killing others in war. This dimension of Just War theory is compromised where decision-makers have multiple reasons for resorting to war, including national interest calculations.

Third, a Just War can only be fought by a legitimate authority that has responsibility for public order. Internationalists would claim that the consent of the United Nations Security Council is a requirement for the right authority condition to be met. The British government believed a UN Resolution permitting war against Iraq in 2003 would be forthcoming, yet the Security Council remained divided and not persuaded by the claim that war was necessary. Fourth, and related, the War on Terror in a general sense has never been a war of 'last resort'. Even the case of Operation Enduring Freedom against Afghanistan fails this test (though it is not obvious what additional measures short of war could have been adopted given al-Qaeda's declaration of war against the West).

The fifth condition is the probability of success: if a state or coalition is going to commit an evil (war) to prevent or avert a greater evil, then there must be a realistic chance of success. The stated goal of the Bush administration, 'to rid the world of evil', pushed this Just War principle to breaking point for the reason that it was too politically obtuse to translate into a military strategy that could be morally justified. Sixth, those responsible for the conduct of the war must act in accordance with an assessment of the proportionality of ends – in other words, the wrong being righted must outweigh the harm likely to be incurred. Again, the America-led War on Terror fails this test, both in terms of resources – 'the three trillion dollar war'[17] – and the harm done to Afghan and Iraqi societies.

Despite the long tradition of Just War thinking, there is also a tradition – identified with Kant – which has been critical of the very notion of 'Just War'. This tradition believes that war should not be legitimised by Just War language, arguing instead that states should go no further than accepting that force is sometimes necessary or excusable. In other words, the Just War paradigm is not well suited to providing moral guidance on when war is permissible and how wars should be fought. But even in its own terms, the disjuncture between Just War principles and the behaviour of the US-led coalition in the War on Terror damages the claim by Elshtain and others that 'our' violence is better than 'theirs'.

New rules and legitimation crisis?

One of the central tenets of the Bush Doctrine was the notion of preventive war. Based on the desire to ensure continued US dominance of world affairs, the preventive war doctrine, as formulated by the Bush administration, was premised on the belief that America cannot rely on deterrence to defend itself from threats from international terrorism and failing states. The costs of inaction, argued its protagonists in and out of government, would be far higher than those of preventive action. When Vice-President Dick Cheney said that Iraq ought to be struck before it acquired nuclear weapons, he was clearly evoking the doctrine of preventive war.[18]

'Pre-emptive' war is one that is initiated when an attack is clearly imminent, such as Israel's strikes against its Arab neighbours in June 1967; preventive war assumes an attack before the target state poses an imminent threat – only a possible attack sometime in the future.[19]

In the previous chapter we outlined the legal and other difficulties with the notion of preventive war; here we want to make the claim that the preventive war rationale used for the invasion of Iraq stands out as the symbolic moment when America lapsed from being a hegemon with a responsibility for maintaining order, to becoming an imperial power bent on changing the rules of the game.

In making this claim it is necessary to appreciate the important difference between the case for war set out by President George W. Bush and that of Prime Minister Tony Blair. For the prime minister, the Iraq War was not about self-defence (despite the intelligence dossier's infamous '45 minute' claim regarding a potential missile attack from Iraq on British forces in Cyprus). The UK case rested on what was considered to be Iraq's consistent breach of disarmament Resolution 1441; consequently, the authority to use force was vested in the 'combined effects' of earlier Security Council resolutions going back to the first Gulf War. For this reason the UK government did not accept the premise of the Bush doctrine that there was a right in international law to act pre-emptively.[20]

The case for war presented by the United States administration was different. 'Evidence' was given to the Security Council, by Secretary of State Colin Powell on 5 February 2003 that Iraq's alleged WMD weaponising constituted a direct threat to US security. Ambassador John Negroponte was but one in the administration who drew the conclusion that America had a right to act if the Security Council failed to comprehend the severity of the threat. In his words, 'If the Security Council fails to act decisively in the event of further Iraqi violations, this resolution does not constrain any member state from acting to defend itself against the threat posed by Iraq'.[21]

Negroponte's claim that conventional understandings of when war is legally permissible are not to be considered impediments to the resort to war is a striking example of an imperialist understanding of the global order. The neoconservative view that sovereign prerogatives of so-called rogue states hostile to the United States should be denied – by force if necessary – set in train the lawless invasion of Iraq by the 'coalition of the willing'. The war did not meet either of the conditions set down by the UN justifying a breach of the general legal ban on force; it was neither an act of self-defence nor was it authorised by the Security Council. In reaction to the Bush doctrine, some international lawyers fear that an imperial system of international law had been summoned into existence in the wake of 9/11.[22] But new rules could only be regarded as legitimate if the United States and its allies could persuade other members of international society to *consent* to the new rules or *exempt* the United States from breaches of existing ones. Neither of these possibilities became a reality.

Washington's assault on the generally understood rules of international politics exposes a central paradox of hegemony. While hegemons possess material capabilities to act unilaterally, they cannot maintain this role if they do so at the expense of the system they are trying to lead. If Iraq was a new front in the War on Terror, then it ended in spectacular failure. As the Appendix at the back of the book reveals, out of the 54 mass-casualty terrorist incidents that took place between 2004 and 2007, 26 were in Iraq (all significantly greater in lethality than the al-Qaeda bombing in August 2003 that killed the United Nations' Special Representative in Iraq Sérgio Vieira de Mello, and 20 others).

Unilateral acts of imperial power are corrosive, as others begin to contrast the exceptionalism of the national security agenda with the exceptional inaction of the American government in response to other major issues of the day, such as the environment and global poverty. The 'two fronts' of the War on Terror have accelerated this dynamic and epitomised the problematic legitimacy of the United States-led world order.

When Barack Obama became president in 2009 most people expected a new start: 'Change' and 'Yes we can' had been the hopeful sound-bites during his election campaign. In foreign and security affairs his liberal language did indeed offer the promise of a new America in a new world. But change proved easier to promise than deliver. The pledge to close Camp Delta (or 'Gitmo' as it is known to the guards and 'detainees') at Guantánamo Bay, Cuba, has not been kept. And when Obama took office in January 2009, the troop deployment to Afghanistan was 32,000; by the end of that year it was 68–70,000 (well over half the number of land forces used in the invasion of Iraq in 2003). The War on Terror against the Taliban was widened to include Pakistan – it is now the AfPak War. It is Obama's War, for he has not only increased troop deployments, he has also massively increased the number of Predator drone attacks begun by Bush.[23] The costs of these attacks are high: they impinge on the sovereign space of other countries and raise various issues of legality and morality (is it state-sponsored assassination and is it acceptable?); they fuel protests against America (is Obama just another liberal-speaking American president who acts with a big stick?); and through extensive collateral damage they provoke anger and the desire for revenge. On the other hand, they have been seen to be very successful in killing al-Qaeda personnel and disrupting its activities. Can America afford not to use effective weapons against its active enemies? The killing of bin Laden (as a result of special operations rather than drone attacks) represents another dimension of US unilateral action. But how long can America continue to tear up the rule book – in this case in apparent disregard of Pakistani sovereignty and governmental sensitivity? Pakistan is an essential ally in the attempt to stabilise the situation in Afghanistan, and potential long-term political costs have to be weighed against what might be short-term military successes. But superpowers will be superpowers. As he comes to the end of his first and perhaps only term as president, Obama's dilemmas have generally been settled in favour of unilateral power rather than world order principles.

According to G. John Ikenberry, one of the leading writers on American hegemony, the failure of the War on Terror is one reason among others why liberal internationalism is in crisis.[24] It is a crisis of authority he said, resulting from the erosion of the norm of sovereignty by humanitarians wanting to protect people against atrocities committed by their own governments, and by US leadership targeting rogue states. This crisis was the result of reactions to the (different) terrors of the 1990s and 9/11. But along came 2011! Despite the catastrophic failings and problems of earlier military interventions – in the name of human rights or disarmament – world opinion turned to America and its allies when a large number of Libyan citizens were terrorised by the threat of slaughter by the Qaddafi regime. The Arab League asked the UN Security Council for direct assistance, leading to Resolution 1973 calling for 'all necessary measures' to protect civilians. This represents the eternal return of the Just War paradigm, but it raises as many questions as it settles. How will it end? Will the intervening forces be sucked in by mission creep? Would there have been an intervention if Qaddafi's regime had a nuclear capability, however primitive? And will Libya be added to the list of failed interventions in the lands of Islam?

Further reading

On Just War theory, see Michael Walzer, *Just and Unjust Wars* (New York: Basic Books, 2000), and specifically in relation to 9/11 see Jean Bethke Elshtain, *Just War Against Terror: The Burden of American Power in a Violent World* (New York: Basic Books, 2003). On US foreign policy and neoconservatism, the literature is vast: see Ivo H. Daalder and James M. Lindsay, *America Unbound: The Bush Revolution in Foreign Policy* (Washington, DC: Brookings Institution, 2003); on torture, and what the Bush administration got up to, see Karen Greenberg and Joshua Dratel (eds), *The Torture Papers: The Road to Abu Ghraib* (New York: Cambridge University Press, 2005), also Philippe Sands, *Lawless World: America and the Making and Breaking of Global Rules* (London: Allen and Lane, 2005). On legitimacy and hegemony in relation to US leadership, see Chris Reus-Smit, *American Power and World Order* (Cambridge: Polity Press, 2004). An excellent critique of the Bush administration's 'preventive paradigm' at home and overseas is David Cole and Jules Lobel, *Less Safe, Less Free: Why America is Losing the War on Terror* (New York: The New Press, 2007).

8   Islam

'What do Muslims really want?' is a question many Americans and others have scratched their heads about when contemplating the landscapes of world order since 9/11. As they, and others, look for answers, the point we want to emphasise in this chapter is that the very question itself is the problem. That so little has been learned over these ten years that the wrong question keeps being asked is testimony to the continuing size of the challenge ahead. To illustrate this claim we begin with a notable attempt by President Obama to reach out from 'the West' to 'Muslims'. Here we see how even the songs sung by the most intelligent politicians can strike false notes.

Obama in Cairo

In June 2009, after just six months in office, Barack Obama made a historic call for 'A New Beginning' between 'Muslims and the West'. His speech was hosted by Al-Azhar and Cairo University; these were two 'remarkable institutions', he said, which together represent 'harmony between tradition and progress'. The president's speech lasted nearly an hour, and was punctuated by enthusiastic applause; still riding a wave of popularity, his words would also have been greeted with enthusiastic applause at most universities in the West, though not always at the same points.[1]

Did this speech, in hindsight, match its billing as 'A New Beginning'? For sure, it felt at the time significantly different from anything delivered by the previous president, but in terms of it being
a radical break, it promised more than it delivered (and, nearly
two years on, it looks far less exciting than it did). On the positive
side, Obama refused to use the term 'terrorist' in a lengthy overview of the relationship between the United States and 'Muslims
around the world' – something that would have been unthinkable
for his predecessor. What is more, Obama started the speech with
the familiar Muslim greeting of peace, '*Assalaamu alaykum*' – a phrase
unlikely to have been contemplated or attempted by President
Bush. Such a start to the speech was only one aspect, in the minds
of the vocal far-right in the United States, of what they regarded
as the president's genuflection in face of the country's enemies;
and for some of them, no doubt, it was further proof that someone with 'Hussein' as his middle name must be a Muslim. What is
important here, however, is not to explore right-wing paranoia,
but to identify some false notes delivered by even a thoughtful
leader trying to hold out the hand of friendship, based on 'mutual
interest and mutual respect'. We identify three false notes, focusing on the misleading identification of Islam with the Arab world,
and the tendency to over-generalise what 'Islam' means and how
'Muslims' think and behave.

First, the choice of location for this 'New Beginning' merits
critical reflection. The reasons why the president chose Egypt were
obvious, according to the influential weekly magazine *The Economist*: 'It is the most populous of the Arab nations adjoining the
Middle Eastern conflict zone, with an ancient tradition of Islamic
scholarship and a citizenry that is tempted by fundamentalism but
also admires some things about the West.'[2] The article went on to
explain that 'not everybody liked his choice'. In particular, some
observers thought the speech would have 'made a better point',
and especially to the domestic audience in the United States, if
he had addressed 'the Muslim world' from a different place such
as Jakarta or Paris. Delivering the speech outside of the Middle
East 'might have challenged the mental association that (judging

by polls) some Westerners still tend to make: Muslim equals Arab equals hostile to the West'. This is an issue to which we will return shortly. But there were also less obvious reasons for the visit, made at the invitation of Egypt's then leader, Hosni Mubarak; these were geopolitical calculations related to legitimising a regime facing increasing human rights criticism, reassuring the second biggest recipient of US aid in the region after Israel, and reinforcing the role of a country united with Washington in its opposition to Iran and Islamist opinion and seen to have a positive contribution to make on Israel–Palestine questions.

A second false note concerns the speech's priorities and its omissions. Many would have liked to have heard Obama speak about Israeli violence against Palestinians, in addition to what he had to say about the historic plight of the Jews: why, in other words, should Palestinians have to continue to be the victims of the wrongs done to the Jews by other people at other times? Other double-standards were apparent. Obama failed to acknowledge the dangers faced by Muslims arising out of US policy in Afghanistan, he focused on Iran as a nuclear pariah while ignoring other states that enriched uranium, and he made no criticism of Israel's possession of nuclear weapons or the fact that it is not a signatory of the Non-Proliferation Treaty (NPT).

A familiar false note was sounded when the president lapsed into the error of talking about Muslim people as an 'object'. He used phrases such as 'the United States and Muslims around the world', and 'Islam and the West'. He took a big misstep in thinking it appropriate to tell Muslims about themselves. Just imagine the negative response that would have been triggered by a speech in 2009 on the need for greater toleration of Islamic minorities delivered in the Reichstag by the Turkish president Abdullah Gül. Or if, in Paris, Colonel Qaddafi (then still in the Western tent) had called for a fresh start in relations between Europe and North Africa, after sketching a picture of Mediterranean history characterised by Christian Europe's domination of its near abroad to the south. The Western media and public opinion would have hit the roof. Critics would have complained that such narratives stereotype 'Christians', 'Westerners', and 'Europeans', and we would have objected to being divided into 'good' and 'moderate' on the one hand, and 'violent extremists' on the other. We are always ready to stereotype, but not to be stereotyped.

This raises critical issues around stereotyping 'Muslims'. Is there a 'Muslim world' to address? And is there an identity – 'Muslim' – coherent enough, and stable enough, to deliver an answer to the question 'What do Muslims want?'

Mapping Islam

Before exploring this further, we need to think a little more about the concept of 'identity' as well as the very term 'Muslim'. To make our point about the general paucity of knowledge about Islam in Western societies, we offer ten short questions on the metrics of Islam:

1 What percentage of the world's population is estimated to be Muslim?
2 What proportion of them live in Asia?
3 Which are the world's most populous Islamic countries?
4 What percentage of the Muslim world is Shi'i, and what percentage Sunni?
5 What is the Muslim population of the United States?
6 What percentage of the UK population is Muslim?
7 Which European state has the largest Muslim population? And does any country in Europe have anything approaching a Muslim majority?
8 How many mosques are there in the United States?
9 How many mosques are there in France, Switzerland, and the UK?
10 How does the estimated growth of the global population of Muslims over the next 20 years compare with non-Muslims? And is it accelerating or decelerating?

The answers are available in the endnotes.[3]

How did you do? Whatever your score, we hope this exercise, as well as providing some basic facts, underlines the global character of Islam and disturbs the Western stereotype that 'Muslim equals Arab' – something correctly pointed out by *The Economist* article mentioned earlier. Equally, we hope that by emphasising the size and geographical and cultural variety of those professing Islam, we place a big warning sign above attempts to objectify 'Muslims', pigeon-hole 'the Muslim mind', or essentialise the 'Muslim world'. With this aim in mind, we turn from (easy-ish) empirical questions to deeper issues.

Islam is as Muslims do

We are scarcely breaking new ground by criticising the objectification, stereotyping, and essentialising of 'Muslims', and by emphasising the diversity of Muslims 'across the world'. Generalising is unavoidable in all aspects of life, of course, but in politically charged matters such as those dealt with in this book, sensitivity, nuance, and particularity must be integral to the way we talk and write (and live) our lives.

The decade since 9/11 has been full of talk about the politics of identity and identity politics, together with a rising chorus of voices claiming that religious beliefs constitute the all-powerful identity marker. One of the most important books on this in these years was also one of the shortest. Written by the leading economist and philosopher Amartya Sen, *Identity and Violence: The Illusion of Destiny* is a civilised plea for a better understanding of identity. An early life experience was pivotal for Sen. As a boy in 1944, at the time of Hindu–Muslim communal riots in India, he witnessed a (then unknown) man stumble into his parents' garden. The man, Kader Mial, had been attacked by 'vicious Hindu thugs' simply because he was a Muslim; he subsequently died in hospital, the victim of having the wrong identity in the wrong place at the wrong time.[4]

In the minds of the Hindu thugs described by Sen, 'no other identity was relevant' save that Kader Mia was 'Muslim'. Such an attitude is aptly described by Sen as the 'miniaturisation of human beings',[5] consigning humans into 'one dominant system of classification'. Such caging of human identities, through history, has been the pleasure and power of tyrants, religious fundamentalists, patriarchs, nationalists, fanatics, liberators, and all those who have an interest in (over)simplifying people. When we stop to think – but that might be asking too much of people under the shadow of 9/11 – we should all know that 'Muslims', like people of other faiths and none, are on different sides of social, political, economic, and other issues; as individuals, they are as likely as any to have complicated characters and multi-faceted 'selves'. Sen's warnings are not meant to criticise people having a sense of identity as such; rather, he reminds us that 'identity can also kill' when it is miniaturised and politicised, when a 'singular and belligerent' identity is imposed on a group. Since 9/11, miniaturisation and politicisation have been widespread, and religion has become an increasingly decisive marker of identity.

Miniaturisation serves various political functions. It can legitimise power and mobilise support for particular policies. Sen rightly criticised those, like Blair, who insisted on putting all Muslims (except those bad people who he deemed not to be 'true Muslims') into one 'community'. Such attitudes force all those so identified into a 'community' whose views become expressed, mediated, and directed by unelected 'community leaders'.[6] Consequently, 'ordinary' Muslims are seen as having access to civil society only *as* 'Muslims', whereas many other identity markers are potentially possible (for example, urban/rural, young/old, feminist/patriarchal, wealthy/poor, liberal/conservative). When Muslim identity is miniaturised, it is a mirror-image of the mindset of those terrorists, claiming to speak in the name of Islam, who characterise 'the West' in one-dimensional (and negative) terms. Identity miniaturisation is vital for terrorists, but irrational for those seeking to overcome them.

In the 1950s, Bernard Brodie used to argue that 'bad anthropology' had often contributed to 'bad strategy' in the past – and continued to do so into the nuclear age.[7] There has been limited progress in the anthropological education of most politicians, unfortunately, when one recalls all their slip-ups, misspeaking, bloomers, and dodgy decisions. It is worth reminding ourselves that those of us in the West – so ready to parade the advances in our knowledge – are still prone when we talk politics to slip into the simplistic categories which feed imperialism and racism and conflict.

If anybody doubts that so many people remain wedded to crude interpretations of world politics, how else can we explain the success in the past 15 or so years of Samuel Huntington's best-seller *The Clash of Civilisations and the Remaking of World Order?*[8] This book, using 'civilisations' as the referent, divided the world in ways that reduced everything to culture and civilisations – inherently vague concepts – and then placed 'religion' at the centre of them. This represented miniaturisation on a global scale.

Other social scientists have been equally sweeping when surveying world politics.[9] In his representation of Islam, Ernest Gellner, a leading sociologist, suggested that it 'has an essence that has remained constant', while the anthropologist Clifford Geertz emphasised the scriptural/theological dimension of Islam as the key to explaining the lives of Muslims. In contrast to such essentialising by academic luminaries, the work of writers who in our view give a truer anthropological and sociological picture of real Muslims in real places has not achieved such prominence.

Gabriele Marranci, an anthropologist who works on Islam, has been prominent in challenging the fallacy of the 'Muslim mind theory', which he sees as having negatively affected both 'academic and popular discourse on Muslims'. According to this theory, Muslims 'believe, behave, act, think, argue, and develop their identity as Muslims despite their disparate heritage, ethnicities, nationalities, experiences, gender, sexual orientations and, last but not least, brains'. In addition to calling for a sophisticated approach to identity markers, Marranci makes a very basic plea, namely for those who talk about Muslims to recognise the 'latent or manifest . . . fact that a Muslim person is primarily a human being'.[10] From an acceptance of the idea that 'Islam' is not the sole variable in a person's personhood, comes the anthropological understanding that Muslims, 'through discourses, practices, beliefs and actions, shape Islam in different times and places'.[11] In brief, Islam is as Muslims do.

Real Muslims in real places

In the long history of bad social science feeding bad policy-making, two issues are always present, if not explicitly. These are crude assumptions about the relationship between religion and politics, and about the place of theology in religious identity.

Some complexities involved in discussing the politics/religion conundrum were outlined in Chapter 5. The main point, it will be recalled, was that to conceive religion and politics as separate spheres requires a distinctly modern view, which involves conceiving 'religion' from a secular perspective. This leads to two starkly different views: a view of life being lived in different bubbles, one called religion and the other non-religion; and a view of the whole of life being considered as a religious experience. In trying to understand these positions, one thing is certain: 'religion' as it is generally understood in the West today is a product of history and politics, and so there can be no 'transhistorical definition' of religion as sought after by contemporary thinkers such as Geertz.[12]

The possibility of separating religion and non-religion in life is not exclusive to modern Western thinking; it has been evident in some Islamic societies and states. Secularisation, for example, was embedded in the new Turkey constructed by Kemal Ataturk in the 1920s. For many Muslims, however, the secularisation and liberalisation which took place in different parts of the world over the past five centuries has not been part of their tradition. For those thinking this way it makes no sense to ask them to respond to the modern liberal imperative to keep religion 'quite separate from politics, law and science'.[13] Their belief is both public and private; it cannot be relegated, as it is largely (but not entirely) in Western liberal societies, to the private sphere. The key point, then, is to recognise that the question 'How does religion motivate politics?' depends on prior assumptions about the religion/politics relationship. If one takes the secular view, the question can be asked, even if it will be difficult to answer. If one takes a traditional view, the question can neither be asked nor answered in the sense it has been meant in modern Western thinking.

But here is a problem for those holding the non-secular view that life is a religious experience. If religion explains everything, does it not equally, at some level, explain nothing? If one believes that religion is life, and life religion, might it not be assumed that all who submit to the same God might think and act in similar ways? But we know that this is obviously not the case, so clearly there are other factors at work, which diversify particular belief systems. These factors belong to time and place, to sociology and politics, and also to personal variables. Believers are individual human beings not exact copies. Before we return to the complex business of tracing multiple causes – which requires concentrating on real Muslims in real places as opposed to abstractions like 'the Muslim mind' – we need to discuss the second set of assumptions, namely those relating to the role of theology in religious identity.

A key concept in understanding these assumptions is the inelegant term 'theologocentrism'; this word refers to the attribution of 'all observable phenomena among Muslims to matters of Islamic theology'.[14] It again derives from modern secular thinking which, through its separation of religion and politics, understands the theology of Islam as the 'blueprint' on which Muslim society is built.[15] Among influential Western intellectuals who have tended to canvass a theologocentric and transhistorical view of 'religion' have been Bernard Lewis and Samuel Huntington.

The Qur'an as the holy book of Islam is the primary (but not only) source of knowledge for Muslims; it was the word of God as transmitted to the Prophet Muhammad between 610 and 631. It is not part of our argument to discuss different interpretations of the text, nor are we competent to judge them. What is clear, however, is the complexity and variety of such interpretations during all the centuries of Islamic theology. It is not surprising since 9/11 that there has been a grasping at straws by non-Muslims in attempting to understand 'the Muslim world'. To give one illustration: Sherifa Zuhur, from within the Strategic Studies Institute at the US Army War College, recently described the problem arising from the lack of information about Islam, and 'insufficient efforts to impart it'. She writes: 'DoD [Department of Defense] programs which typically provide some 3 hours of instruction on various aspects of Islam have no time to go into any detailed explanations of the Qur'an.'[16] Centuries are allocated three hours of classroom time: tick the box and move on. It is not clear which is more dangerous: ignorant naivety or a little learning. Whatever, the scope for misunderstanding is great.

In times of danger a little knowledge has to be puffed up into being the best available. This has led some, with their understanding of politics and religion as separate, to posit 'Judeo-Christian' culture 'as the foundation of freedom, and Islam tending towards violence because it has been unable or unwilling to emulate such a separation'.[17] Such views about Islam have been popular among some influential voices in the United States; this was evident for example in the forceful arguments in 2002–03 by the journalist Charles Krauthammer on 'Islam's bloody borders', a phrase first used by Huntington.[18]

Earlier, we argued that Islam is what Muslims do. Such a perspective does not weaken the importance of the Qur'an in the lives of those who consider themselves Muslims; it is simply a way of drawing attention to the multiple understandings of the Qur'an across space and time, and to the multiple patterns of behaviour by Muslims that appear to be unrelated to scriptural explanations. In an influential critique of Geertz's attempt to propose a 'universal (i.e. anthropological) definition' of religion, Talal Asad has emphasised the importance for students of 'particular religions to unpack the comprehensive concept which he or she translates as "religion" into heterogeneous elements according to its historical character'.[19] Simply put, even the all-powerful word of God is heard differently by different people at different places and times.

That said, analysts are confronted by a challenge in trying to avoid essentialism while taking account of the persistent appeals to Islam, to the *umma* (the global community of Muslims), and to other signifiers of shared identity by people who describe themselves as Muslims.

The label 'Muslim' is complex, and much more so than the great-stereotypers in high political positions who divide human beings into 'moderates' and 'extremists'. But there is a prior question: when we talk about Muslim identity, do we even know what we mean when we invoke the term *identity*? What does it mean, for example, to say that somebody *shares* an identity with somebody else? How many 'definite characteristics' add up to a shared identity? Are they all in play equally, or is their prioritisation variable? And so on. Identity is a beguilingly simple word; it is also a trendy buzz word in the social sciences; but 'identity' is a fuzzy concept, as unhelpful as it is unavoidable. On the negative side, it is one of those vague concepts, like culture, that spawn simplistic analysis. On the positive side, as Sen shows, identity can be a source of pride and joy, and strength and confidence for people. But remember, he also went on to say that 'identity can also kill – and kill with abandon'.

The task of understanding real Muslims in real places – their varied attitudes and behaviour – requires endless accounts of specific Muslim societies: their geographical situation, the way nationalism developed locally, state formations under Muslim rulers, the cultural traditions of different places where Islam became settled, levels of economic development, class, ethnic composition and characteristics – and on and on. In addition to general contextual variables, one must also think about more contingent factors affecting individual Muslims, such as age and sex, and whether the individual is a migrant or citizen, a male street-cleaner or a princess, a political leader or a criminal, a citizen of Saudi Arabia or the United States. All such issues have been further complicated by globalisation. Today, Muslim communities have a markedly different political geography than at the start of the previous century. Complexity grows in other ways. While violent tensions erupted between Shi'i and Sunni Muslims in Iraq during the chaos of the postwar occupation, it has been recorded that in some parts of the world – the UK, for example – Muslims of different persuasions have forged greater unity as a consequence both of their shared experiences as immigrants but also as a defensive response to growing Islamophobia.[20]

Islamophobia feeds on the stereotype of Muslims as 'fundamentalists'. But we never hear about 'fun loving Muslims'. It might seem trivial in a book on as weighty a topic as terror in our time to digress for a moment to discuss Muslim dating sites, but this is what Theodore Dalrymple asks us to do in a recent book.[21] The phrase 'fun loving' comes from a woman who wrote to a Muslim dating site advertising herself as follows (the spelling is the original): 'Hello all im a fun loving woman, im down to earth and do not judge people.' This particular person (like some others) was looking for a 'partner' rather than a spouse; Dalrymple considered this an interesting choice of term as it has connotations with equality rather than subordination in a relationship. From his deconstruction of the self-advertising taking place in searches for a significant other, Dalrymple offered a profound but trivial insight: as they appear on dating websites, Muslims are revealed 'to be just as shallow as everyone else'. (When one considers the beauty of some of the architecture, calligraphy, painting and other dimensions of the art produced by Muslims, it is equally apparent that 'Muslims' are also as talented.) The point of arguments like these is to emphasise that behind labels there are human beings in all their varieties.

Some of the arguments above might be seen as endorsing the (controversial) general theory called 'Orientalism'. This is the explanation of Western thinking associated with the Palestinian-American cultural critic Edward Said.[22] It referred to 'a style of thought' that was based upon an 'ontological and epistemological distinction' between 'the Orient' and the West. As a result of this style of thought, Said argued, stereotypes were built up over time, and were influential in policy-making and everyday social discourse. The 'East' – comprising ideas such as 'Muslim culture' and the 'Arab mind' was represented as the exotic, the deficient, and one that was to be contrasted with, and subordinated by, the West. Without doubt, some of the problems identified by Said still exist in some English-language fiction and cinema dealing with the Middle East and its Islamic neighbourhood; they have attracted the label 'neo-Orientalism'. According to Zuhur, works in the past decade such as Azar Nafisi's *Reading Lolita in Tehran: A Memoir in Books* (Random House, 2003), Khaled Hosseini's *The Kite Runner* (Riverhead Books, 2003), and Åsne Seierstad's *The Bookseller of Kabul* (Little Brown, 2003) all 'offer the dichotomy of the modern West posed against a traditional, cruel, and backwards East'.[23] Such traditional Orientalism, she said, seems to hold out much greater interest to American readers than the cosmopolitan, urbanised, technocratic face of the Muslim world to which Zuhur also drew her readers' attention. There is also a parallel countertrend that must be noted – an 'Occidentalism' essentialising the West. But this is not an equally powerful countertrend, for as Zuhur correctly observes, there is 'a lack of symmetry' given the West's 'stronger economic, political, military, and cultural status'.

Both Occidentalism and Orientalism, when they occur, should be rejected for their miniaturisations of swathes of humanity, as well as biases of one sort or another. But let us not exaggerate the problem. Important aspects of Said's interpretation of Orientalism are flawed, both empirically and ethically. For one, his main works do not give appropriate credit to those European scholars who did so much to develop a sophisticated understanding of Islamic culture.[24] Not only does Said's work do a disservice to history, but it has fed analyses and politics that are prejudiced against the fostering of cross-cultural understanding and harmony. In a powerful critique of Said's central argument, and especially his assertion of a 'fundamental ontological distinction' between the so-called West and the so-called Rest, Kenan Malik writes that 'theoreticians of difference' have become mirror-images of those they ostensibly challenge. For Malik, the theorists of difference, like 'advocates of racial thinking' seem 'equally indifferent to our common humanity'. They place identity before equality. Such thinking can be the route, Malik argues, by which 'difference becomes resolved into indifference'.[25]

This chapter opened by asking 'What do Muslims really want?' and in engaging it we have questioned whether there is an identity – 'Muslim' – coherent enough, and stable enough, to deliver a sensible answer. We have shown that real Muslims in real places are humans as varied as any, badged as they are by gender, nationalism, class, race, and all the other political, social, and economic constructions history has imposed on humans. Without in any way minimising the place Islam occupies in the life of any individual Muslim, it is our contention that anthropological, sociological, and political analysis must insist that Islam is not an 'it'; Muslims are not a 'they'; Islam is not anti-modern but can offer (or not) a different path to modernity; 'essentialism' should be resisted; theology does not equal identity; and there is no 'Muslim mind' as opposed to minds that are Muslim.

Muslims might worship in different ways to believers of other faiths, and authenticate ideas in different ways, but – like most people of faith and no-faith – they do not turn to terror to achieve their ends first, or even easily under any circumstances. This is a simple point, to do with 'the facts of human existence' but one with profound implications for combating terrorism. Out of better anthropology will come better strategy. One way to begin is by asking better questions, and this thought brings us back to where the chapter began. Our own response to the question 'What do Muslims really want?' is that it is the wrong question. Its foolishness is evident if we insert the name of another major world religion. Can we, for example, sensibly ask or answer the question 'What do Christians really want?' when we know the label 'Christian' embraces someone who is a pacifist community worker today and a Crusader King a thousand years ago? Questions that can be answered must be more precise: What does that person who is a Muslim want? What does that Islamicist government want? What do those Muslim immigrants in country 'x' want? At least with such questions we can make a stab at a researchable answer; to go broader is an intellectual stretch too far, for Muslims want as Muslims are.

Some Muslims, modern and educated, want democracy. Others, Muslim tyrants, want to maintain their authoritarian regimes. In Cairo in 2009 where we began this chapter, President Obama spoke powerfully about democracy. The ghosts of the Iraq War – the deaths, the costs, the mistakes, and the controversies – hovered around him throughout, and he said (somewhat disingenuously) that America did not presume to know what is best for everyone. He insisted that 'no system of government can or should be imposed upon one nation by any other', but he also affirmed his own belief in governments 'that reflect the will of the people'. Eighteen months later, changes in the Arab world began to test Washington's thinking about democracy in ways that had been quite unpredictable when Obama made his speech.

Further reading

On identity and culture, see Amartya Sen, *Identity and Violence: The Illusion of Destiny* (London: Allen Lane, 2006). On the separation of religion and politics in Western thought, see Michael Walzer (1984) 'Liberalism and the Art of Separation', *Political Theory*, 12(3): 315–30, and on comparative world religions, see Talal Asad *Genealogies of Religion: Discipline and Reasons of Power in Christianity and Islam* (Washington, DC: Johns Hopkins Press, 1993). On the sociology and anthropology of Islam, see Gabriele Marranci, *The Anthropology of Islam* (London: Berg, 2008) and *Understanding Muslim Identity, Rethinking Fundamentalism* (Houndmills: Palgrave Macmillan, 2009). Theologocentrism is deployed by Sherifa Zuhur, *Precision in the Global War on Terror: Inciting Muslims through the War of Ideas* (US Strategic Studies Institute: Carlisle, 2008). On contemporary Islam as a faith and a way of life see Oliver Roy, *Globalised Islam: The Search for a New Ummah* (Hurst: London, 2006).

9 Governance

Governance is an over-elaborate term for the everyday ways that individuals and institutions 'manage their common affairs'.[1] In our globalised world, where hopes for tomorrow are invariably far more ambitious than achievements today, managing our common affairs is complex and critical. This is particularly the case with governance on a global scale, which frequently reveals a rupture between ambition and capacity. Beneath this capacity deficit run deep fault-lines in world order, reflecting value-conflicts and different historical experiences. The governance agenda relating to counter-terrorism sometimes reflects these cleavages, for example between those institutions pursuing order and those pursuing justice.

Homeland security and human rights rollback

The 'governance' response to terrorism has been wide-ranging and complex. Familiar debates about 'going it alone' versus enhancing the multilateral responses have been a common feature. So have debates about the application of different kinds of power, between those favouring the 'hard' institutions of the inter-state system – the UN Security Council, NATO, and coalitions of willing powers – versus 'soft' institutional responses focusing on diplomacy, aid, and stopping the financing of terrorism.

Prior to 9/11, multilateral cooperation with regard to international terrorism was virtually non-existent. States that experienced terrorist atrocities tended to deal with them unilaterally. The sarin gas attack on the Tokyo subway posed a security problem, but only for the Japanese government and its people; acts of terror by deranged individuals, such as the Oklahoma bomber Timothy McVeigh, posed a threat to America alone. Terrorism remained largely an intra-state problem. Joining up the transnational dots between acts of terror, identifying patterns, and projecting future possibilities – this was the preserve of scholars specialising in terrorism and intelligence, it was not a priority for policy-makers, not the core business of governments. The realisation, after 1998, that al-Qaeda and its affiliates could cause catastrophic damage to people and property, anytime, anywhere, was transformational: here was an organisation that was seeking the violent overthrow of world order.

The Prologue queried the image of 9/11 being a complete bolt from the blue, though Chapter 1 pointed to the difficulties of predicting the timing and particularities of spectacular terrorist events when information is sketchy (though giving visas to jihadists applying for pilot training courses was, at best, careless!). The early Bush administration and both preceding Clinton administrations were complacent with respect to the strategic challenges that were looming. This realisation, after the event, informed the recommendations of the 9/11 Commission which argued that an effective counter-terrorism strategy required significant institutional reform, including the creation of a Department of Homeland Security.

The UK response and that of America's most ardent allies in the War on Terror – including Israel, India, Singapore, Malaysia, and Australia – was not to reconfigure domestic institutions along this 'homeland security' model. Yet in terms of doctrine, it is evident that governments have indeed followed America in rebalancing what is often characterised (wrongly in our view) as the simple choice between liberty and security. Such a shift was evident in the new political vocabulary that emerged after 9/11. Government officials told their citizens to report 'suspicious activity'. It became respectable to treat followers of Islam as 'enemies' who 'hate our freedoms'. Phrases such as 'in the interests of security' were seen and heard whenever one entered a railway station, got ready to board a plane, entered a public building, or applied for a new credit card. This new vocabulary became a standard repertoire of politicians, police chiefs, organisations of all sorts, and journalists. As it did so, words became deeds, suspicion matured into conviction, and 'sexed-up' evidence by a politicised intelligence community became a *casus belli*. Conor Gearty, a leading human rights lawyer, described this process as one that has more in common with a 'moral warrior' than it does 'a court of law'.[2]

Enhanced anti-terror legislation was passed in many countries. Widespread powers were granted to the police and security services to apprehend, control, and transfer those deemed to be a potential threat to the state. Just a month after 9/11 the US attorney general, John Ashcroft, announced the 'paradigm of prevention', the 'single objective' of which was to 'prevent terrorist attacks by taking suspected terrorists off the street'. The Justice Department later found that few of the suspects had anything to do with terrorism, but were seen as suspects because of their ethnic and religious identity.[3] Part of the new 'paradigm' was the US Patriot Act, which gave executive powers for detention, surveillance, and interrogation. Comparable legislation has been introduced in many other countries, including Britain, where extended periods of detention (before being charged) are lawful. The notional safeguard of a 'judicial officer' examining the evidence, and interpreting it according to criteria that is favourable to the doctrine of 'state necessity', has been likened to 'confetti at a funeral'.[4]

What marks out the contemporary challenge as being of particular significance is that the assault on established norms about human rights and the rule of law is being led by Western governments whose political culture rests on rights-based principles. It is not being led, as in the past, by communist states regarding individual liberty as a bourgeois sham, or by apartheid South Africa wanting to exclude peoples on grounds of race, or by Asian states claiming that community must precede liberty. The post-9/11 challenge was typified by the response of British prime minister Tony Blair to the terror attacks on the London transport network on 7/7. His words reflected the scepticism in certain Western governments towards the validity of certain human rights norms: 'The rules of the game are changing', he said.[5]

Governments led by George W. Bush, Tony Blair, and other Western leaders such as Australia's John Howard called for a reappraisal of certain core civil and political rights. These included (among others) the right not to be tortured or suffer degrading treatment, the right not to be detained without trial, and the right of refugees and asylum seekers not to be returned to any country where their life would be threatened. Human rights experts refer to these as *fundamental* human rights – fundamental in the sense that they are highly legalised. Such rights are a different order of magnitude to some of those listed in the 1948 Universal Declaration; this includes, for example, the right to a holiday, something we can all appreciate but should not expect our sovereign state to guarantee.

The extent of the measures, taken in the name of 'security', which threatened fundamental freedoms, prompted doubting liberals such as Michael Ignatieff to ask whether it was 'the end of the human rights era'.[6] Before discussing this, it is important to remember that all rights-claims imply a duty-bearer: in the case of human rights, the state is the bearer of the responsibility to implement the principle of humanitarian protection.

Despite the normative power of the idea that human rights are the best way to realise human dignity, the institutional mechanisms for enforcing compliance has been chronically weak from the beginning. Responses to 9/11 illustrate how states – particularly those countries with individual rights-based political orders in Western Europe, Israel, and the United States – have been backsliders in relation to their pre-commitments. The claim to respect the rights of detainees will be forever tainted by the images of human pyramids made up of naked prisoners stripped of everything including their dignity. The problems at Abu Ghraib were more fundamental than the Bush administration's claim that responsibility lay with 'a few bad apples' running amok on the night shift. It reflected a changing culture about security/liberty and us/them.

The 1984 UN Convention against Torture and Other Cruel, Inhuman or Degrading Treatment or Punishment (CAT) was previously thought to be one of the most robust norms in the human rights regime. It defines torture as 'any act [committed by a public official or with their consent] by which pain or suffering, whether physical or mental, is intentionally inflicted on a person for such purposes as obtaining from him or a third person information or a confession'.[7] The strength of the prohibition on torture is such that it has the status of a 'peremptory norm' that is binding on all states, and does not permit any exceptional circumstances to be invoked 'as a justification for torture' (Article 2.2).

Despite the robust legal character of the CAT, and the extremely high levels of legitimacy accorded to the ban internationally, the Bush administration offered a new take on the norm. In what has become known as the infamous 'torture memo', drafted by John Yoo and signed by Office of Legal Council head Jay S. Bybee, the bar for what was considered torture was raised significantly.[8] The infliction of physical pain was said to amount to torture only when it is equivalent 'to the pain accompanying serious physical injury, such as organ failure, impairment of bodily function, or even death'.[9] Bybee's memorandum was repudiated after the Abu Ghraib scandal, but by then a 'torture culture'[10] had evolved such that arguments regarding executive authority, and the non-application of the convention to off-shore territory, were repeatedly proffered.

It ought to be self-evident that when leaders begin to question what had previously been seen as uncontested, those directly below them in the institutional hierarchy will follow suit. Administration officials expressed consternation at the 'news' that torture had become institutionalised in their detention centres. This was like the scene from *Casablanca* where Captain Renault expressed shock and indignation to 'discover', as he pocketed his winnings from the croupier, that 'gambling was going on' in Rick's casino.

The 'new paradigm' for US security set out by the Bush administration sought not only to revise the prohibition on torture but also to find 'workarounds' of their obligations under the Geneva Conventions. In the words of the US deputy assistant attorney general, 'what the Administration is trying to do' in Guantánamo and other detention centres 'is create a new legal regime'.[11] Three arguments underpinned this new legal regime. First, the president's memo of 7 February 2002 determined that the Geneva Convention on the treatment of prisoners (Geneva III) did not apply to the conflict with al-Qaeda as it was a non-state actor. Although it was seen to apply in principle to Afghanistan, Taliban captives must be denied prisoners-of-war status as they did not meet the conditions of lawful combat. Yet Article 5 of the Geneva III maintains that the status of captives is to be decided by a 'competent tribunal', which ought to be promptly convened. The status of detainees, if it is to be determined in ways that are consistent with international humanitarian law, cannot be decided by presidential decree. Second, the detainees at Camp Delta in Guantánamo could be held without charge or access to a lawyer, or receiving a public hearing in court, because they were not held on sovereign US territory, hence the International Covenant on Civil and Political Rights was not applicable (implying that no official could ever be responsible for crimes committed on non-sovereign territory). Third, there was the related point that human rights treaties did not generate obligations beyond those already set out in American law.

The reluctance on the part of the United States to internalise various human rights commitments often provokes the charge of double-standards, particularly as moralistic language is used when justifying military interventions. But this charge is misleading. America does not 'reject' the basis of the human rights regime per se: its position is one where 'we think the values are right but they do not apply to us'.

What are the grounds for claiming exemptions in relation to fundamental rights? The US government has claimed it does not need to accede to international jurisdiction because of its special status in the hierarchy of states. This practice is centuries old. The difference today is that non-Western states, and peoples around the world want a fairer world order. Such a sentiment was neatly captured by Ramesh Thakur: 'Washington cannot construct a world in which all have to obey universal norms and rules, while it can opt out whenever, as often, and for as long as it likes.'[12]

The British government, with its very different international status, has adopted a modified position in relation to fundamental human rights since 9/11; this is because it cannot go it alone, at least not without paying a high price for challenging accepted human rights norms. In the eyes of the Labour government under Blair in 2005, the new context of catastrophic terror threats meant that 'the circumstances of our national security have self evidently changed'.[13] If the 'rules of the game' were new, how did they manifest themselves in the changed situation? Significantly, the Labour government adopted a position on torture that was distinct from their Republican allies in the United States. They did not seek to defend interrogation methods which openly flouted international humanitarian law, yet there is much circumstantial evidence that they were complicit in US breaches of it – though this has been consistently denied. Assisting in 'extraordinary rendition' is a case in point. In the years following 9/11, the US government transferred hundreds of suspected terrorists from its sovereign territory to other countries where they faced interrogation, detention, and torture. Article 3 of the CAT prohibits rendition where there is a substantial risk that the individual would be tortured; the United States has interpreted this prohibition in ways that are enabling for torturers, arguing that the CAT only applies if it is 'more likely than not' that the individual will be tortured.[14]

Allegations that the UK government assisted the United States in rendition flights were categorically dismissed by ministers. On 13 December 2005, Foreign Secretary Jack Straw told the Foreign Affairs Select Committee that 'there simply is no truth in the claims that the United Kingdom has been involved in rendition full stop'.[15] On February 2008, the new Foreign Secretary David Miliband made a statement that showed Straw to have been wrong. He apologised to MPs for the misinformation, and went on to detail how the CIA had informed the government that Diego Garcia, the British overseas territory that had been leased to the United States in the early 1970s, had twice been used for refuelling rendition flights. Such an admission adds credence to the persistent allegations that the British government assisted many more rendition flights than had touched down in Scotland en route to picking up detainees.

In claiming that under new circumstances 'new paradigms' had to be invented and 'new rules' elaborated, some types of internationalists on both sides of the Atlantic – the muscular liberal type in Britain, and the neoconservative type in America – interpreted security governance in ways that were damaging to fundamental human rights. Authoritative sources reported copy-cat behaviour in China, Pakistan, Russia, Israel, Egypt, and elsewhere. Egypt, prior to the 2011 revolution, routinely used torture, but as one State Department official described the diplomatic dilemma: 'How can we raise it [with Egyptian counterparts] when the Bush administration's policy is to justify torture?'[16]

The failure of British political leaders, especially in the Blair years, to establish support for 'new rules' was detrimental to counter-terrorism. Apart from ethical objections, complicity in torture is bad governance: it weakens the distinction between Western claims to be a 'force for good' and the tactics of their adversaries. This hypocrisy is then of considerable propaganda value for jihadists, and it alienates domestic constituencies (and notably the non-violent Muslim communities that are vital in the struggle to weaken al-Qaeda). Moreover, there is no body of evidence that supports the view that information gained through torture and intimidation is reliable.

Intriguingly, in the rollback of fundamental rights by the US and UK governments, domestic law courts emerged as sources of resistance. The US Supreme Court dealt the Bush administration a blow on 29 June 2006 when it ruled – by a 5:3 majority

– that the executive had over-reached its authority in seeking to try suspects by military tribunal. In the UK, the case of unlawful detention at Camp Delta opened up further questions about legality. Lawyers working for detainee Ferroz Abbassi claimed that his imprisonment was in breach of the 1966 Covenant, and that the UK government had a duty to protect those rights. In advancing this argument, Nicholas Blake QC dismantled the claim by government lawyers that the UK can have no view about what happens in US jurisdiction; he referred to this as 'an old view which takes no account of modern developments in international law and human rights'.[17] There has been a firm view that the British response to terrorism, despite all such concerns and failings, has been more restrained and fastidious; this is generally explained by the experience in Northern Ireland, where suspected terrorists were treated as suspected criminals, not combatants. It is also claimed that this approach may have contributed to what seems to have been the greater success of the UK in disrupting plots and charging terrorists.[18]

A further example of judicial censure over the UK government's complicity in torture concerns the former Guantánamo prisoner Binyam Mohamed, who claims he was tortured in a variety of locations as a result of rendition. The UK government denied the charge. In delivering the verdict against the government, Lord Neuberger (head of civil justice in England and Wales) noted that security officials 'appear to have dubious records when it comes to human rights and coercive techniques'. This led him to conclude that their information with respect to Mohamed's mistreatment could not be trusted, a damning conclusion that seemed to be confirmed by the way in which the chief government lawyer, Jonathan Sumption QC, sought to have the criticism removed before the judgment was handed down by the court. This attempt at interfering with the judicial process was resisted, and the principle of 'open justice' and the 'rule of law' were reasserted.[19]

An important conclusion about governance follows from these deviations from human rights commitments in the name of security. The cases of rendition, detention without trial, water-boarding, institutionalised bullying, sexual humiliation, inhumane treatment, are a reminder that the direction of the 'human rights caravan', as advocates like to think of it, is not moving ineluctably forwards; it can be halted, and sometimes, reversed. Think of how many authoritarian leaders have embraced a culture of counter-terrorism as a convenient fiction for consolidating their domestic power base by cracking down on the civil liberties of opposition groups. Yet to suggest this is the 'end of the human rights era', as Ignatieff did, is an overstatement. There has been significant pushback against cases of inhumane governance by domestic law courts and campaigning NGOs and civil society, by scrutiny and censure from the media, and by political inquiries and hearings by various constitutional bodies in the UK and the United States. The activism in the public sphere on behalf of the rule of law is a check against undue pessimism about the setbacks since 9/11. It continues to be a struggle, but as General MacArthur reminded his troops in the War in the Pacific, retreating can also be a way of going forward in a different direction.

Governance and international institutions

What, then, of the governance initiatives that have been taken at the inter-state level? Here we see how several institutions have combined in ways designed to manage the threat from al-Qaeda and its affiliates.

All governance arrangements require a system of rules that tell states – the main parties to international legal agreements – 'how to go on', as the philosopher Ludwig Wittgenstein said of the function of rules in everyday life. It is in the body of international law where prescriptive rules of international conduct are codified. The self-binding character of international law derives from the absence of a global government that has universal jurisdiction, and the capacity to enforce the law. Instead of this power of com-pellence, rule-following in international relations is mainly driven by the expectation of reciprocity and a realisation that a political order without rules is one that is without the minimum conditions for social life to flourish. Global rules are fragile, elaborate, sometimes labyrinthine, and always prone to the play of power and self-interest.

War is a long-standing institution of international politics. Since the emergence of 'the law of nations' in the eighteenth century, philosophers and lawyers have argued that war can be a lawful and appropriate redress for a 'wrong' inflicted. Over time, ever greater restrictions have been placed upon the resort to force (jus ad bellum) and its application (jus in bello). While grounded in customary international law, the principal modern legal source of jus ad bellum derives from the Charter of the United Nations, which maintains, in Article 2 that '[a]ll members shall refrain in their international relations from the threat or the use of force against the territorial integrity or political independence of any state'. The reasonable exceptions to this prohibition are twofold. Article 51 of the Charter permits 'the inherent right of individual or collective self-defense if an armed attack occurs against a Member of the United Nations'. The second exception is where the UN Security Council (UNSC) resolves to use force in order to restore international peace and security. Respecting the rule of law in these ways is critical to the moral case for responding to terror attacks with violent means. Western governments cannot fight terror with more terror without becoming seen as barbarians themselves.

On the morning after the September 11 atrocities, both the UN General Assembly (UNGA) and the UNSC adopted Resolution 1368; this condemned the acts of terror, affirmed the right to take action in individual and collective self-defence, and demanded that states cooperated to bring the perpetrators to justice. This abrogation of oversight in relation to a possible military response to 9/11 was in stark contrast with UNSC Resolution 1373 (28 September 2011) which deemed all terrorist acts to be a threat to international peace and security, and imposed requirements on member states in terms of dealing with terrorist threats in their domestic jurisdiction.

It is a twist of international history that the legal basis of the invasion of Afghanistan is seldom questioned (outside discussions among public international lawyers), due to it being overshadowed by the diplomatic and legal debacle that developed on the road to the invasion of Iraq. *Jus ad bellum* considerations in relation to Afghanistan were also mitigated by the fact that 9/11 was so exceptional that diplomats were more willing than usual to give the state that had been attacked greater scope to use force itself. Interpretations have differed among specialists on what was permitted by the various UN resolutions relating to the war in Afghanistan. Yet from a technical legal point of view, the best that could be said for the covering resolutions was that they provided the United States with a tenable argument for the war.[20]

If legality in relation to the first terror war was tenuous, it was non-existent in relation to Iraq. The best legal opinion that London and Washington could come up with was that authorisation was 'implied' by a particular reading of Security Council resolutions going back to the Gulf War. The reading of these resolutions was sufficient for pro-war political leaders and their supporters to dismiss the legal concerns of their opponents on the grounds that legal arguments were evenly weighted for and against war. Such a conceit has been delivered a knock-out blow by evidence put before the Chilcot Inquiry into the conduct of the UK government prior to the 2003 war. Declassified documents show that the attorney general, whose legal opinion was put before parliament, switched his position right on the eve of war. Tellingly, the documents suggest that the prime minister ignored his legal counsel's earlier warnings about the need for a second UNSC resolution if the war was to be legal.

On 30 January 2002, in a note marked 'secret', Lord Goldsmith wrote to the prime minister in advance of his meeting with the US president on the following day. It repeated Goldsmith's long-standing view that Security Council Resolution 1441 'does not authorise the use of force without further determination by the security council'. This prompted an impatient response from Blair, who wrote in the margin 'I just don't understand this'. Another document disclosed to the Inquiry, tells us what happened next. This one was from the prime minister's senior foreign policy advisor, David Manning. He recorded how Bush told Blair at the meeting in Washington on 31 January that military action would happen with or without a second resolution. Manning's note affirms that '[t]he prime minister said he was solidly behind the president'[21] despite the clear steer from his chief law officer that a second resolution was a necessary condition for the war to be legal. Six weeks later, as troops amassed on the Iraqi border, the attorney general flipped his argument. It was this short statement on the legality of the war that was heard by parliament in the critical debate about Britain's participation in the war, and which led Elizabeth Wilmshurst, legal counsel in the Foreign and Commonwealth Office, to resign on the grounds that the imminent forcible action constituted 'a crime of aggression'.[22]

One school of thought in relation to governance maintains that there are always costs associated with breaking the rules. A great deal was made at the time of the invasion of Iraq about the 'costs' that Britain and the United States would pay for their norm violation. Evidence to sustain this argument in terms of state interests is hard to find. Yes, individual leaders have paid a price (witness the reputational damage to Bush and Blair, Powell and Straw, Rumsfeld and Hoon); the claim of the UN to manage global security has been further damaged; but did the states themselves get away with it? And if so, was this because they skilfully used hard and soft power instruments to ensure sufficient 'buy-in' to the broader strategic goal of ensuring compliance to a doctrine that puts security before the rule of law? Not only did particular states 'get away with it', but rules and prerogatives pertaining to sovereignty have been strengthened by the governance changes after 9/11.

'New rules' and 'old rules'

Leaders in the West used al-Qaeda's declaration of war against them as an opportunity to dismantle some of the foundations of human rights law. The clamour to make 'new rules' was led by

Bush and Blair, and endorsed by the political leadership of Burma, Israel, Libya, and Zimbabwe.

The 'old rules' adopted by states after 1945 had the virtue of dispensing with ideas associated with superiority (of race, civilisation, or creed). A universal conception of justice and community – 'we the peoples' – began to erode the singular and exclusionary power of the sovereign state. Within the UN order, international humanitarian law represented the apogee of this civilising process, in which rules were grounded in procedural fairness,[23] and not which side of a cause you were on (or as neoconservatives saw it, whether you were 'with us or with the terrorists').

The initial years after 9/11 saw the pluralist basis of the UN legal order coming under strain, though they did not 'snap' entirely due to the countervailing power exerted by various actors in domestic and transnational public spheres. Where previously Western powers had been pushing the idea and relevance of a global human rights culture, the necessity of defeating global terrorists was a pretext for the evolution of governance norms that strengthened state capacity for controlling 'enemies within' and disciplining enemies of 'the civilised world'.

Rather than seeing one form of governance being replaced by another (as advocates of 'new rules' tried to achieve), a more subtle picture emerges in which new rules came to overlie the old. A good example here is the way in which 'state necessity' arguments post-9/11 converged with the humanitarian intervention doctrine of the 1990s. Both came to regard sovereignty in the global south as conditional and potentially extinguishable; both doctrines believed in the utility of force; and neither regarded the prohibitions on the use of force in the UN Charter as an impediment to action. Sovereignty, once eclipsed in weak and failing states, was being reaffirmed by the governance arrangements put in place by the strongest powers (and their institutions and alliances) of the global North.

Further reading

For an account of the impact of the War on Terror upon law and justice see Conor Gearty, 'Human Rights in an Age of Counter-Terrorism', *Oxford Amnesty Lecture*, 23 February 2006. Available at http://www2. lse.ac.uk/humanRights/articlesAndTranscripts/Oxford_Amnesty_ Lecture.pdf (accessed 11 April 2011). For a range of views on how to respond to governance challenges in relation to international terror, see Phillip Bobbitt, *Terror and Consent: The Wars for the 21st Century* (New York: Random House, 2009); Adrian Guelke, *Terrorism and Global Disorder* (London: I.B. Tauris, 2006); and David Cole and Jules Lobel, *Less Safe, Less Free: Why America is Losing the War on Terror* (New York: The New Press, 2007). Documents and testimonies at the UK Iraq Inquiry on the invasion of Iraq can be found at http://www.iraqinquiry.org.uk/ (accessed 6 June 2010).

10 Democracy

Is 'democracy' the best answer to the bomber? A popular argument, advanced by politicians, officials, INGOs, and many commentators is that the progressive spread of democracy does indeed provide the long-term solution to the threat of politically motivated terror. By addressing grievances through negotiation and compromise, democracy offers the promise that the support for terror networks will evaporate and the money dry up. An equally popular argument is that terrorism is organically linked to authoritarian regimes. We want to question both arguments, and begin by calling for some sharper thinking: about the *types* of states (can we meaningfully divide the world into 'democracies' and 'non-democracies/authoritarian states', as is often done?), the conduct of the different types of states (do democratic countries criminalise terrorism while non-democratic countries harbour it?), and the relationship between democratic norms and cultures (is 'the Islamic state' compatible with democracy?). Before simply accepting that democracy is the answer to terrorism, we need to consider terrorism's relationship with authoritarian states.

Regime type and terrorism

In one of his hate speeches to the American people, and all those categorised as part of the 'Zionist crusader alliance', bin Laden said that had America been Sweden, there would have been no

9/11. But why should Sweden have been spared (assuming that we know why America had been punished)? Subsequently, of course, Sweden has not been spared. On 11 December 2010, Taimour-al-Abdaly set off two bombs in downtown Stockholm. He was the only fatality. Carl Bildt, Sweden's foreign minister, warned, however, that 'it could have been truly catastrophic'. An email received by the press only minutes before the bombs exploded blamed what was about to happen on Sweden's military presence in Afghanistan (it had around 500 troops there at the time), and the caricatures of the prophet Muhammad drawn by Swedish artist Lars Vilks five years previously. The journey that had been taken by Taimour-al-Abdaly had been similar to that of the 7/7 London bombers. An Iraqi-born Swede, he had spent time in the UK, having graduated from the University of Bedfordshire. He had travelled to Jordan; and al-Qaeda in Iraq claimed he was one of their 'brothers'.

This botched terror attack reveals the scope and reasoning behind al-Qaeda's choice targets. It also draws attention to issues relating to democracy and terrorism, and particularly to assumptions about the vulnerability of democratic states. Sweden is often mentioned when discussions arise about ideal societies; its per capita income is high, its involvement in inter-state wars has been low historically, and the protection for fundamental rights and freedoms has been unstinting. Even so, for the citizens of Sweden – and their privileged neighbours in Scandinavia – the rise of radicalised jihadists, willing to use terror, poses a threat, just as al-Qaeda has done to other open societies. The premise that democratic systems of governance are inhospitable to terrorism is based on the belief that opposition parties or groups can take up many voice opportunities to air their grievances. Why plant bombs, or wrap yourself in explosives, if political goals can be sought through political processes such as voting, lobbying, or standing for an election?

Democratic peace theory has been an influential idea in Western political circles through the past quarter of a century.[1] It claims that democracies are more peace-prone because they have institutional and legal processes that enable negotiated settlements of even the most hardened and opposed views. A narrower version of the theory holds that democracies are peace-prone only in their interactions with other democratic governments. In relations with what the philosopher Immanuel Kant called 'unjust enemies', democracies are seen to be as war-prone as any other regime type. Indeed, the relationships between democracy and violence in general belie simple formulae.

Those who juxtapose 'terror' and 'democracy' imply that liberal practices and institutions can help to minimise, if not eradicate, the underlying conditions which enable transnational jihadist groups to survive and proliferate. Such a view was influentially expressed after 9/11 in the book *The Case for Democracy* written by the former Soviet dissident, Natan Sharansky. As he simply and ardently put it: 'all free societies will guarantee security and peace'.[2] History suggests reality is more complex: terror (often) made democracies, and democracies (sometimes) make terror. The very word *terror* entered the political vocabulary to describe the violent overthrow of the *ancien régime* in France at the end of the eighteenth century. Subsequently, many democratic regimes owe their existence, in part, to successful campaigns of terror, with Israel and South Africa being two examples.

To this day, many 'local' terror campaigns are only intelligible in relation to unrealised claims to freedom and political autonomy made by particular ethno-national groups: we are thinking in recent years particularly of the Liberation Tigers in Sri Lanka, Hamas in Palestine, the Chechens in Russia, and Islamist separatists in South-East Asia (part of the region-wide network Jemaah Islamiya).

In addition to being potential drivers of democratisation, terrorist movements have also found democracies to be accommodating political systems. In Western Europe in the 1970s and 1980s, lethal terrorist groups – the Red Brigades in Italy, the Baader-Meinhof Gang in West Germany, and the IRA in Northern Ireland – took advantage of liberal political orders so they could organise, proselytise, recruit, strike, and hide. Indeed, a study of terrorist incidents in the early 1980s found that terrorist groups were more likely to be found in democracies by a factor of three and a half.[3] It is simply bad history to declare, as former president Bush did, that 'stable and free nations do not breed the ideologies of murder'.[4]

History records that the fate of democracies and that of terrorist movements have been interwoven; if it was so in earlier times of terror, why should it be different today? One continuity with the past is the relative freedom of association afforded by democratic societies, though as previous discussions have shown, this is a space that has narrowed with the rolling out of 'anti-terror' legislation since 9/11. Even so, countries that jealously guard freedoms of speech and association, and set limits on police and judicial interventions, remain vulnerable to the abuse of such freedoms by those whose actions undermine the liberties of all. To put the point another way: *a society cannot be open and democratic unless it provides for the conditions in which terrorists can act.* Freedom of speech, thought, assembly, and in the case of America, the constitutional right to bear arms, all enable the contemplation and carrying out of terror as surely as Americans believe them to be fundamental to the protection of civil liberties.

It has been pointed out in several chapters that terrorism is a form of communication − a particularly brutal and not always coherent form, but nonetheless a medium for messages. The global media is, therefore, a critical force multiplier for terrorists. The newsworthiness of human slaughtering − visceral scenes of severed limbs and bloodied bystanders − guarantees suicide and other types of terrorist an audience; this is one reason why terrorists seem to prefer targeting democracies.[5] Faisal Devji puts an ironic twist onto this argument by suggesting that a terror attack only becomes 'real' if it is aired on a global news network such as Al Jazeera or CNN, and downloadable from YouTube.[6]

While democracies, because of their openness and freedoms, do appear to be uniquely vulnerable to the harbouring of violent jihadist extremists, the reality is more complex. Governments in advanced liberal states have learned to manage the threat of international terrorism with some success; this is evident in the security of air travel and the protection of their national infrastructures. It is not inconceivable, of course, that a group of jihadists could acquire a surface-to-air missile and target a large passenger aircraft as it takes off; equally, a 9/11-style suicide flight could be flown into a stadium packed with sports fans. But these days such horrific scenarios are deterred or prevented by a range of (so far) effective counter-terrorism measures. This is why democratic societies in Europe and North America do not seem to be the political system of choice by al-Qaeda's headquarters and training camps when it comes to targeting; and why there has been a shift from spectaculars to microterrorism, as discussed in Chapter 4.

Despite the historical interplay of democracy and terror, and the presence of both international and home-grown jihadists in the world's most stable democratic states, there remains a great deal of faith in the mantra 'democracy is the answer'. Earlier in the decade, Bernard Lewis, an American scholar who exercises considerable influence on the policy agenda, declared that 'the war on terror and the struggle for freedom' are 'inextricably linked' and that neither can survive without the other. We agree with Lewis's premise though not his conclusion: the War on Terror (albeit in the name of the struggle for freedom) has unleashed profoundly undemocratic dynamics in world politics.[7]

Democracy and terror in the Arab and Islamic worlds

Academic thinking about the relationship between the promotion of democracy and the prevention of terrorism has found many echoes in the policy documents of leading states, international organisations, and INGOs. It has been the latest in a series of 'paradigm fixes' for the countries of the Middle East and North Africa, following on from the commitment to 'developmentalism' in Western policy-making during the Cold War.

Developmentalism hoped that economic growth and large-scale investment would lead to political stability (ideally democratisation), meet growing human needs, and promote pro-Western policies.

Across the Arab states in the Middle East since 1945 this trajectory proved problematical to say the least, though by 2011 the region appeared to be undergoing an 'Arab reawakening'. By the early 2000s, for sure, money did not equate with democracy in the Arab world. Per capita income levels in many Arab countries were comparable to successful and stable democracies in the global North: Kuwaitis were as rich as Swedes, Bahrainis were on a par with New Zealanders, Saudi Arabians with Portuguese, and Lebanese with Argentinians. The people of Egypt, Jordan, Morocco, and Syria were at the lower end of the distribution, although they were wealthier in per capita terms than either India or Indonesia, two of the world's largest democracies.[8]

Rather than being a locomotive for democracy in the region, the form of economic development that has taken place in the Arab world has been closely co-related with 'unfreedom' throughout the 18 countries in the region. According to the INGO Freedom House, only one country is 'free', and that is Israel (and only two countries are partially free – Lebanon and Kuwait – the remainder are considered not free).[9] This situation prompted Fareed Zakaria, doyen of Newsweek and CNN, to conclude in 2003 that 'almost every Arab country is less free than it was forty years ago'.[10] We will shortly discuss whether such categories – 'free', 'not free', 'partially free' – are useful, or whether they can be misleading. For the moment, let us look into the conditions of unfreedom in Muslim-majority countries.

One convincing explanation is 'the oil curse'. This emphasises the connection between the economic model of an 'extractive state' and the institutional arrangements that are designed to ensure that this wealth bolsters the power of the regime. The dynamics of the oil curse were neatly captured two decades ago by Samuel Huntington, then one of the leading American theorists on development, democracy, and big-picture world politics (before he became almost entirely identified with the Clash of Civilisations thesis). Huntington wrote:

> Oil revenues accrue to the state: they therefore increase the power of the state bureaucracy and, because they reduce or

eliminate the need for taxation, they also reduce the need for the government to solicit the acquiescence of its subjects to taxation. The lower the level of taxation, the less reason for publics to demand representation. 'No taxation without representation' was a political demand; 'no representation without taxation' is a political reality.[11]

Adding weight to this argument, Larry Diamond, founding editor of the journal *Democracy*, offers the striking claim that 'none of the 23 countries that derive most of their export earnings from oil and gas is a democracy today'. The only states that have succeeded in profiting from their extractive industries, without undermining their governance and legitimacy, have been countries such as Norway and the UK. This does not undermine Huntington's general explanation about extracting states. Rather, it shows that liberal and democratic principles need to be firmly embedded in a society prior to the accrual of windfall profits from oil and gas.[12] Democracy, if it is to be more than a slogan, involves a historical process requiring the building of respected institutions and the evolution of a sophisticated language of politics; it is a way of life, not an event that can be guaranteed by wealth or fiat.

The institutional order established by extraction states has been profoundly authoritarian. The elites owe their status to the state, and not to voters or shareholders; the rulers, in turn, rely on patronage to maintain power, not the legitimacy of the people. Power, a great deal of it, is essential for maintaining an authoritarian state, and three mechanisms in particular have been primarily responsible for their durability in modern times. The first is the size and scale of internal security services tasked with monitoring opposition groups and any 'enemies within'. The second is 'great and powerful' external allies such as America and the most powerful European states. These allies confer some legitimacy on autocracies through development assistance, trade deals, and multilateral arrangements. This provides 'regional strongmen' with international status despite the internal democratic deficit of their countries. The third mechanism has been the persistence of an elite consensus among Arab rulers fortified by a pan-Arabic identity; the latter itself is forged by a common language, shared history and religion, and a united posture towards the common enemy, the state of Israel.

In the past decade, Libya's regime has shown the many and complex ways in which 'the War on Terror and the struggle for freedom' have been linked; but they have not been positively co-related in the manner Bernard Lewis and others assert. During its first four decades after independence, Libya became one of the world's most repressive regimes. Under Qaddafi, detention without trial, torture, and execution became routine. There was no institutionalised protection for individuals and social groups from arbitrary abuse by government agents. In 2009, Fred Halliday, an acute exposer of gaps between rhetoric and reality, noted: 'Libya is not a state of the masses' as its promoters infer, 'it is a state of robbers, in formal terms, a kleptocracy'.[13]

In Qaddafi's Libya, terror at home accompanied terror abroad. On 21 December 1988, a Pan-Am jumbo jet with 259 passengers was blown up by Libyan agents and crashed into the Scottish town of Lockerbie, leaving no survivors; there were also 11 casualties on the ground. This act was a retaliation on the part of Qaddafi's regime for the bombing of Tripoli two years previously (which resulted in the death of his adopted daughter among others), when the United States sought retribution for the killing of one of its servicemen by the Libyan secret service in a Berlin nightclub. In 1984, a British policewoman, Yvonne Fletcher, was shot dead while she was controlling a small demonstration outside the Libyan diplomatic bureau in central London – an outrage for which, years later, Qaddafi accepted responsibility and paid damages to the family.

By the end of the Cold War, Qaddafi's Libya was regarded by Western governments as one of the leading sponsors of state terrorism. The UNSC itself had imposed sanctions on Libya after Lockerbie, in the light of Qaddafi's failure to cooperate with an investigation into the causes of the destruction of Pan-Am flight 103. Sir David Hannay, then UK ambassador to the United Nations, emphasised that Libya's terrorist activity had led to deaths of people from more than 30 countries; accordingly, he declared, 'The whole world has an interest in combating Terrorism'.

Paradoxically, 9/11 signalled the start of a significant change in Libya's international standing. After nine months of secret talks, in December 2003, Libya renounced its programme for the acquisition of chemical, biological, and nuclear weapons, and it permitted inspections of its facilities. Shortly afterwards, the British prime minister, Tony Blair, went to Tripoli to personally endorse the return of Libya to diplomatic normality. Blair said that he had been struck by how Qaddafi wanted to make 'common cause with us against al-Qaeda, extremists and terrorism'.[14] It must be noted that the Libyan regime had sought on several previous occasions to negotiate a similar deal (in 1999 and 2000) 'but it did not find a receptive audience'.[15] The world order agenda fashioned by the United States and its leading allies after the destruction of the Twin Towers became much more accommodating to tyrants.

Alliances with strange bedfellows, of course, are nothing new in international politics. It is one of the standard plays of *Realpolitik*. It is, therefore, not surprising to hear conservative opinion in the United States claiming that the critical test for its external support should not be such basic indicators of democracy as competitive elections, the rule of law, and fundamental freedoms, but whether a country is aligned with US grand strategy. From this viewpoint, great power interests always trump democracy. However, opinion poll data consistently show the popularity of democracy as a system of government in Muslim-majority countries in the Middle East and South-East Asia. The problem has not been that Arabs do not like democracy, or that democracy (in some form) is 'incompatible' with Islam; the problem is that governments in the world's most powerful state have not approved of the governments that the people have chosen.[16] This has been the case in Palestine, in Algeria, and elsewhere. Green shoots of democracy have been trying to break through in the Arab Middle East for many years. For example, the Iraqi turnout in successive elections after 2003 has been impressive, despite the internal turmoil and ever-present threat of violence.

In the first months of 2011 the authoritarian politics of the Middle East and North Africa characteristic of the Cold War and post-Cold War world order was challenged by publics on the move. Having toppled the Mubarak regime, Egyptian pro-democracy supporters campaigned outside the Libyan embassy in Cairo, carrying banners reading 'free Libya' and chanting 'the people want Arab nations united against military regimes'. It is too soon to tell whether this will turn out to be a '1989 moment' for the Arab Middle East – there are in any case significant differences between 2011 and the challenges faced in the achievement of democratic systems in central and eastern Europe 20 years earlier. While every state in the region has its own characteristics, there are grounds for thinking that change is possible in those places where the three mechanisms of authoritarian state control are in crisis: the crony model of patriarchal leadership; the unchecked power of the security services; and external support by powerful Western governments.

A striking feature of the political and social revolutions that began to grip North Africa and the Middle East has been the virtual absence of al-Qaeda's ideology, strategy, or tactics. What has animated the demonstrators does not appear to have anything to do with al-Qaeda's mission to defeat the Far Enemy and establish a transnational Islamic state. To the contrary, the revolutions have been targeting the Near Enemy, and for their denial of democratic rights and freedoms, not the absence of Islamic purity. It is amusing to record that al-Qaeda's chief appearance in the revolutions in 2011 was as a scare word by Qaddafi; facing a powerful rebellion in eastern Libya, Qaddafi made the improbable claim that the people of Zawiyah had 'turned to bin Laden'. This claim was as incredible as his allegation that the demonstrators against him had a drug problem. On top of the declining legitimacy of al-Qaeda over a number of years, the progress made by popular revolutions against local despots – something al-Qaeda signally failed to do in the 1990s – further challenges its leaders to demonstrate their relevance to the overwhelming majority of the Islamic world. While al-Qaeda has been marginalised, it is nonetheless expected that Islamic parties will play some role in the future governance of these countries once the dust settles, and perhaps a significant one. What is critical to the future of the region, if democracy does spread, is that these parties work through the institutions of the state and renounce terrorism in all its forms.

Survey data underscore the general acceptance of the view that Islam must play a 'strong role' in political life. Surveys in Egypt, Indonesia, Lebanon, Nigeria, and Pakistan returned figures of over 70 per cent holding such views. This is not surprising, and one might even think the figures low, given the understanding discussed in Chapter 5 that in Islamic countries politics is part of life as a religious experience. What should also be recognised is the priority accorded to Muslim identity and Islamic institutions in these countries, over and above their identity as citizens of particular states.[17] These survey data also give indicative reasons for thinking democratic reforms can co-exist with Islamic state structures.

Discussion about democracy in the Middle East, as with much else, must eventually come round to Israel. In this case the view of many people in the West is that Israel is a regional 'beacon of democracy'. Israel might be Freedom House's most-favoured state in the Middle East but this should give us reason to reflect on the limits of this debate, for its neighbours and many critics throughout the world consider Israel an international pariah; this is because of its repeated breaches of UN resolutions on Jewish settlements on Palestinian land, the building of its massive 'security fence', the ruthless siege of Gaza,[18] and its revisionist stance on its internationally agreed boundaries. The War on Terror accentuated the dynamic of law-breaking on the part of both the Israeli and Palestinian authorities; this suggests that democracies can be war-like as well as peace-prone, and can connive in terror attacks as well as seek negotiated compromises.[19] The future of democracy, terrorism, and the international politics of the region depends critically on these two countries.

Simple associations are best avoided when considering the Middle East. Israel has a brave peace movement as well as a tough military machine. And Hamas is not simply a terrorist organisation. In that regard, there are reasons for thinking that terrorist activity by supporters of Hamas would diminish if there was a negotiated solution to the Palestine question. Hamas has a political and social programme and a constituency of supporters who share these general goals and who are not 'terrorists'. In 2009 its Interior Minister, Fathi Hamad, declared: 'Claims that we are trying to establish an Islamic state are false . . . Hamas is not the Taliban. It is not al-Qaeda. It is an enlightened, moderate Islamic movement.'[20] Hamas, we believe, underlines the point that there is no meaningful parallel between political movements that resort to a contingent strategy of terror in their struggle against a specific enemy, and the absolutism of bin Laden's revolutionary jihadists. As we discussed in Chapter 4, al-Qaeda's identity is built on what is claimed to be a pure version of Islam, where sovereignty in all its manifestations comes from God. Democracy, being based on civil laws, is therefore regarded as a 'deviant system'. Consequently, al-Qaeda members and supporters regard democracy promotion as an attempt to supplant the rule of God by the rule of secular institutions and leaders. It is almost impossible, therefore, to comprehend how any of the opportunities enabled by democratic societies would not be viewed as a sham, whether this is to change government, to tolerate dissent, to conduct politics within a legal framework, or to inculcate shared values (such as freedom of speech) based on democratic ideals.[21] In this regard, note al-Zarqawi's rejection of the 2005 election result in Iraq, on the ground that in a democracy it was the legislator who had to be obeyed, 'and not God'.[22]

Such beliefs as al-Zarqawi's help explain why so many people in the Muslim-majority world are on the move, while al-Qaeda is being left behind as a political force. Democracy and Islam are not incompatible. Indeed, a striking feature of political systems in the Arab and Islamic worlds has been the popularity of 'moderate' Islamic parties. The trend started with the Algerian elections of 1990, and it has continued. Of the three Islamic states that have embraced recognisable democratic systems, two provide successful models for their co-existence (Turkey and Indonesia) while a third (Pakistan) has lurched from crisis to crisis as it has become part of the 'front-line' in the War on Terror. Even if state–society relations in the Islamic world continue to reform such that they are better able to provide for the good life of their publics, the power of Islam as a transnational community is unlikely to diminish in the foreseeable future, even if its political expression – as in the 'Arab spring' of 2011 – becomes less assertive. One of the striking features of the second half of the decade of the War on Terror has been the diminishing legitimacy among Muslims everywhere of using terror.

There is much that can be learned from a dialogue between scholars writing on Islamic and liberal-democratic modes of governance, their underlying political theories, and their histories. Convergences are evident in that both share experiences of multiculturalism (the Ottoman empire's model predated that of Europe), both have a conception of ethical citizenship (charity being one of the five pillars of Islam), and both have exhibited the principle of tolerance and even secularism (the Indian Muslim Emperor Akbar defended the need for the state to be 'equidistant from different religions' at a time when the Inquisition was inflicting religious terror on Europe).[23] In the settled systems of the developed, democratic world – where excessive self-regard can sometimes obscure reality – we all know about the tensions in multiculturalism, failures in ethical citizenship, intolerance, and secular norms being challenged by the co-mingling of faith and politics. The foundations for such a dialogue are much stronger than the extremists and pessimists on both sides since 9/11 allow; as Susan Buck-Morss, an American political theorist keen to promote *Thinking Past Terror* has written, 'we cannot allow our identities to hold us apart'.[24]

Further reading

For an optimistic account of the relationship between democracy and security, see Natan Sharansky and Don Dermer, *The Case for Democracy: The Power of Freedom to Overcome Tyranny and Terror* (New York: Public Affairs,

2004). Works focusing on the question of renewal in the Islamic world include Noah Feldman, *The Fall and Rise of the Islamic World* (Princeton: Princeton University Press, 2008); Ali A. Allawi, *The Crisis of Islamic Civilization* (Yale: Yale University Press, 2009). For an outstanding comparative political analysis of democracy, see Charles Tilly, *Democracy* (Cambridge: Cambridge University Press, 2007). On democracy promotion, compare Thomas Carothers, *Critical Mission: Essays on Democracy Promotion* (Washington: Carnegie, 2004) with the critical essays included in A. Geis, L. Brock, and H. Müller (eds), *Democratic Wars: Looking at the Dark Side of Democratic Peace* (Houndmills: Palgrave, 2006).

11   Security

Security is the essential concept in every discussion about terrorism. Security, its presence or absence, is a 'fact of human existence', and as such is at the very heart of politics both within and between states. In the practices of foreign and defence policy, and in maintaining state sovereignty, the achievement of the goal of 'security' is the benchmark of success. This leads some to argue that security *must come before* politics; in other words, something called security must be established before politics can meaningfully take place. This is not our view. Instead, security should be understood as an intrinsic value within politics: what security *is*, how it is *achieved*, and *against* which threats it defends, are all derivative of particular conceptions of politics. Security is politics (and, therefore, ethics) not a mode of conduct outside politics, and is integral to our conception of world order.

Geopolitics: 9/11 v. 2011

If security is the heart of politics among nations, geopolitics is the heart of traditional thinking about security. Geopolitics can be considered to be international politics in the raw: that is, 'power politics', material strength, military potential, the strategic significance of location, the distribution of resources, and a state's ability to manipulate balances of power. For the student of geopolitics, power is destiny. It is also the level of policy-making where, if governments get the big picture wrong then 'stuff happens', to use the notorious phrase of the former US defense secretary Donald Rumsfeld.[1]

Traditionally, geopolitics has been considered to be the terrain of exponents of *Realpolitik* and 'realism' in international politics. The watchwords of these traditions have been prudence, sensitivity to power, feasibility, caution when contemplating war, avoiding moralising in foreign policy, rejecting Manichaean thinking. The mindset of the US and UK leaders after 9/11 represented a radical departure from these traditions. Instead, it was ideology that was doing the work not prudence, and faith not feasibility. As the coalition of democracies rushed to war against Iraq in 2003, a group of leading realists put their names to a letter warning against what was being planned. It was headed 'war with Iraq is not in America's national interest'.[2] It was ignored. Stuff happened.

If the big picture in geopolitics is wrong, it is predictable that things will go wrong in detail. In big-picture thinking, an old and familiar danger is that of 'fighting the last war'. In the present context, that means the risk of the world's leading power remaining too wedded to seeing the challenges of world order too much through the lens of 9/11. We think there is such a risk, though hope previous chapters leave readers in no doubt about how dangerous we think terrorism can be. One major entry into this debate, which frames the future too strongly through the lens of the recent past, is *Terror and Consent* by Philip Bobbitt, a senior adviser to the White House and other branches of the US government.[3] This book, which has received glowing endorsements from leading political figures and opinion-makers, advances the *everything has changed* narrative discussed in Chapter 3, and projects a picture of wars in the rest of the century through a 9/11 lens.

According to Bobbitt, each type of state through history has provoked its own form of terrorism. In this era we are moving from the traditional nation-state to the 'market state', and so the threat is 'market state terrorism', with the confrontation being between terror or consent as the basis for a state's legitimacy.[4] This new form of terrorism – market state terrorism – will be just as global, networked, decentralised, and devolved as the market state itself; and will rely just as much on outsourcing and incentivising.[5] Compared with its predecessor (nation-state terrorism), Bobbitt says it is more lethal, better financed, often outsourced, more decentralised, less hierarchically structured, more adept at modern communications technology, more likely to seek and use WMD, more theatrical, and 'no longer simply a technique but . . . also an end in itself'. Al-Qaeda, for example, is said to be distinct from nation-state terrorism by not wanting simply to seize a particular state; instead, Bobbitt explains al-Qaeda as a reaction to globalised market states of consent, and incompatible with international regimes of human rights. As a result, he suggests there will be 'attempts to achieve a constant state of terror' in pursuit of the goal of establishing a global caliphate.

Whatever one thinks of his characterisation of al-Qaeda, a more significant issue at this point is the way Bobbitt lumps al-Qaeda with the whole gamut of terrorist organisations. He writes:

> The goals of ecoterrorists (whose desired world is incompatible with the consumption patterns of the developed world, and indeed of the desires of peoples generally throughout the world), animal-rights terrorists (whose desired world gives a political voice to nonhumans that can overrule the democratic determined wishes of any society), antiglobalization terrorists (who define themselves against the currents that are bringing the market state itself into being), and groups that have yet to gel have this in common: they cannot accept the existence of market states of consent, and thus will be at perpetual war with them that make terror an end as well as a means. The requirement for perpetual conflict translates in light of how armed conflict is developing . . . into a requirement for a continual state of terror.[6]

This bundling of terrorisms is breathtaking. It is reminiscent of the loose use of the label 'communist' in the Cold War, when superficial similarities were allowed to obliterate significant

differences between groups, such that their Marxisms were elevated far above their nationalisms. Bad strategy followed bad
analysis, and the failure of US governments to impose democracy
in South Vietnam and elsewhere in South-East Asia remains a tes-
tament to the dangers of flawed big-picture thinking. The terrorisms bundled together by Bobbitt have even less in common than
did the 'Marxists' whose commonality existed only in the anti-
communist mindsets of Cold War hawks.

The danger here is of the world's most powerful state engaging
the future through a 9/11 mindset when world order dynamics
are visibly moving on, with the lens of 2011 offering glimpses of
different opportunities and dangers, not least in the Arab world.[7]
The decades ahead will be tumultuous, as human society will
predictably come face-to-face with historic challenges arising out of global business-as-usual: climate change, population
expansion, food insecurity, energy pressures, water shortages,
the spread of WMD, the destruction of the natural world, and
the gaps between the haves and have-nots.[8] In addition, policy-
agendas will include old geopolitical issues such as power transi-
tions, security dilemmas, and inter-state conflict. Terrorism can
have a role in these issue-areas as a spoiler and a distractor. Recall,
for example, the discussion on p. 35 of the way acts of terror
have, on several occasions, set back the prospects of dialogue
between Iran and the United States. Recall also the way preoccu-
pations with terrorism have distracted the attention of the White
House: how the obsession with Saddam Hussein and his fictional
association with al-Qaeda allowed the real al-Qaeda leadership
to escape into the mountains of Afghanistan and Pakistan, and
how the obsession with Saddam Hussein and his fictional WMD
allowed the real nuclear programmes of North Korea and Iran to
accelerate.

In the geopolitical churn of the near future, the danger exists
that the 9/11-lens could distract Washington from what many
consider to be the central issue of the day, that of 'power transition' between an ostensibly declining United States and a rising China. Periods of power transition are often thought to be

particularly dangerous in international relations. Consequently, appropriate attention and resources are essential if dangers are to be minimised. In this regard, it is noteworthy that China is not a central player in Bobbitt's scenario of market state terrorism. At another level, the kaleidoscope of international affairs is throwing up Russia, India, and Brazil as major players – and each of them has to be carefully integrated into the emerging multipolar world dominated by the United States and China. The United States' relationship with China is not only critical globally, but also in key geopolitical regions. Not least of these is what in many ways has been the epicentre of 9/11 + 10: it is often overlooked that China shares borders with Afghanistan and also with Jammu and Kashmir (the area disputed between Pakistan and India, and partially occupied by China since 1962).

In earlier chapters we drew attention to Pakistan, and claims that it is probably the world's most dangerous geopolitical place. Its security agenda is indeed a witch's brew: the presence of al-Qaeda and the Taliban in the north; the frequent use of terror as a continuation of politics; the continuing disputes with India (Kashmir, nuclear rivalry, and Indian suspicions about Pakistani involvement in terrorism within India); renegade nuclear scientists; growing religious intolerance characterised by an 'infamous' blasphemy law that has resulted in the assassination of several politicians and others; the overspill of the conflict in Afghanistan, with incursions by US special forces, al-Qaeda activity, attacks by US drones; widespread suspicion outside Pakistan of the role of state institutions and individuals in terrorism (heightened by the discovery in Abbottabad of bin Laden); and on top of all this there has been a series of natural disasters and continuing widespread poverty. Pakistan is a precarious polity, but so far (and perhaps indefinitely) the worst has been avoided by stubborn politicians keeping the creaking democratic institutions alive, by an elite committed to maintaining the nation's reputation and integrity, and by a resilient population.

But let us not forget the extreme crisis potential represented by Pakistan's situation. However remote, we showed in Chapter 3 that the occurrence of low-probability catastrophic events is not unknown. In his scenario 'A Brilliant Yellow Light', Brian Michael Jenkins sits his readers at the desk of a US president faced by an incident of nuclear terrorism in Manhattan. As the crisis escalates, Pakistan figures prominently, as the president is faced by conflicting information, mixed advice, and only terrible choices. Towards the end reports come in of 'intense fighting at Pakistan's main nuclear weapons sites', and of Indian military aircraft being 'in the air'. 'We may have little time . . .'.[9]

Nuclear weapons and terrorism have also figured among geopolitical concerns in the Middle East, but with the additional ingredient of oil in this witch's brew. As Dick Cheney once cynically remarked, 'The Good Lord didn't see fit to put oil and gas only where there are democratically elected regimes friendly to the United States'.[10] While much discussion in earlier chapters has focused on the power of ideas (jihadi beliefs and neoconservative ideology, for example) we should never overlook the geopolitical interest of all states in energy security; and this has been a central feature of US grand strategy ever since its rise to superpowerdom.[11] Energy security ties US grand strategy to the Middle East for the foreseeable future, regardless of any other considerations. But, of course, there are other considerations, with one in particular not being explicable in traditional geopolitical 'power politics' terms, namely the relationship with Israel.

The special relationship between America and Israel is critical to world order and international terrorism because of the Palestine question. At the outset of the War on Terror it was well understood that future relations between Israel and Palestine would be central to making progress in the management of jihadist terrorism. Despite such an understanding, the past ten years have seen a lack of progress along the 'road maps' promised, and in the peace processes initiated or revived. Given the character of the special US/Israel relationship, relatively few Americans would identify with the impassioned fury of the journalist Robert Fisk on the importance of the Palestine question. On the ninth anniversary of September 11 he wrote: 'The madness of 9/11 is more entrenched than ever'. At the centre of his argument was the Palestine question, which he introduced in relation to 'the one taboo subject of which we must not speak – Israel's relationship with America, and America's unconditional support for Israel's theft of land from Muslim Arabs'. He insisted that while many in the West preferred to ignore it, the War on Terror is 'also about Israel and "Palestine"'.[12]

Fisk is right. The history of Israel and Palestine cannot be isolated from future questions of international terrorism and world order. This history, from the Palestinian side includes: al-Nakba ('The Catastrophe') which resulted in the establishment of the state of Israel and the beginning of the continuing Palestinian refugee crisis; the Israeli occupation of additional territory since 1967; the suffering of Palestinians on the West Bank and in Gaza; the endless failure of external bodies to bring peace; Israeli defiance of UN resolutions; the brutal actions of the government of Israel – all these things and more engage the sympathies of Muslims everywhere, as well as a substantial body of non-Muslim opinion. This history has been central in the transformation of some moderately religious, generally apolitical young men in some Western cities into jihadists, as we noted with Mohammed Siddique Khan, one of the London bombers.[13] But while Fisk is right to remind us of what is involved in the Palestine question, it does not follow that if peace could somehow be achieved between Israel and Pakistan the leaders of al-Qaeda would decide to call it a day.

The popular uprisings that spread through several Arab countries in early 2011 confront both al-Qaeda and Israel with dilemmas. We will discuss the former in the next chapter. Israeli leaders, like their US backers, have generally been more comfortable with Arab dictators prioritising order rather than the volatile 'Arab street' – whose priorities have often seemed threatening. This is just one of the uncertainties introduced into the politics and security issues of the Arab world by the spirit of democracy that finally began to rattle the cages of old thinking about the Middle East and North Africa at the turn of 2010–11.

'Bread, freedom, social justice!'

This so-called Arab spring brings together questions of security at the level of geopolitics (the prospect of different sorts of relations between governments) but also security at the level of individuals and groups (the hope of better lives). One of the major developments in thinking about international relations since the Second World War has been the conceptual broadening of security to include not only the defence of state sovereignty but also the improvements of the lives of individuals and groups. In this section we focus on the human security level, where the picture since 9/11 has been of almost unremitting insecurity. We offer four snapshots.

First: the disruption of ordinary lives

The widespread human insecurity caused by the different versions of the 'paradigm of prevention' resulted in the rule of law, in the view of two senior US law professors, becoming 'virtually unrecognizable'.[14] Processes that had been central to civilised life were set aside as counter-terrorist measures were justified on the grounds of security. The measures ranged from the relatively harmless, such as surveillance cameras, to depriving individuals of their liberty without charge or adequate information. The excesses fed hostile propaganda by opening up the self-styled champions of freedom to charges of hypocrisy. Some measures, and the way they were implemented, were wrong both in principle and prudentially. In the words of lawyers David Cole and Jules Lobel, 'Abandoning the rule of law is not just wrong as a matter of principle. It is wrongheaded as a practical matter of security. The administration's turn to preventive coercion has actually made us more vulnerable to attack, not more secure.'[15]

Throughout many parts of the world people have been made to feel more insecure not so much by any direct experience of terrorism as by their direct experiences of counter-terrorism. It sometimes seems as if people feel scared because they are protected, rather than feel protected because they are scared. These measures of protection include the by-now familiar menu of surveillance activities, legal innovations, police with heavier firepower, additional security checks, more robust police methods, and so on. In Britain after 2003 a key manifestation of the developing culture of counter-terrorism was the coordination of government activities under the CONTEST strategy ('Pursue, Prevent, Protect, Prepare'); this culture of counter-terrorism became normalised in national life.

Counter-terrorism measures raise the old issue of the need to 'balance liberty and security'. In our view, as moral values, liberty and security cannot be separated (even if implementing counter-terrorist policies requires thinking carefully about their relative priority in specific instances). We cannot have liberty and security domestically without free speech, and we cannot have human rights and security overseas without the rules of international law. The package is inseparable. So, when somebody asks for 'liberty' to be sacrificed for 'security' we must interrogate the values of the politics behind the claim.

Second: host communities

The feelings of insecurity arising out of the growing risk of direct terror attacks were obviously intensified by images of explosions and accounts of foiled attacks in major cities throughout the world. The uncertainty of life became normalised at a higher register in 9/11 + 10. The old concept of the 'security dilemma' is relevant here, namely the uncertainties we have from not knowing the intentions of others, and the uncertainty of not knowing how best to act to minimise bad possibilities. Horrific terror attacks have resulted in the concept of the security dilemma (originally developed to explain problems in relations between governments) becoming individualised. Security dilemmas now board buses and subway trains in the daily rush-hour. Minds occupied by knowledge of terror will closely examine a fellow passenger who looks different, and they will wonder what might be hidden in the backpack on the floor.[16] Such suspicions have been heightened by the terrifying knowledge that terrorists are not bogeymen from 'over there', but come in home-grown varieties. They are 'like us', except they have been radicalised by preachers, the internet, life experiences, what they regard as hateful foreign policies and counter-terrorist measures, and the feeling they are targets of blatant anti-Muslim prejudice.

'Multiculturalism', once seen by many in host communities as a progressive policy, has increasingly become a negative term. The UK prime minister David Cameron voiced his criticisms of it in March 2011. Such concerns on the part of the host community, even if expressed in sober language at the highest level, easily feed the forces of extremism, from far-right groups marching in the street, to the mindless burning of a Qur'an in a church in Florida, to the publication of a book by a former head of the Bundesbank, Thilo Sarrazin, attacking the intelligence of immigrants, and to the complaints of Peter King, chair of the House Homeland Security Committee, that Muslims in America are not doing enough to counter radicalisation. Words, sometimes, are equivalent to deeds.

Third: immigrant communities

The radicalisation of Muslims, in turn, is fed and legitimised by what is seen – in some cases rightly, in some quite misguidedly – as 'Islamophobia'. This refers to the extreme suspicion of Islam on the part of host communities, and of the Muslim population which is feared to be growing in numbers and vociferousness.[17] For their part, Muslim communities since 9/11 in many Western countries fear victimisation simply because of their religion's identification with terrorism.

The situation of Muslim communities in the West varies greatly between countries, yet despite problems, individuals prefer to remain there rather than in Muslim-majority states elsewhere. In the Netherlands, Muslim immigrants are mostly of Indonesian origin and are generally 'law-abiding and religiously undemanding', reflecting their origins, while in France one-fifth of Muslims marry outside their religion.[18] But no country in the West where there is a large Muslim population has been free of tension, including the Netherlands (symbolised by the murder of the filmmaker Theo Van Gogh in Amsterdam) and France (where a 2004 law banned girls from wearing headscarves in public schools). Tensions inflame passions, and the worrying fact is, as we pointed out on p. 60, that a terrorist group requires only a minute proportion of an immigrant community to become radicalised, in order for it to pursue its objectives.

When immigrant communities are not being victimised they feel they are being patronised; as we explained in Chapter 8, this occurs when individuals believe themselves 'miniaturised', to use Sen's term, by being seen as having one identity and belonging only to one 'community'. Equally objectionable is being patronised by political leaders (gesturing towards 'the Muslim community') who choose unelected 'community leaders' with whom to consult.

'Islamophobia' finds many sources of fuel: terrorism conducted explicitly in the name of Islam, reports of extremist teachings, attacks on Christian churches by Islamic militants in various countries, expressions of conservative attitudes towards women and so on. The list is familiar. But those of us who reject Islamophobia should not allow empathetic impulses toward fellow citizens who are Muslims to dull the critical senses, for there is a great deal to criticise in the behaviour of many across the world who act in the name of Islam. In a generally sympathetic article about Baroness Warsi, Britain's first Muslim cabinet minister, Andrew Anthony recently drew attention to her own criticism of the 'intolerance of secularist fundamentalists'. He wrote:

> This is the kind of language that plays well among many religious activists. However, there is a hidden paradox in Warsi's position. She wants to give greater voice to religion in the political arena, yet she also wishes there to be less criticism of religion, in other words, power without scrutiny.

Anthony insisted that she should recognise the distinction between reservations people might have about particular aspects of Islam (as practised) and blanket condemnation of all Muslims: the latter is 'Islamophobia', the former is not. He commended Warsi for defending Muslims against discrimination, but 'not for placing Islam beyond critical debate'.[19]

Fourth: 'Beautiful Souls' and 'Just Warriors'

In her path-breaking book of the 1980s, Women and War, Jean Bethke Elshtain described how ideas about gender have been deeply rooted in the mythology of war, with Man as 'Just Warrior' and Woman as 'Beautiful Soul'.[20] Elshtain argued that these myths, while still influential, did not match the realities of modern war; the same is true with terrorism and wars to counter it.

Men as Just Warriors? During 9/11 + 10, many fine men carried out their duty as soldiers, acting honourably according to the norms of war, and risking all for their countries. Regrettably, their governments have not risked all for them; this is an old story in contemporary guise. Andrew J. Bacevich, West Point-trained former officer in Vietnam and the Gulf War, now a Professor of History and International Relations, is but one who has criticised his government for the 'cavalier' attitude towards volunteer soldiers: they 'fight our battles out of sight and out of mind'; for a while they returned in coffins 'in the shroud of night'; and they have sometimes 'endured inhumane treatment in military hospitals'.[21] There is more still.

Just Warriors can morph into brutal and remorseless killers. A microcosm of this is 'The Wounded Platoon'.[22] A typical 'Band of Brothers' from Fort Carson, Colorado, went to fight in a war they hardly grasped, in a place they understood even less. Alongside accounts of heroism, a much darker story unfolded of alcohol, drugs, shootings, murder, violence, and trauma. As has happened so often in the past, the war in the men's heads did not stop when they returned home. Seventeen soldiers from Third Platoon, Charlie Company, had by 2010 been convicted of murder, manslaughter, or attempted murder.

Women as Beautiful Souls? Women are no longer forgotten in the study of war; and they have attracted research attention in the study of contemporary terrorism. The phenomenon of female suicide terrorists has been an issue of shocked interest among researchers (and also people at large); and women have been seen to play supportive roles in organisations where terror is employed, such as Hezbollah. Women also have featured as agents of state policy, and the war in Iraq created conditions whereby two in particular will stand forever as objects of enquiry in the study of gender. The first involved the saving of Private Lynch. This was a story of attractive Jessica Lynch being saved by brave (male) US soldiers, except it was later exposed (unknown to Private Lynch) to have been staged. Jessica later said, 'They used me as a way to symbolize this stuff'. The other case is Lynndie England, who was centrally involved in the abuse of Iraqi prisoners, including their sexual humiliation, at Abu Ghraib in 2004. She was subsequently convicted of prisoner mistreatment and sentenced to prison. What the stories of the two women show is that gender stereotypes are alive and well, with one woman (falsely) exploited for Beautiful Soul propaganda, and the other exhibiting the very opposite of Beautiful Soul behaviour.

The dominant image of women in war has been as victims, and rape as a political tactic has had more publicity since the early 1990s than ever before – consistent with the developing human security agenda. Alan Dershowitz has described rape as terrorism, following a case in which a group of Palestinians had raped teenage Israeli girls. One of the Palestinians said: 'We are raping Jews because of what the Israel Defense Forces is doing to the Palestinians in the territories.' Press reports of the case indicated they showed no remorse: 'They feel they are entirely justified as acts of political revenge.' Dershowitz also said that Palestinian terrorists had raped Palestinian women to make them become suicide terrorists. 'I often wonder', he reflected, 'how any feminists can support one of the most sexist regimes in the world, namely the Hamas controlled Palestinian Authority, while opposing one of the most gender integrated regimes in the world, namely Israel.'[23]

Among the iconic images of 9/11 + 10, those of prisoner abuse in Abu Ghraib are incomparable; but a close contender is a photograph of Aisha, a beautiful young Afghan woman aged 18, which was the front cover of *Time* magazine in the summer of 2010. On orders from the Taliban, her nose and ears had been cut off. *Time's* cover story was entitled 'What Happens if We Leave Afghanistan'.[24] The magazine was accused by feminists among others of complicity in justifying occupation, through the cynical exploitation of a woman victim of the war (this was an accusation that was also levelled against the US government, and Wikileaks documents are reported to confirm CIA endorsement of using the plight of Afghan women to rally public support for the war).

In criticising the exploitation of images such as that of Aisha, the Cambridge academic Priyamvada Gopal took the opportunity to criticise the affluent West not only for having nothing substantial to offer Afghanistan, but also for failing at home. Her words deserve quoting at length:

> In the affluent west itself, modernity is now about dismantling welfare systems, increasing inequality (disproportionately disenfranchising women in the process), and subsidising corporate profits. Other ideas once associated with modernity – social justice, economic fairness, peace, all of which would enfranchise Afghan women – have been relegated to the past in the name of progress.

Gopal's comments in a curious way bind people in very different geopolitical settings into a community of human insecurity caused by the dynamics and oppressions of the world order. The political values she noted have been the rallying cries across the world and across the centuries when people have been oppressed. In Britain in the nineteenth century calls for emancipation were associated with the Chartists. One of their leading figures, William Lovett, summed up his goal in the title of his book *The Pursuit of Bread, Knowledge, and Freedom*.[25] These words evoke the desire for material well-being; the desire for freedom from ignorance, superstition, and lies; and the dream of liberation from political tyranny and economic exploitation. Such political values echo down the centuries, and sometimes in almost exactly the same word order. So it was in Tahrir Square in Cairo in January 2011, the focal point of popular revolution in the Arab world. Among the massed crowds calling for the fall of the brutal dictatorship was the chant: 'Bread! Freedom! Social justice!'[26]

Here we see the potential of security at the human level to transform not only the lives of ordinary people, but also through changes at the highest level bring about reconfigurations of relations in international politics. In the expression of such shared political values can be glimpsed the realisation – 'thinking past terror'[27] – of the possibility of shared identities and interests across the traditional walls built up by religion, nationalism, race, culture, class, and gender. 9/11, Lower Manhattan, was a shared place for common humanity. 2011, Tahir Square, was another.

Further reading

On *Realpolitik*, realism, and geopolitics, the best contemporary work is John Mearsheimer, *The Tragedy of Great Power Politics* (New York: Norton, 2001). For an overview of US grand strategy, the best book is G. John Ikenberry, *Liberal Leviathan: The Origins, Crisis and Transformation of the American World Order* (Princeton, NJ: Princeton University Press, 2011). A feminist theory perspective on women and violence is Laura Sjoberg and Caron Gentry, *Mothers, Monsters, Whores: Women's Violence in Global Politics* (London: Zed, 2007). For a comprehensive framework for understanding security as a political value as represented in this chapter see Ken Booth, *Theory of World Security* (Cambridge: Cambridge University Press, 2007).

12 Endings

'De quoi s'agit-il?' The simplest questions can be the biggest. 'What is it all about?' is the question Marshal Ferdinand Foch, one-time allied Commander-in-Chief in the First World War, used to ask his subordinates.[1] In this final chapter we want to think about that simple yet profound question in relation to the on-going struggle against terrorism since 9/11.

In the course of 9/11 + 10 influential opinion in the West offered a range of answers to Foch's question. These included: it is about reinvigorating US global hegemony and democracy promotion (the Bush doctrine); about defending civilised values against evil (the Just War doctrine adopted by liberal internationalists); about retaliating against new threats before they take place (the prevention paradigm); and about the clash of civilisations (in which religion featured more or less prominently). From the earliest days after 9/11 there were radically different answers to these big-picture perspectives. For one, the eminent military historian Michael Howard reminded everyone that terrorism is something we had experienced before, and advised that the optimum strategy would be to coordinate an international policing policy to contain and prevent future threats. Cool and considered words such as these were spoken by a number of voices in the initial weeks after 9/11, but were not heard by policy-makers in the dominant states and international organisations.

As was argued throughout Part I (Terror and danger), *pathologies in world order* provide our basic answer to the question 'What is it all about?' Before discussing these further, let us consider the purpose of world order: to provide for the conditions in which basic human rights to life, freedom, and equality (within practical limits) are respected by the strong and extended to the weak.

To evaluate whether or not contemporary world order is achieving the purpose we have indicated, it is necessary to consider the pillars that produce and sustain it. World order is 'all about' the political struggle over dominant ideas, the institutional rules in relation to the control and regulation of violence, and the unequal local and global power relations. In the course of our book, the focus has been on dominant ideas and rules, and responses to them, in the aftermath of 9/11, and how these have informed practices taken up by states, organisations, and civil society. The political economy of world order, a companion book in itself, has not been the primary concern here.

World order, as it was practised by the leading powers after 9/11, failed to promote the conditions of security considered in all its dimensions and levels. These are the failings we refer to as the pathologies of world order. Richard Falk, a leading thinker on these matters, has criticised the world order that developed historically for not supporting 'an invariable practice of nonviolence'. 'Will it ever?' many people ask. If business-as-usual mindsets continue to rule the conduct of politics among nations, there can be only one, pessimistic answer. In this regard, we must not lose sight of the important fact that the challenge of global jihadist terrorism has been one more variation on a history of private forms of violence, albeit with greater lethality. All previous world orders have been subject to the sometimes deadly consequences of organised violence, whether public (states) or private (be they revolutionaries, insurgents, pirates, or terrorists).

Specific pathologies of world order have been conspicuous since 9/11; as a result, the achievement of world security remains elusive. We have not tempered our criticism of the choices that were made and the paths not taken, though we emphasised in Chapter 1 that we recognised that international crises place particular pressures on governments to react quickly and decisively, and that some of the loudest calls they face for quick and decisive action are from those who bear little or no responsibility for the consequences.

Resisting the clamour to take military action after the 9/11 attacks would have been almost impossible, given the tide of public opinion in favour of the War on Terror. The pressures to rush forward were multiple, and among them were pathological mindsets parading prejudices about the terrorist perpetrators of the attacks, and towards the communities with which they were identified.

Prejudice was one aspect of a broader pathology of ethnocentrism that has been evident in the book. During 9/11 + 10 Islam has often been represented as a degenerate civilisation that has proven unable to adapt to modernity. Closely related to this has been the pathology of exceptionalism. This has been evident in relation to complicity in torture and the rewriting of rules over the use of force rather than respect for the law; in the excessive faith shown in militarised responses to terrorism rather than fighting clever; and in militant democracy promotion yet not always respecting the will of the people when the people speak what one does not want to hear. The book has also given numerous examples of the pathology of hypocrisy in which leaders enhanced their authority by inflating threats and inventing enemies in a way that generated insecurity rather than resilience.

It is through examining such pathologies that we have sought to understand complex questions about contemporary terrorism. It was beyond the scope of this book to embrace the broadest sweep of history, and discuss the centuries of decline of Islam and the domination of world order by the West. Our focus has been more specifically on the world order that emerged after the end of the Cold War, and which enabled the United States and its allies to implement a grand strategy that was highly antagonistic to Muslim minorities in the West, as well as to Islamic states and Muslim-majority countries in Africa, the Middle East, and South and East Asia. These failings were exacerbated in their impact on world order by the serious divisions between, and weaknesses within, Islamic states, and problems among Muslims themselves.

Recapping the book's approach to understanding jihadist extremism enables a consideration of the ideas and dynamics that might shape a different order – together with the opportunities presented for containing current terrorist threats, bringing about the dissolution of groups, and discouraging the growth of future ones. We argue not only that the most powerful states can do better in terms of creating an order less conducive to international terrorism, but that it is a strategic priority, because al-Qaeda and its affiliates are unlikely to decay of their own accord. This world order perspective is certainly not to suggest that al-Qaeda and other terrorists are merely the products of inhospitable global structures. We have not flinched from blaming jihadists for the many atrocities for which they have been responsible. They made their choices; they chose their particular 'march of the mind', to use John Adams' words. It has been a march, we have also made clear, that very few Muslim believers or communities have been prepared to join.

Declining support among Muslim people – who after all have suffered the largest number of victims during 9/11 + 10 – poses the gravest threat to al-Qaeda. Is this likely to bring about the organisation's demise? The United States National Intelligence Council (NIC), an influential think-tank inside government, believes this will be the case. Its projections on world trends suggest that by 2025 al-Qaeda could be about to 'decay into marginality'.[2] Their 2008 rationale for this prediction was based upon social scientific data on 'waves' of 'terror cycles'. In each wave, terror groups share common ideologies, be they the leftist groups that asserted independence after 1968, or the violent extremism that has been unleashed among factions in Islamic and Muslim-majority countries from the 1980s. Over the years, many of the terrorist groups that began in Western Europe and Latin America in the late 1960s and 1970s failed and disappeared, including Sendero Luminoso in Peru, the Baader-Meinhof gang in Germany, and the IRA in Northern Ireland (but not all its affiliates). Will groups proclaiming a global jihad go the same way in the next decade or so?

While we share the NIC's ultimate conclusion about the long-term failure of al-Qaeda, we offer a different account of why the global jihad might fail. Instead of looking only at the network's internal dynamics – al-Qaeda leaders being captured, killed, or dying, or the movement stumbling and fracturing through ideological divisions and political turf battles – attention should turn to the direct and indirect leverage that Western states, international institutions, and governments in Muslim-majority countries can exercise to bring about the organisation's failure. Again, it is useful to think about this as a world order strategy, and not simply in terms of specific policies.

The road ahead is not without grounds for rational hope, though there are more crossroads than open highways. The Arab spring of 2011, for example, offers some promise that the resentment that fuelled Islamist extremism will be mollified to a significant degree; if so, fewer and fewer potential junior jihadists will be provoked into taking the step from being political moderates to extremists to terrorists. In the protest movements that grew across North Africa and the Middle East at the turn of 2010–11 there were no placards identifying Usama bin Laden as their leader. Being a bystander in these upheavals will have damaged al-Qaeda's standing. Those previously sympathetic to its goals but dubious about its strategy will have seen how coordinated mass protests brought some previously strong governments to their knees. Social networking media and universal desires for 'Bread, Freedom, and Social Justice!' inspired mass mobilisation in ways that no amount of al-Qaeda 'doctrines' about 'Islamic purity', or bomb-making manuals, ever managed to achieve.

Even if bin Laden's voice was not heard and his face was not seen in the Arab spring before his death, it is too soon to tell what kind of governance is in transition throughout the Arab world. Fears about al-Qaeda infiltration have been aired. Admiral James Stavridis (Supreme Allied Commander Europe) told the Senate Armed Services at the end of March 2011 that 'flickers' of al-Qaeda and Hezbollah had been seen in the Libyan opposition to Qaddafi, though he did say that there was no evidence of a significant presence.[3] Nonetheless, such qualifications are likely to be of little comfort to those in Israel, Turkey, and beyond, who fear the prospect of any rising movement in the Arab world being a Trojan horse for jihadists.

The pace of change in the Middle East and North Africa has been breathtaking, given how embedded autocrats like Mubarak appeared only months before they were challenged. 'All that is solid melts into air', as Marx said. Perhaps: but the picture across this vast region is complex. The popular uprisings happened at different times and have taken different trajectories. The early revolutions, in Tunisia and Egypt, attracted great hope for more of the same (the promise of speedy, peaceful change) but other regimes have been less ready to melt into history: Saudi Arabia continued to look relatively stable, mixing its own repressive methods with the military capability to shore-up the ruling elite in neighbouring Bahrain; Yemen's prospects remained predictably unpredictable; the regime in Syria showed itself determined to stand firm (and tough) against all dissidents; and Qaddafi turned peaceful rebellion into civil war in Libya. Other Muslim-majority countries (such as Turkey, Lebanon, Malaysia, and Indonesia) offered different models of political systems wrestling with allegiances to religious principles in the context of broadly secular political institutions. When, as the tenth anniversary of 9/11 approaches, we contemplate the mix of Islam globally, 'democracy', the changing Arab world, the uncertain prospects for familiar US domination of world order, variable 'Western' policies in the Middle East, and the dubious path of jihadism, it is evident that discussions of what it is 'all about' must be more complex and radically different than those that framed world order postures and posturing in the immediate aftermath of 9/11.

In addition to changes in the Arab world more conducive to human security, another source of hope about positive change in the spring of 2011 was the support for preventive intervention given by the Arab League to the UNSC – a coalition not seen since the 1991 Gulf War. While tensions in this alliance emerged very quickly following the start of US-led air attacks on Qaddafi's defences, and there were some notable absentees in terms of offering material (military) help, in the early stages of the intervention members of the Arab League did not view America and its European allies (with Britain and France taking the lead) as being unremittingly imperialist – the dogmatic view maintained by revolutionary Iran since 1979. Here again there are crossroads as circumstances change very rapidly. Regional support for intervention could solidify, or it could collapse. While 'regime change' was, from the start, seen as a potential side-benefit of NATO's protective intervention, and would rebound positively across the region, there is a less-welcome scenario: if Qaddafi survives, the West will look weak, intervention will be discredited, and the remaining autocrats will be emboldened in the face of public clamour for change.

As we contemplate the tenth anniversary of 9/11, what is remarkable is that those governments with the primary capacity to steer world order have a second chance to decide what it has all been about. The future is not inevitably one of War on Terror v. Jihadism, or a world order constructed out of the pathologies of the last decade. Choices can be made to promote the purposes outlined at the start of this chapter. Critical among these second chances is democracy.

Western governments committed to democracy are now confronted by a familiar crossroad arising out of the fact that the arrival of popular sovereignty does not necessarily mean that pro-Western preferences will be the outcome. Western governments must learn to listen when democracy has spoken elsewhere. If the events in the Arab world do settle in a progressive democratic direction, then it will finally be time for the West, and especially Washington, to attempt to become comfortable with the fact that democracies will (and should) make their own choices and might follow different paths. It is better in principle and practice to identify with the calls elsewhere for universal values of democracy, freedom, and social justice than to engage in the discredited diplomacy of the past. But it is not only those outside the region who are being called upon to change old thought-ways. Even more so, Islam is engulfed in a crisis of its own, and is struggling to bridge the tensions between faith and the values required for public fairness.[4]

In talking of 'Islam' and 'outsiders' like this, we are aware that we risk treating civilisations as closed entities with unchanging institutions and values. This picture of world politics was false when it was first proposed by Huntington and has always been dangerous, not least because of the self-interest of traditional power structures. We will shortly emphasise the importance of qualities of political leadership not generally in evidence after 9/11, but here we want to appeal to the importance of improving inter-cultural dialogue – an activity in which we are all (or can be) foreign policy practitioners. The phrase 'inter-cultural dialogue' is a somewhat grandiose term (and some might dismiss it merely as 'warm thoughts') for trying to normalise life between people through deepening understandings of diversity in our globalised world, and how these can be negotiated to resolve shared problems and threats. A critical ingredient to *doing* inter-cultural dialogue is abandoning stereotypes. Dialogue begins with human interactions, rather than categories of identity; it seeks to understand political struggles in relation to the interpretations that actors bring to their situation; and it recognises that deliberation must take account of the needs and interests of all those who will be affected.

There is great scope for people to reason together across traditional identity-markers in the common good; only traditional power-brokers have an interest in stopping it. We can, for example, reason together about the fact of *cruelty* or *poverty* or *oppression* in human existence (in capital punishment or global economics or political systems) regardless of the name of our 'maker', or whether we hold faith-based or secular foundational beliefs. Shared identities around common norms (against cruelty, poverty, and oppression) can be solidified, even while we accept different metaphysical sources for them.[5]

At the level of political leadership, building a more just world order requires that the material and non-material claims of the currently marginalised across the world are listened to; it will be a slow process – involving upheavals, reversals, and perhaps violent eruptions – and so will require virtues of patience and caution. The 'prevention paradigm' put in place in 2001 was the antithesis of this, as the rush to war in Iraq showed. The first years of the occupation of that country yield many lessons. Above all, if the Western powers are fighting to rescue and protect people from the threat of weak or failing states and terrorist networks, they must do so without devastating the local infrastructure and causing mass casualties among civilian communities. If they fail to take heed of this they forfeit the right 'to be there at all'.[6]

Leaders must also recognise how words matter in world matters. Language shapes and limits possible political responses to terror. On 9/11 the United States was on a war footing before it really knew who the perpetrators were and what their political aims might be. It is difficult to conceive how an attack from a conventional enemy state could have triggered such an immediate conjoining of 'terror', 'horror', 'this is war', 'War on Terror'.[7] One lesson from the 9/11 decade is that language matters critically in the struggle over ideas in politics, from who gets to be called an 'enemy' to how the confrontation as a whole is described (and, therefore, what it is supposed to be 'all about').

Inter-cultural dialogue is likely to be long-term in its benign effects, but negotiations are potentially more immediate in their results. But here there are impediments generated by self-righteous leaders all over the world who claim 'we do not talk to terrorists'. This latter assertion is one of the biggest deceits in the history of words on terror, terrorism, and terrorists, but one feature of the global War on Terror has been the way in which leaders have reinforced this deceit in their declaratory policies. Vladimir Putin, when he was the Russian president, suggested that 'an unconditional refusal to hold any dialogue with terrorists' had become 'an accepted international principle'. Such 'principled' statements have usually been justified by leaders on the grounds that to talk to terrorists is to reward them for their barbarity and thus signal an incentive to perpetrate 'new, even bloodier crimes' (in Putin's words). Former British prime minister Margaret Thatcher used to rationalise not talking to Irish Republican terrorists in order to deny them the 'oxygen of publicity'. In practice, however, research suggests that concessions to terrorist groups have in many instances not led to increased incidents of violent attacks.[8]

The slogan 'we don't talk to terrorists' is a reminder of the problem of hypocrisy on the part of world leaders − another pathology obstructing the creating of a just world order. The record shows that governments frequently talk to groups that they classify as terrorists. Hamas appears on the State Department list of terrorist groups, yet communication channels between their leadership and Western governments have been maintained for years.

To know whether the opening of talks will be promising requires an understanding of the centre of gravity of a terror network or group. The bad news for those who believe dialogue is always the answer is that some terrorists see violence as being indistinguishable from peace. As we noted in Chapter 4, the organisational survival of al-Qaeda is identified with the utopian goal of establishing a global caliphate under shar'ia law. Dialogue, on the face of it, is inconceivable. This prospect is not unusual, though al-Qaeda's ambitions are. Research shows that the vast majority of terrorist groups do not live up to the liberal expectation that diplomacy and dialogue can bring about an acceptable outcome. Eighty-two per cent of the 457 groups listed in the Michigan global terrorism database did not enter negotiations.[9] Among those that did go down the path of seeking a negotiated settlement, the vast majority of cases, according to Audrey Kurth Cronin, 'yield[ed] neither a clear resolution nor a cessation of the conflict'. The usual outcome was for negotiations to drag on, 'occupying an uncertain middle ground between a stable cease-fire and high levels of violence'.[10]

Whether negotiations can help to transform a conflict is one of the possibilities importantly affected by the role of world order dynamics in enabling or preventing a solution. In the case of the three-decade struggle against terrorism in Northern Ireland, two exogenous factors had a big impact on the normalising of the problem. After 9/11, American sympathy for any kind of terrorist attacks evaporated, even when there remained support for the political goals of the Republican movement. The winds of change were blowing from the East as well as the West: the European political project of 'ever closer union' produced a realignment of state–society relations that significantly impacted upon the Irish question. In the case of the Republic of Ireland, the economic advantages of Europeanisation heightened its interest in a resolution to 'the troubles' in the North. Similarly, as the North benefitted from inward investment from both London and Brussels, parties to the conflict (and their constituencies) realised they had more to lose by fighting than they had to gain from negotiating.

World order realities are thereby changed by the ideas that create them. A different yet realistic ordering framework to that of the post-Cold War era could lead to the decline and dissolution, whether voluntary or coerced, of the al-Qaeda threat, and in so doing bring to an end the most lethal period in the history of international terrorism. But each configuration of world order contains its own potential for oppression, and the possibility that new patterns of violence will emerge. Such violence might not be rational or excusable or justifiable but, rather, the outcome of perverted politics, extravagant revenge, deluded idealism, or militant religiosity. The present is not the exclusive 'age of risk' some commentators describe it as; life has always been a risky business, though the dangers in some world orders are much more bearable than others.

Terror is eternal, it is a 'fact of existence', and it opens up the possibility of a strategy that can never be disinvented. Particular terrorisms can be made politically irrelevant, and terrorism as a strategic choice can be made anachronistic. Cronin's verdict, based on impressive research, is encouraging here: 'The good news is that terrorism virtually always fails.' But her rider is less encouraging, namely that for this to be the case policy-makers must be 'wise enough' to learn the right lessons.[11] Terrorist groups failing, however, is not always, or even often, the same as coming to an 'end'; this is why we prefer to talk about the 'endings' of terrorism rather than its end. This is for two main reasons. First, the idea of an 'end' encourages focusing on an 'endgame', but what we are talking about is less a strategic endgame and more a political way of life – constructing and reconstructing world orders that are not conducive to terrorism. Second, our preference for 'endings' challenges the mindset, in operation immediately on 9/11, that the grand strategy for countering the terrorist attack was a war conducted according to familiar militarised priorities. Wars in the traditional way ended with a great battle, surrender agreements, and victory parades. Confronting terrorism throws up different patterns when it comes towards the reckoning: think Cold War not Second World War. The Cold War had multiple endings in practice,[12] and so do terrorist campaigns. The case of Northern Ireland is revealing. Although Sinn Fein turned away from terrorism, and the Good Friday Agreement was signed, the 'troubles' did not end, they only experienced serial (and still on-going) endings. Going back many years now, these endings consisted of secret talks here, negotiations there, a cease-fire, a treaty, some disarming, an official apology, terrorists becoming politicians, and infamous 'hard men' settling back into ordinary jobs. In-between times, there were, and continue to be, backsliders and spoilers, dissidents acting unhelpfully, ultras planning outrages, explosions, and murders – people choosing to keep terror alive, wrecking trust, and doing their best to stop normality breaking out.

The terrorist campaign of al-Qaeda will not 'end' in 2025 or any other specific point in time in quite the truncated way envisaged by think-tank staffers. Perhaps its end will never really be known, even by future historians, because its jihadist narrative will outlive the killing or capture of any individuals. Nevertheless, we are confident that global jihadism's terrorist project will not prosper, as governments learn and avoid predictable mistakes, while Muslims as a whole explore much better ways of living, dying, and doing politics than terrorism. But there will be many endings on the way, as well as the risk of future spectaculars and microterrorism.

Terror in our time is not over, but a time of endings is a real possibility if the pathologies of world order are reduced. Do not think of preparing victory banners, for success is a process not an event. If all goes well, one day, a reporter will file a story wondering what has happened to al-Qaeda: he or she will speculate about the long time that has elapsed since anybody has suffered a terrorist outrage in its name; and wonder whether there is still anybody, anywhere, who even remotely wants to identify with its impossible aims, remorseless violence, and atrocious crimes.

Epilogue

In his novel *The Plague*, published in 1947, Albert Camus tells of a horrific disease that grips the townspeople of Oran in Algeria, and condemns its victims to a quick and nasty end. After it has passed, Dr Rieux contemplates what the celebrating crowd of survivors does not know:

> that the plague bacillus never dies or vanishes entirely, that it can remain dormant for dozens of years in furniture or clothing, that it waits patiently in bedrooms, cellars, trunks, handkerchiefs and old papers, and that perhaps the day will come when, for the instruction or misfortune of mankind, the plague will rouse its rats and send them to die in some well-contended city.[1]

The bacillus never dies, but whether plague strikes depends largely on the care humans take in looking after each other and their environment: the disease is, to a degree, a choice. Likewise the emotion of terror is immanent in human existence, but whether it is politicised, and terrorism strikes is an explicit human choice – a choice about ends and means. Whether the choice becomes active depends in part on the care taken by humans in looking after each other, and in particular in the ways in which they organise and conduct themselves politically, socially, and economically.

Historically, down to the present, injustice – real and imagined

– has been widespread in world affairs; this has led some to be roused and to move beyond the bedrooms and cellars in which plotting stereotypically takes place, and then decide to spread terror in 'some well-contented city'. Sometimes that sense of injustice will be understood by the well-contented (as it was in the fight against institutionalised racism in apartheid South Africa); often it will seem to be perverted religious fervour or idealism (as is the case with al-Qaeda). But sometimes, terror is plotted not in bedrooms and cellars but in government offices, and the state inflicts it upon its own citizens, holding up sovereignty as its shield.

As well as understanding that the plague had endings, but not an end, Dr Rieux also learned that each person, faced by the terrifying disease, reacted in their own way. Fear, revenge, resignation, small heroisms, and decency were some of the ways people reacted. So it is with reactions to political terror. We have emphasised, ultimately, that it is our own fear we must fear, not terrorism itself. When we contemplate some ghastly future 10/11 – the day after – the greatest danger is the nature of the reaction of the powerful rather than the act of political terror itself. Something must always be done, of course, and we have discussed multi-level responses, from governments eschewing all forms of terror in their own policies, to using multilateral institutions, to the building of networks of identity and interest across traditional divides of nationhood and religion, and to the embedding of decency and a sense of hope in the daily business of the world.

Strategies of terror cannot trump human decency indefinitely, which is one of the reasons why the reach of al-Qaeda never matched the prophecies of Western fear-mongers and jihadist myth-makers. With the killing of the organisation's dominating figure, it is tempting to see al-Qaeda's '1 May 2011' and the spectacular bin Laden orchestrated against the United States on September 11, 2001 as forming a nice ten-year symmetry. But this must be resisted. While the plans of al-Qaeda have been disrupted, bin Laden's successors will continue to offer violent strategic visions to their followers; the militant jihadist narrative will remain; cells exist in a variety of countries; lands without governance promise a base for striking out at the Far Enemy; bin Laden's iconography in martyrdom might exceed that of his life as a fugitive; and it remains far more difficult, yet far more critical, to destroy a dangerous idea than it is to kill a dangerous man.

Nonetheless, the signs are promising, and have been for some time – though more the result of the weaknesses and terrorist strategies of al-Qaeda than the wisdom of some of its opponents. Above all, al-Qaeda has become increasingly unpopular among the overwhelming majority of Muslims across the world, and this has been evident in the way it was marginal and marginalised during the first stirrings of the Arab spring. Though al-Qaeda may have been out of touch with these developments in the Arab world, its presence in South Asia is still a factor in that precarious region, and violent extremists, as we have shown, do not need mass armies to ignite massive destruction. Potential targets should not therefore lower their guard, for 9/11 is still a time we all inhabit. The decline of al-Qaeda represents one of the endings of that period, not its end, while the Arab spring promises, but does not guarantee, one of the beginnings of a world order less prone to terrorism.

The possibility of terror remains eternal, but the risk of terrorism could be made infinitesimal. The chief lesson of 9/11 + 10 is that too many of the reactions to the atrocity and its aftermath incubated the metaphorical bacillus they were supposed to eradicate. The challenge is not to expand counter-terrorism techniques and strategies, though some of these must remain in place indefinitely, or to strike grandiloquent postures and give criminality a part in a heroic narrative, but rather to build a world order, step by step, in which terrorism is progressively delegitimised as a choice, and so becomes relegated to being a mere chapter in the history of political violence.

Appendix

Statistical analysis of terrorist incidents[1]

The data in this Appendix shows the following:

1 non-state terror deaths as a total figure, in the eight years prior to 2001 and the eight years after and including 2001;
2 state terror deaths in the eight years prior to 2001 and the eight years after and including 2001;
3 details of each incident of mass atrocity terrorism since 9/11;
4 comparison of the lethality of state terrorism with that of non-state terrorism.

We are utilising the open-source Global Terrorism Database (GTD) held at the University of Maryland, and the Uppsala Conflict Data Programme (UCDP) which provides data for state terrorism (though Uppsala refer to this as 'one-sided violence').

The GTD database includes information on terrorist events around the world from 1970 through to 2008 (with annual updates planned for the future).[2] For each GTD incident, 'information is available on the date and location of the incident, the weapons used and nature of the target, the number of casualties, and – when identifiable – the group or individual responsible'.

Table A.1 examines 'the rise of mass-casualty terrorism 2001–2008'. We have filtered the GTD information to show only those terrorist incidents in which fatalities have exceeded 50 (which we present as 'mass-casualty terror incidents'). Focusing only on the mass-casualty terror data has strengths and weaknesses. A strength is that the information can be presented economically; without the body-count threshold, the number of incidents increases from 160 to 16,626 (a 103-fold increase). Additionally, in the case of mass-casualty terrorism, it is highly likely that, even if military installations were targeted, there would have been death or injury to civilians, thereby masking over the differences we have with the GTD dataset on this issue. For the purposes of this book the time period that is tabulated is 2001 to 2008 – the GTD data for 2009 onwards has not been released.

Table A.2 looks at 'state terrorism 2001–2008'. These data do not exist in a manner that is directly comparable to the GTD (or other databases such as RAND, and ITERATE) – neither are state terror deaths integrated into any of the other major databases. As we have made it clear in the book, we believe it is important to consider state and non-state terrorism. To record cases of state terrorism, and achieve some kind of comparison with the datasets for non-state terrorism, we have used the UCDP[3] which collects empirical information on 'one-sided violence', i.e. intentional and harmful attacks on civilians by governments and formally organised armed groups. We have filtered the data such that only government 'one-sided violence' appears in this table.

Table A.3 compares 'incidents of state and non-state terrorism after 9/11'. The table examines the total deaths in terrorist incidents by non-state terror groups without the 50-death threshold in place. This figure is compared with state terrorism as provided by UCDP (with a 25-death threshold in place in relation to one-sided violence). Figure A.1 represents the data in a different form, showing the two trajectories intersect in 2003 as state-based terrorism is surpassed in lethality by non-state terror. The graph plots the relationship between the number of fatalities caused by state and non-state terrorism. Note that because these data come from different sources with different coding methods, *cross data comparisons are only indicative of trends.*

The rise of mass-casualty terrorism by non-state actors, 2001–2008[4]

Figures in column 4 of Table A.1 include deaths and (injured). Where the GTD has 'unknown' in the 'Perpetrator' column, we have rectified this in a few cases where the identity was traceable through other databases, notably RAND; where this has happened, (RAND) appears after the name of the perpetrator. Finally, where two events occur in the same country, on the same day, in order to differentiate them we have placed in brackets the city in which each particular event occurred.

Table A.1 The rise of mass-casualty terrorism by non-state actors, 2001–2008

Date	Country	Perpetrator	Deaths & (injured)	Target type
9/04/2001	Angola	National Union for the Total Independence of Angola (UNITA)	129 (Unknown)	Military
18/07/2001	Angola	UNITA	70 (15)	Private citizens & property
11/08/2001	Angola	UNITA	259 (160)	
11/09/2001	United States	Al-Qaeda	2,949 (Unknown)	Private citizens & property
19/11/2001	Philippines	Moro National Liberation Front (MNLF)	52 (40)	Military
17/02/2002	Nepal	Maoists	102 (Unknown)	Government (general)
11/04/2002	Nepal	Unknown	170 (Unknown)	Military

Table A.1 Continued

Date	Country	Perpetrator	Deaths & (injured)	Target type
2/05/2002	Colombia	Revolutionary Armed Forces of Colombia (FARC)	119 (80)	Religious figures/ institutions
7/05/2002	Nepal	Maoists	140 (Unknown)	Military
12/10/2002	Indonesia	Jemaah Islamiya (JI)	202 (300)	Tourists
23/10/2002	Russia	The 29th Division	129 (Unknown)	Private citizens & property
27/12/2002	Russia	Chechens	57 (121)	Government (general)
18/02/2003	South Korea	Individual	192 (149)	Private citizens & property
12/05/2003	Russia	Chechens	59 (197)	Government (general)
16/06/2003	Congo (Kinshasa)	Other	70 (Unknown)	Private citizens & property
4/07/2003	Pakistan	Lashkar-e-Jhangvi	53 (53)	Religious figures/ institutions
25/08/2003	India	Students Islamic Movement of India (SIMI)	52 (150)	Other
29/08/2003	Iraq	Al-Qaeda	100 (200)	Religious figures/ institutions
5/02/2004	Uganda	Lord's Resistance Army (LRA)	56 (70)	Other

10/02/2004	Iraq	Al-Qaeda	71 (150)	Private citizens & property
27/02/2004	Philippines	Abu Sayyaf Group (ASG)	116 (Unknown)	Maritime
2/03/2004	Iraq (Karbala)	Al-Qaeda	110 (233)	Private citizens & property
2/03/2004	Iraq (Baghdad)	Al-Qaeda	58 (167)	Private citizens & property
11/03/2004	Spain	Abu Hafs al-Masri Brigades	135 (900)	Private citizens & property
21/03/2004	Nepal	Communist Party of Nepal-Maoist (CPN-M)	518 (216)	Government (general)
21/04/2004	Iraq	Al-Qaeda	74 (100)	Police
24/06/2004	Iraq	Tawhid and Jihad	60 (220)	Private citizens & property
28/07/2004	Iraq	Al-Qaeda	70 (56)	Police
1/09/2004	Russia	Chechens	344 (727)	Educational institution
19/12/2004	Iraq	Unknown	62 (130)	Religious figures/ institutions
28/02/2005	Iraq	Al-Qaeda in Iraq (RAND)	110 (130)	Private citizens & property
19/03/2005	Pakistan	Unknown	51 (Unknown)	Religious figures/ institutions
4/05/2005	Iraq	Ansar al-Sunna	60 (150)	Police
6/05/2005	Iraq	Unknown	59 (44)	Private citizens & property
6/06/2005	Nepal	Maoists	53 (72)	Military

Table A.1 Continued

Date	Country	Perpetrator	Deaths & (injured)	Target type
7/07/2005*	United Kingdom	Other	56 (700)	Private citizens & property
16/07/2005	Iraq	Unknown	54 (82)	Private citizens & property
23/07/2005	Egypt	Al-Qaeda in Levant and Egypt	91 (110)	Private citizens & property
14/09/2005	Iraq	Al-Qaeda in Iraq	160 (542)	Private citizens & property
29/09/2005	Iraq	Tanzim Qa'idat al-Jihad fi Bilad al-Rafidayn (Al-Qaeda Affiliate) (RAND)	65 (70)	Private citizens & property
29/10/2005	India	Lashkar-e-Taiba (LeT)	55 (155)	Private citizens & property
18/11/2005	Iraq	Unknown	77 (90)	Religious figures/ institutions
28/02/2006	India	Communist Party of India-Maoist (CPI-M)	55 (20)	Private citizens & property
12/03/2006	Iraq	Unknown	62 (250)	Private citizens & property
7/04/2006	Iraq	Al-Qaeda in Iraq	90 (90)	Private citizens & property

11/04/2006	Pakistan	Lashkar-e-Jhangvi	57 (125)	Private citizens & property
12/05/2006	Nigeria	Movement for the Emancipation of the Niger Delta (MEND)	200 (Unknown)	Utilities
15/06/2006	Sri Lanka	Liberation Tigers of Tamil Eelam (LTTE)	64 (80)	Private citizens & property
16/06/2006	Sri Lanka	Liberation Tigers of Tamil Eelam (LTTE)	63 (71)	Private citizens & property
1/07/2006	Iraq	Sunni Supporters	77 (96)	Private citizens & property
12/07/2006	India	Lashkar-e-Taiba (LeT)	187 (817)	Transportation
17/07/2006	Iraq	Unknown	56 (67)	Private citizens & property
18/07/2006	Iraq	Mujahedeen Shura Council	59 (132)	Other
5/08/2006	Sri Lanka	Liberation Tigers of Tamil Eelam (LTTE)	100 (Unknown)	Private citizens & property
14/08/2006	Sri Lanka	Unknown	61 (150)	Private citizens & property
16/10/2006	Sri Lanka	Liberation Tigers of Tamil Eelam (LTTE)	103 (150)	Military
29/10/2006	Sudan	Unknown	63 (0)	Police
11/11/2006	Sudan	Unknown	80 (0)	Private citizens & property

Table A.1 Continued

Date	Country	Perpetrator	Deaths & (injured)	Target type
20/11/2006	Sudan	Unknown	80 (0)	Private citizens & property
23/11/2006	Iraq	Unknown	202 (257)	Private citizens & property
3/12/2006	Iraq	Unknown	112 (182)	Private citizens & property
12/12/2006	Iraq	Unknown	61 (148)	Private citizens & property
16/01/2007	Iraq	Unknown	65 (123)	Private citizens & property
22/01/2007	Iraq	Unknown	88 (160)	Private citizens & property
1/02/2007	Iraq	Unknown	57 (150)	Private citizens & property
3/02/2007	Iraq	Unknown	120 (246)	Private citizens & property
12/02/2007	Iraq	Unknown	66 (150)	Private citizens & property
18/02/2007	Iraq	Unknown	56 (127)	Private citizens & property
19/02/2007	India	Unknown	66 (Unknown)	Private citizens & property
19/02/2007	Chad	Union of Forces for Democracy	63 (45)	Private citizens & property

		and Development (UFDD)		
6/03/2007	Iraq	Islamic State of Iraq (ISI)	92 (200)	Private citizens & property
15/03/2007	India	Naxalites	55 (12)	Police
27/03/2007	Iraq	Other	63 (Unknown)	Private citizens & property
30/03/2007	Iraq	Unknown	145 (170)	Private citizens & property
30/03/2007	Iraq (Baghdad)	Unknown	72 (130)	Private citizens & property
30/03/2007	Iraq (Al-Khalis)	Unknown	53 (103)	Private citizens & property
30/03/2007	Iraq (Tal-Afar)	Unknown	145 (170)	Private citizens & property
31/03/2007	Iraq	Unknown	152 (347)	Private citizens & property
15/04/2007	Sudan	Janjaweed	73 (0)	Private citizens & property
18/04/2007	Iraq	Al-Qaeda in Iraq	127 (148)	Private citizens & property
24/04/2007	Ethiopia	Ogaden National Liberation Front (ONLF)	74 (0)	Utilities
28/04/2007	Iraq	Unknown	69 (178)	Private citizens & property

Table A.1 Continued

Date	Country	Perpetrator	Deaths & (injured)	Target type
2/06/2007	Sri Lanka	Liberation Tigers of Tamil Eelam (LTTE)	62 (20)	Military
19/06/2007	Iraq	Unknown	79 (200)	Private citizens & property
7/07/2007	Iraq	Unknown	150 (250)	Private citizens & property
10/07/2007	Pakistan	Other	96 (35)	Private citizens & property
18/07/2007	Iraq	Unknown	80 (183)	Private citizens & property
15/08/2007	Iraq	Unknown	200 (170)	Private citizens & property
16/08/2007	Iraq	Unknown	200 (Unknown)	Private citizens & property
28/08/2007	Greece	Unknown	63 (Unknown)	Private citizens & property
18/10/2007	Pakistan	Harkatul Jihad-e-Islami	141 (250)	Government (general)
2/11/2007	Ethiopia	Al-Shabaab	100 (Unknown)	Military
6/11/2007	Afghanistan	Unknown	64 (95)	Private citizens & property
18/11/2007	Pakistan	Unknown	90 (150)	Private citizens & property

11/12/2007	Algeria	Al-Qaeda in the Lands of the Islamic Maghreb (AQLIM)	67 (100)	Private citizens & property
21/12/2007	Pakistan	Unknown	72 (101)	Religious figures/ institutions
18/01/2008	Iraq	Unknown	70 (Unknown)	Private citizens & property
1/02/2008	Iraq	Al-Qaeda	90 (130)	Private citizens & property
17/02/2008	Afghanistan	Taliban	101 (100)	Military
24/02/2008	Iraq	Unknown	64 (68)	Private citizens & property
6/03/2008	Iraq	Al-Qaeda in Iraq	56 (130)	Private citizens & property
10/05/2008	Sudan	Justice and Equality Movement (JEM)	134 (0)	Private citizens & property
17/06/2008	Iraq	Unknown	63 (75)	Private citizens & property
7/07/2008	Afghanistan	Unknown	58 (141)	Government (diplomatic)
21/08/2008	Pakistan	Tehrik-i-Taliban Pakistan (TTP)	64 (100)	Business
20/09/2008	Pakistan	Unknown	60 (200)	Business
26/11/2008	India	Deccan Mujahideen	126 (152)	Private citizens & property
11/12/2008	Iraq	Islamic State of Iraq (ISI)	56 (120)	Other

Table A.1 Continued

Date	Country	Perpetrator	Deaths & (injured)	Target type
26/12/2008	Congo (Kinshasa)	Lord's Resistance Army (LRA)	89 (0)	Private citizens & property
27/12/2008	Congo (Kinshasa)	Lord's Resistance Army (LRA)	60 (0)	Private citizens & property

Total mass-casualty fatalities of attacks by non-state terror groups is 13,557 when threshold for terror deaths is 50 and over for an incident.

* The London bombings have been inserted into these data even though they do not show up in the GTD data due to the fact that each incident was coded separately. We have consolidated other terror attacks similarly (e.g. 9/11 is represented as one and not four attacks); only in the case of the 7/7/2005 London bombings does combining the incident data push the fatalities into the over-50 bracket.

State terrorism 2001–2008

Unlike the GTD data in Table A.1, in Table A.2 UCDP incidents are not punctuated in time; instead, their figures give 'annual' lethality numbers (making comparison between state an non-state terrorism indicative rather than absolute). In mitigation, government violence against civilians is likely to be sustained and lower in intensity as governments are more sensitive to censure than non-state terrorist groups. The data have been filtered so only those government/years that exceed 50 deaths and over are listed, enabling comparison with GTD figures.

Table A.2 State terrorism 2001–2008

Actor	Year	Fatality best estimate	Fatality highest estimate	Location
Government of Afghanistan	2001	142	1003	Afghanistan
Government of Nepal	2001	74	76	Nepal

Government of Nigeria	2001	150	209	Nigeria
Government of Russia (Soviet Union)	2001	188	389	Russia (Soviet Union)
Government of Burundi	2002	218	315	Burundi
Government of Cote d'Ivoire	2002	228	279	Cote d'Ivoire
Government of Democratic Republic of Congo (Zaire)	2002	114	114	Democratic Republic of Congo (Zaire)
Government of Indonesia	2002	50	651	Indonesia
Government of Nepal	2002	274	278	Nepal
Government of Russia (Soviet Union)	2002	205	380	Russia (Soviet Union)
Government of Sudan	2002	55	55	Sudan
Government of Angola	2003	59	74	Angola
Government of Burundi	2003	86	163	Burundi
Government of Cote d'Ivoire	2003	73	73	Cote d'Ivoire
Government of Ethiopia	2003	509	513	Ethiopia
Government of Indonesia	2003	235	310	Indonesia
Government of Myanmar	2003	72	77	Myanmar
Government of Nepal	2003	197	269	Nepal
Government of Nigeria	2003	50	113	Nigeria
Government of Sudan	2003	1,776	12,470	Sudan
Government of Democratic Republic of Congo (Zaire)	2004	130	130	Democratic Republic of Congo (Zaire)
Government of Ethiopia	2004	244	1,252	Ethiopia
Government of Nepal	2004	176	251	Nepal
Government of Sudan	2004	2,593	15,377	Sudan
Government of USA	2004	101	142	Iraq, Afghanistan
Government of Iraq	2005	72	134	Iraq
Government of Myanmar	2005	132	133	Myanmar
Government of Nepal	2005	108	136	Nepal
Government of Sudan	2005	403	707	Sudan
Government of Central African Republic	2006	102	139	Central African Republic

Table A.2 Continued

Actor	Year	Fatality best estimate	Fatality highest estimate	Location
Government of Democratic Republic of Congo (Zaire)	2006	111	119	Democratic Republic of Congo (Zaire)
Government of Israel	2006	182	221	Lebanon, Israel
Government of Laos	2006	73	73	Laos
Government of Myanmar	2006	211	344	Myanmar
Government of Sudan	2006	252	362	Sudan
Government of Ethiopia	2007	143	224	Ethiopia
Government of Iraq	2007	63	109	Iraq
Government of Myanmar	2007	205	405	Myanmar
Government of Sudan	2007	88	134	Sudan
Government of China	2008	51	151	China
Government of Kenya	2008	64	205	Kenya
Government of Nigeria	2008	123	199	Nigeria
Government of Sudan	2008	186	357	Sudan

Summary
- Best estimate total state terror deaths 2001–2008   10,568
- Lowest fatalities of state terror deaths 2001–2008   10,400
- Highest fatalities from state terror 2001–2008   39,155

Comparing state and non-state terror deaths pre- and post-9/11

Table A.3 compares the total fatalities of state and non-state terrorism without the mass-casualty threshold of 50 being applied to non-state terror acts. It shows that, for the years since 9/11, as far as the statistics allow, non-state forms of terrorism have been a more significant killer than state terrorism. Note, however, the important caveat that state-based forms of terror elicit significant variances, with 10,568 being the best guess and 39,155 the highest guess (see summary of Table A.2 above). The variance between the lowest, highest, and best estimates for number of deaths can best be explained by the type of violence being explored. Darfur, for example, can have significant variance in the number of deaths between 'best' and 'highest' due to the poor conditions for reporting events among other things. The converse is not necessarily the case: microterrorist incidents in Israel or Europe take place in societies where both the perpetrators and the 'host' country have a convergent interest in recording the event. Uppsala's best guess reporting is generally conservative to ensure that the data is capturing the specific phenomenon of one-sided violence.

Table A.3 Comparing state and non-state terror deaths pre- and post-9/11

Time period	Non-state terror deaths (GTD)	State terror deaths (Uppsala)
1993–2000	42,812	534,723 (to 883,424)
2001–2008	54,569[5]	12,176 (to 43,850)

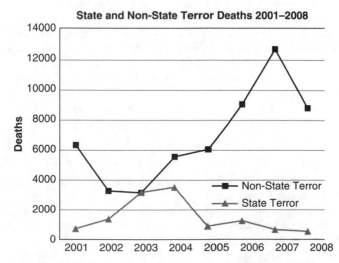

Figure A.1 Tracking state and non-state terror deaths post-9/11

Notes

Prologue

1 Some of these episodes are described in Joanna Bourke, *Fear. A Cultural History* (London: Virago, 2005), pp. 356–91.

1 9/11 + 10

1 'What Price to Stay Free of Terrorism?', *New York Times*, 5 October 2010.
2 In the opening paragraph, we used the phrase 'War on Terror' to underscore this was a term that political leaders – especially in Washington, London, Tel Aviv, and elsewhere – were using to describe the 9/11 attacks and their responses to it. Hereafter, we will not use the phrase with speech marks but we retain the use of capital letters as this signals an official status that some leaders have given to the phrase.
3 'Sharon Condemns Attacks in USA, Declares Day of Mourning', *BBC Monitoring Middle East – Political*, 12 September 2001.
4 Kate Kelland, 'Blair Works to Build Anti-Terror Coalition', *Reuters News*, 17 September 2001.

2 Terror

1 Nelson Mandela, http://www.notable-quotes.com/t/terrorism_quotes.html (accessed 5 November 2010).
2 Don DeLillo, 'In the Ruins of the Future', *The Guardian*, 22 December 2001. Each of the subheading titles in this chapter is from this article, as are other references to DeLillo.
3 Ken Booth and Nicholas Wheeler, *The Security Dilemma: Fear, Cooperation and Trust in World Politics* (Houndmills: Palgrave Macmillan, 2008), pp. 62–80.

4 Stuart Walton, Humanity: An Emotional History (London: Atlantic Books, 2004), p. 23.

5 Elaine Scarry, The Body in Pain: The Making and Unmaking of the World (New York: Oxford University Press, 1985), p. 162.

6 See, in particular, Philippa Foot, Natural Goodness (Oxford: Oxford University Press, 2001), Chapter 1: 'A Fresh Start?'

7 Geoffrey Warnock, Contemporary Moral Philosophy (London: Macmillan, 1967), p. 60.

8 Raymond Aron, Peace and War: A Theory of International Relations (New York: Doubleday, 1966), p. 170.

9 We have consulted numerous definitions. Our short version is close to that of M.C. Bassiouni, quoted in Albert Bandura, 'Mechanisms of Moral Disengagement', in Walter Reigh (ed.), Origins of Terrorism (Washington, DC: Woodrow Wilson Center Press, 1998), p. 163.

10 Audrey Kurth Cronin, How Terrorism Ends: Understanding the Decline and Demise of Terrorist Campaigns (Princeton, NJ: Princeton University Press, 2009), p. 7. Alex Bellamy, Fighting Terror: Ethical Dilemmas (London: Zed Books, 2008), p. 31.

11 This distinction is taken from the discussion of 'power' by Terence Ball: see his essay on 'Power' in Robert E. Goodin and Philip Pettit (eds), A Companion to Contemporary Political Philosophy (Oxford: Blackwell, 1993), pp. 553–4, and Terence Ball, Transforming Political Discourse (Oxford: Blackwell, 1988).

12 Statistical support for this is given by Alex P. Schmid and Albert J. Jongman, Political Terrorism: A New Guide to Actors, Authors, Concepts, Databases, Theories and Literature (Amsterdam: North Holland Publishing Co., 1988), pp. 5–7.

13 See, among others, Talal Asad, On Suicide Bombing (New York: Columbia University Press, 2007), and Robert A. Pape, Dying to Win: The Strategic Logic of Suicide Terrorism (New York: Random House, 2005).

14 Quoted by Tzvetan Todorov, Hope and Memory: Lessons from the Twentieth Century (Princeton, NJ: Princeton University Press, 2003), pp. 33–4.

15 Churchill's final speech in the House of Commons, 1 March 1955, quoted by Lorna Arnold, Britain and the H Bomb (Houndmills: Palgrave Macmillan, 2001), p. 65.

16 Usama Bin Laden, 'In His Own Words: Statements by Osama Bin Laden', in Karen Greenberg (ed.), Al Qaeda Now: Understanding Today's Terrorists (Cambridge: Cambridge University Press, 2005), p. 185.

17 In addition to Mandela, the other terrorists/Nobel Peace Prize winners are Yasser Arafat, Menachim Begin, and Sean McBride.

18 Paul Lacey, The Unequal World We Inhabit: Quaker Responses to Terrorism and Fundamentalism: Swarthmore Lecture, 2010 (London: Quaker Books, 2010), pp. 16–17.

19 Some of the arguments in the remainder of this section are based on Ken Booth (2008) 'The Human Face of Terror: Reflections in a Cracked Looking-Glass', Critical Studies on Terrorism, 1 (1): 65–79.

20 Mark Twain, *A Connecticut Yankee in King Arthur's Court* (New York: The Modern Library, 2001; 1st pub. 1899), p. 114.

3 Dangers

1 National Commission on Terrorist Attacks Against the United States. *The 9/11 Commission Report: Final Report of the National Commission on Terrorist Attacks Against the United States* (Washington: U.S. Government Printing Office, 2004), pp. 1–2. 'More than 2600 died at the World Trade Center; 125 died at the Pentagon 256 on all the four planes'. This total of 2,981 fatalities differs marginally from that of the Global Terror Database. For reasons of comparability, we use the GTD fatality figure for 9/11 in the Appendix, p. 187.

2 'President Bush to Address the Nation', *Washington Post*, 20 September 2001.

3 Kenneth N. Waltz, 'The Continuity of International Politics', in Ken Booth and Tim Dunne (eds), *Worlds in Collision: Terror and the Future of Global Order* (Houndmills: Palgrave Macmillan, 2002), pp. 348–53; and 'Foreword', in Ken Booth (ed.), *Realism in World Politics* (Abingdon: Routledge, 2011), p. xiv.

4 Louise Richardson, *What Terrorists Want: Understanding the Terrorist Threat* (London: John Murray, 2006), pp. 182–3.

5 According to December 2010 Pew Survey, 59 per cent say they are 'very' or 'somewhat' worried there will be another terrorist attack on the United States. See 'Despite Years of Terror Scares, Public's Concerns Remain Fairly Steady', http://pewresearch.org/pubs/1815/poll-worried-about-terrorist-attack-america-anti-terror-campaign (accessed 6 March 2011).

6 Magnus Ranstorp, 'Mapping Terrorism Studies After 9/11: An Academic Field of Old Problems and New Prospects', in Richard Jackson *et al.*, *Critical Terrorism Studies: A New Research Agenda* (London: Routledge, 2009), pp. 13–33, esp. pp. 17, 30.

7 This understanding of security was first formulated by Ole Waever. For an early account see his 'Securitization and Desecuritization', in Ronnie D. Lipschutz (ed.), *On Security* (New York: Columbia University Press, 1995), pp. 46–86.

8 Rumsfeld's own account of the origin of this phrase is in his *Known and Unknown: A Memoir* (New York: Sentinel, 2011), pp. xiii–xv.

9 See 'Table 6.3: The Terrorist Threat in Empirical Context', in Richard Jackson *et al.*, *Terrorism: A Critical Introduction* (Houndmills: Palgrave Macmillan, 2011), pp. 132–3.

10 The Archduke was not a 'civilian' as such, but the Head of State in the Austro-Hungarian Empire. We still define this as a 'terrorist' attack, though concede it is a grey area. Nine out of ten IRA attacks were against military or state targets, as opposed to civilians.

11 Jessica Wolfendale (2007) 'Terrorism, Security and the Threat of Counter-terrorism', *Studies in Conflict and Terrorism*, 30(1): 75–92.

12 John Tirman (2009) 'Diplomacy, Terrorism, and National Narratives in the United States–Iran Relationship', *Critical Studies on Terrorism*, 12(3): 527–39.

13 Jason Beattie, 'Terrorist Nuclear Threat "Real and Imminent"', *The Evening Standard*, 22 June 2004: http://www.thisislondon.co.uk/news/article-11493436-terrorist-nuclear-threat-real-and-imminent.do (accessed 22 March 2011).

14 BBC News, 'MI5 Tracking "30 UK Terror Plots"', 10 November 2006: http://news.bbc.co.uk/1/hi/uk/6134516.stm (accessed 22 March 2011).

15 John Mueller, *Obsession: Nuclear Alarmism from Hiroshima to Al-Qaeda* (Oxford: Oxford University Press, 2010), Part III.

16 Brian Michael Jenkins, *Will Terrorists Go Nuclear?* (Amherst, NY: Prometheus Books, 2008).

17 Mueller, *Obsession*, pp. 193–4.

18 Andrew Silke, 'Retaliating Against Terrorism', in Andrew Silke (ed.), *Terrorists, Victims and Society: Psychological Perspectives on Terrorism and its Consequences* (Chichester: John Wiley & Sons, 2003), pp. 230–1.

19 Jackson *et al.*, *Critical Terrorism Studies*, p. 134.

20 Title 22 of the United States Code, Section 2656f(d). That statute contains the following definitions:

- The term 'terrorism' means premeditated, politically motivated violence perpetrated against noncombatant targets by subnational groups or clandestine agents, usually intended to influence an audience.
- The term 'international terrorism' means terrorism involving citizens or the territory of more than one country.
- The term 'terrorist group' means any group practicing, or that has significant subgroups that practice, international terrorism. (http://www.state.gov/s/ct/rls/crt/2000/2419.htm (accessed 28 October 2010)).

21 Colin Wight (2009) 'Theorising Terrorism: The State, Structure and History', *International Relations*, 23(1): 100–3.

22 Robert E. Goodin, *What's Wrong with Terrorism?* (Cambridge: Polity, 2006), pp. 55–6.

23 See Richardson, *What Terrorists Want*, discussion at pp. 72–7.

24 Colin Wight's description of those who take seriously the problem of state terrorism; see 'Theorising Terrorism', p. 101.

25 Quoted by Ken Booth and Nicholas Wheeler, *The Security Dilemma* (Houndmills: Palgrave Macmillan, 2008), p. 71.

26 Audrey Kurth Cronin, *How Terrorism Ends* (Princeton, NJ: Princeton University Press, 2009), p. 1.

27 Dominique Moïsi, *The Geopolitics of Emotion* (London: The Bodley Head, 2009), p. 31.

28 Moïsi, *The Geopolitics of Emotion*, p. 90.

29 S. Walton, *Humanity: An Emotional History* (London: Atlantic Books, 2004). See also Dan Gardner, *Risk: The Science and Politics of Fear* (London: Virgin Books, 2009), pp. 5–6. Compare Moïsi's superficial interpretation, p. 94.

30 Gardner, *Risk*, pp. 5–6.

4 Base

1 Among other discussions of the origins of the term, see Jason Burke, *Al-Qaeda: The True Story of Radical Islam* (London: I.B. Tauris, 2003), pp. 1–2; and Reza Aslan, *How to Win a Cosmic War: Confronting Radical Religion* (London: Arrow Books, 2009), pp. 124–5.

2 Fawaz Gerges, *The Far Enemy: Why Jihad Went Global* (Cambridge: Cambridge University Press, 2005), p. 24.

3 Lawrence Wright, *The Looming Tower* (London: Vintage, 2007), p. 79.

4 Susan Buck-Morss, *Thinking Past Terror: Islamism and Critical Theory on the Left* (London: Verso, 2006), pp. 98–9.

5 Sayyid Qutb, *Social Justice in Islam* (New York: Oneonta, 2000).

6 Wright, *The Looming Tower*, p. 30.

7 Lawrence Wright, 'The Man Behind Bin Laden', *The New Yorker*, 16 September 2002.

8 The term hybridisation is Aslan's, *Cosmic War*, p. 30.

9 Wright, *The Looming Tower*, p. 127.

10 Max Rodenbeck, 'The Truth about the Jihad', *New York Review of Books*, 52, 3 August, 2005.

11 Quoted in Aslan, *Cosmic War*, p. 119; see also pp. 25, 30, 118, 120, and Jason Burke, *Al-Qaeda*, pp. 72–6, 82. These two authors disagree on whether bin Laden or al-Zawahiri was behind the car bomb that killed Azzam.

12 Rodenbeck, 'The Truth about the Jihad'.

13 This argument is made by Faisel Devji in his *Landscape of the Jihad: Militancy, Morality and Modernity* (Ithaca, NY: Cornell University Press, 2005).

14 Wright, *The Looming Tower*, p. 302.

15 See Audrey Kurth Cronin (2007) 'Ending Terrorism: Lessons for Defeating Al Qaeda', *Adelphi Papers*, 47(394): 60.

16 For a detailed analysis of Jihadism, see, among others, Jarret M. Brachmen, *Global Jihadism: Theory and Practice* (London: Routledge, 2009), Chs 3 and 4; quotation at p. 51.

17 Quoted in Peter Bergen, 'What Osama Wants', 26 October 2006. http://www.nytimes.com/2006/10/26/opinion/26bergen.html (accessed 16 March 2011).

18 Life in an al-Qaeda camp is described by Shadi Abdallah, who was in the al Farouq camp in Afghanistan before being arrested in Germany in 2002; Peter Bergen '"The Front": The Taliban-Al Qaeda Merger', *The New Republic*, 19 October 2009.

19 Wright, *The Looming Tower*, p. 178.

20 Wright, *The Looming Tower*, p. 308.

21 Gerges, *The Far Enemy*, p. 206.

22 Jarret Brachman, *Global Jihadism: Theory and Practice* (London: Routledge, 2009), p. 14.

23 Quoted in Gerges, *The Far Enemy*, p. 264.

24 The interview was conducted by Peter Taylor, 'The Secret War on Terror', BBC 2, 7 March 2011.

25 Aslan, *Cosmic War*, pp. 52–4.

26 Quoted in Brachman, *Global Jihadism*, p. 182.

27 Quoted in Cronin, *Ending Terrorism*, p. 68.

28 Cronin, *Ending Terrorism*, p. 70.

29 90 per cent, according to a Gallup Poll quoted in Gerges, *The Far Enemy*, p. 294.

30 Craig Whitlock, 'On Tape, Bin Laden Warns of Long War. He Accuses the West of Acting as "Crusader"', *Washington Post Foreign Service*, 24 April 2006.

31 Paul Cruickshank examines the link between these serious planned attacks and al-Qaeda Central. He argues that the Base had 'operational ties' in 38 per cent of the cases examined. See his *The Militant Pipeline Between the Afghanistan-Pakistan Border Region and the West* (Washington, DC: American Enterprise Foundation, 2010).

32 Both quoted in Dan Gardner, *Risk: The Science and Politics of Fear* (London: Virgin Books, 2009), p. 302.

33 Bruce Riedel, *Deadly Embrace: Pakistan, America, and the Future of the Global Jihad* (Washington, DC: Brookings Institution Press, 2011), pp. 97–105. Unless indicated otherwise, the following paragraphs are based on this overview.

34 Useful surveys include: Julie Cohn, 'Islamist Radicalisation in Yemen', Council on Foreign Relations Backgrounder, 29 June 2010. Available at http://www.cfr.org/yemen/islamist-radicalisation-yemen/p9369 (accessed 24 March 2011); 'Factbox: "Al Qaeda's Yemen-based wing"', Reuters, 22 March 2011, http://www.reuters.com/article/2011/03/22/us-yemen-president-aqap-idUSTRE72L3QK20110322 (accessed 24 March 2011); and Gregg Miller and Peter Finn, 'CIA: Al Qaeda in Yemen Now Biggest Threat', *Washington Post*, 25 August 2010.

35 'Al Qaeda New Online English Magazine Inspire Launched 7 January 2010', http://globaljihad.net/view_news.asp?id=1535 (accessed 24 March 2011). The 2nd edition was available on 10 November 2011.

36 Fareed Zakaria, 'The Year of Microterrorism', *Time*, 27 December 2010.

37 Senate Committee on Homeland Security & Government Affairs, 'Violent

Islamist Extremism and the Homegrown Terrorist Threat', 15 February 2011, http://hsgac.senate.gov/public/index.cfm?FuseAction=Home.ViolentIslamistExtremism (accessed 24 March 2011).

38 Quoted by Aslan, *Cosmic War*, pp. 4, 7.

5 Evil

1   These points are based on 'This 9/11 Obama Has the Bullhorn on Terrorism', *US News*, 11 September 2009: www.msnbc.msn.com/id/32783395/ns/us_news (accessed 9 March 2011).

2   The McCain quotation is from 2008, Boykin's from 2003: both are taken from Reza Aslan, *How to Win a Cosmic War Confronting Radical Religion* (London: Arrow Books, 2010), p. 9.

3   Tony Judt, 'Goodbye to All That? Leszek Kołakowski and the Marxist Legacy', in Tony Judt (ed.), *Reappraisals: Reflections on the Forgotten Twentieth Century* (London: Vintage, 2009), p. 135.

4   Terry Eagleton, *On Evil* (New Haven, CT: Yale University Press, 2010); see also A.C. Grayling (2010), 'On Evil', *New Humanist*, 125(3), available at www.newhumanist.org.uk/2290/book-review-on-evil-by-terry-eagleton (accessed 9 March 2011).

5   Philip Cole, *The Myth of Evil* (Edinburgh: Edinburgh University Press, 2006).

6   Aslan, *Cosmic War*, pp. 2, 5.

7   Yehuda Bauer, *Rethinking the Holocaust* (New Haven, CT: Yale University Press, 2002), quotation at p. 16.

8   This is elaborated in David Cole and Jules Lobel, *Less Safe, Less Free: Why America is Losing the War on Terror* (New York: The New Press, 2007).

9   A classic study is Robert J. Lifton and Eric Markusen, *The Genocidal Mentality: Nazi Holocaust and Nuclear Threat* (London: Macmillan, 1990).

10 Bauer, *Rethinking*, p. 22.

11 Louise Richardson illustrates this well in relation to the bomb outside the Old Bailey in 1973: see *What Terrorists Want: Understanding the Enemy, Containing the Threat* (London: John Murray, 2006), pp. 41, 50, 243–5.

12 Primo Levi, *The Drowned and the Saved*, trans. Raymond Rosenthal (New York: Vintage International, 1989), p. 202.

13 Paul Lacey, *The Unequal World We Inhabit: Quaker Responses to Terrorism and Fundamentalism* (London: Quaker Books, 2010), p. 1.

14 Richard T. Antoun, 'Fundamentalism', in Bryan S. Turner (ed.), *Sociology of Religion* (Chichester: Wiley-Blackwell, 2010), pp. 529–31; see also Richard T. Antoun, *Understanding Fundamentalism: Christian, Islamic, and Jewish Movements*, 2nd Edition (Lanham, MD: Rowman & Littlefield, 2008).

15 Karen Armstrong, *The Battle for God: Fundamentalism in Judaism, Christianity and Islam* (London: HarperCollins, 2001), pp. 199–201.

16 Antoun, 'Fundamentalism', p. 520.

17 Antoun, Understanding Fundamentalism, pp. 3, 117–32.

18 Antoun, Understanding Fundamentalism, pp. 73–84.

19 Antoun, Understanding Fundamentalism, p. 165.

20 Lacey, Unequal World, pp. 32–3.

21 This paragraph is based on Bettany Hughes, The Hemlock Cup: Socrates, Athens and the Search for the Good Life (London: Jonathan Cape, 2010), p. 24.

22 Colin Wight (2009) 'Theorising Terrorism: The State, Structure, and History', International Relations, 23(1): 104.

23 Walter Lacquer, The New Terrorism: Fanaticism and the Arms of Mass Destruction (Oxford: Oxford University Press, 2000).

24 Lacey, Unequal World, p. 28.

25 Harold D. Lasswell, Politics: Who Gets What, When, How? (New York: Peter Smith, 1950).

26 Richard Falk, Revolutionaries and Functionaries: The Dual Face of Terrorism (New York: E.P. Dutton, 1988), p. xvii.

27 Audrey Kurth Cronin, How Terrorism Ends: Understanding the Decline and Demise of Terrorist Campaigns (Princeton, NJ: Princeton University Press, 2009); Walter Laqueur, No End To War: Terrorism in the Twenty-First Century (New York: Continuum, 2003); Adrian Guelke, Terrorism and Global Disorder (London: I.B. Tauris, 2006).

28 See, for example, Sarah Kershaw, 'The Terrorist Mind: An Update', New York Times, 9 January 2010, http://www.nytimes.com/2010/01/10/weekinreview/10kershaw.html (accessed 11 January 2011).

29 Robert Pape, Dying to Win: The Strategic Logic of Suicide Terrorism (New York: Random House, 2005), p. 4.

6 Wars

1 Quoted by Thomas J. Schoenbaum, International Relations: The Path Not Taken (Cambridge: Cambridge University Press, 2006), p. 3.

2 The International Security Assistance Force (ISAF) was created in December 2001. ISAF, which NATO assumed leadership of in August 2003, aimed to work in partnership with the Afghan Transitional Authority and the UN Assistance Mission in Afghanistan (UNAMA) to bring about peace and stability in postwar Afghanistan.

3 'War Logs', The New York Times, http://www.nytimes.com/interactive/world/26warlogs.html#report/15A27543-B022–4736-AC31–71006B18794E (accessed 1 November 2010).

4 Peter Bergen, 'Why Afghanistan is Far from Hopeless', Time, 28 March 2011.

5 Joe Klein, 'Finishing the Job in Afghanistan. Needed: Security, Development and a Stable Pakistan', Time, 17 January 2011.

6 Bergen, 'Why Afghanistan'.

7 Ken Booth, *Strategy and Ethnocentrism* (London: Croom Helm, 1979), pp. 102, 152.

8 Mehdi Hasan, 'The NS Interview', *The New Statesman*, 23 August 2010.

9 See, Philip Everts and Piernagelo Isernia (2006) 'The Polls-Trends: The War in Iraq', *Public Opinion Quarterly*, 69(2): 264–323. In the UK, opinion moved from being opposed to being in favour in the week before and after combat operations began (see p. 320). In the US, opinion was more consistently favourable.

10 Everts and Isernia, 'The Polls-Trends', see p. 269.

11 Key references to US policy-making on Iraq are: Bob Woodward, *Plan of Attack* (London: Simon & Schuster, 2004) and Ivo Daalder and James Lindsay, *America Unbound: The Bush Revolution in Foreign Policy* (Washington, DC: Brookings Institution, 2003).

12 Donald Rumsfeld, *Known and Unknown: A Memoir* (New York: Sentinel, 2011), p. 425.

13 For UK policy, see Kampfner *Blair's Wars* (London: Free Press, 2003). On the diplomatic failure, see Christopher Meyer, *D.C. Confidential* (London: Orion Publishing, 2006).

14 David Cole, *Justice at War: The Men and Ideas that Shaped America's War on Terror* (New York: New York Review Collection, 2008).

15 Richard Norton-Taylor, 'Iraq Doubts Kept from Cabinet', *The Guardian*, 29 January 2011.

16 Booth, *Strategy and Ethnocentrism*.

17 Eric Schmitt and Joel Brinkley, 'State Dept. Study Foresaw Trouble Now Plaguing Iraq', *New York Times*, 19 October 2003.

18 Anne Penketh, 'Backlash begins against "camel corps" plotters', *The Independent*, 24 April 2004. See also, 'Number 10 loyalist defends Blair', *BBC News*, 28 April 2004, http://news.bbc.co.uk/2/hi/uk_news/politics/3661877.stm (accessed 26 March 2011).

19 Philip Bobbitt, *Terror and Consent: The Wars for the Twenty-First Century* (London: Penguin, 2008), pp. 299, 334.

20 National Commission on Terrorist Attacks Against the United States. *The 9/11 Commission Report: Final Report of the National Commission on Terrorist Attacks Against the United States* (Washington, DC: US Government Printing Office, 2004), p. 334.

21 Richard A. Clarke, *Against All Enemies: Inside America's War on Terror* (New York: Free Press, 2004), p. 267.

22 Compare the critical position of Schoenbaum, *International Relations*, with Bobbitt, *Terror and Consent*.

23 Ron Suskind, *The One Percent Doctrine: Deep Inside America's Pursuit of its Enemies Since 9/11* (London: Simon & Schuster, 2006).

24 According to the Iraq Body Count, between 101,000 and 109,500 civilians

were killed between 2003 and 2011, http://www.iraqbodycount.org/ (accessed 28 March 2011).

25 Bergen, 'Why Afghanistan'.

26 See, Ken Booth, *Theory of World Security* (Cambridge: Cambridge University Press, 2007), pp. 254–6, 428–41.

7 America

1 Reza Aslan, *How to Win a Cosmic War: Confronting Radical Religion* (London: Arrow Books, 2010), p. 160.

2 Jean-Marie Colombani, 'We Are All Amercians', *Le Monde* (Liberal), 12 September 2001.

3 Jean-Marie Colombani, 'Are We Still "All American"?', *The Wall Street Journal*, 13 March 2004.

4 *London Review of Books Letters*, 18 October 2001. http://www.lrb.co.uk/v23/n20/letters (accessed 9 April 2011).

5 Giovanna Borradori, *Philosophy in a Time of Terror: Dialogues with Jürgen Habermas and Jacques Derrida* (Chicago, IL: Chicago University Press, 2003), p. 107.

6 'America is founded on genocide', Susan Sontag wrote: quoted in Gary Younge, 'The Guardian Profile. Susan Sontag. The Risk Taker', *The Guardian*, 19 January 2002.

7 Madeleine Albright, 'Interview on NBC-TV', *The Today Show* with Matt Lauer, 19 February 1998.

8 'The Bush Legacy: Bush's Final Approval Rating, 22 percent', *CBS News*, 16 January 2009, http://www.cbsnews.com/stories/2009/01/16/opinion/polls/main4728399.shtml (accessed 29 October 2010).

9 Ken Booth, *Theory of World Security* (Cambridge: Cambridge University Press, 2007), p. 357.

10 President George W. Bush, 'State of the Union Address', 29 January 2002, available at http://archives.cnn.com/2002/ALLPOLITICS/01/29/bush.speech.txt/ (accessed 26 July 2010).

11 Cited in Robert Jervis (2003) 'Understanding the Bush Doctrine', *Political Science Quarterly*, 18(3): 368.

12 Stockholm International Peace Research Institute (SIPRI), *SIPRI Yearbook 2009* (Stockholm: SIPRI, 2010), http://www.sipri.org/yearbook/2009/files/SIPRIYB0905.pdf (accessed 26 July 2010). Parts of this discussion on America, especially in relation to Iraq, are taken from Tim Dunne and Klejda Mulaj (2010) 'American After Iraq', *International Affairs*, 86(6): 1287–98.

13 Michael Cox (2005) 'Empire by Denial: The Strange Case of the United States', *International Affairs*, 81(1): 15–30, see p. 26.

14 'Poll: Confidence in Iraq War Down Sharply', *CNN Politics*, 18 March 2007, http://articles.cnn.com/2007–03–18/politics/poll.wars_1_iraq-war-sampling-error-poll?_s=PM:POLITICS (accessed 30 October 2010).

15 Jean Bethke Elshtain, 'How to Fight a Just War', in Ken Booth and Tim Dunne (eds), *Worlds in Collision: Terror and the Future of Global Order* (Houndmills: Palgrave Macmillan, 2002), pp. 263–70, p. 264.

16 Elshtain, 'How to Fight a Just War', p. 265.

17 Joseph Stiglitz and Linda Bilmes, 'The Three Trillion Dollar War', *The Times*, 23 February 2008. 'The cost of the Iraq and Afghanistan conflicts have grown to staggering proportions.'

18 See, for instance, his speech at the Veterans of Foreign Wars 103rd National Convention, Nashville, TN, 26 August 2002, available at http://www.mtholyoke.edu/acad/intrel/bush/cheneyvfw.htm (accessed 26 July 2010).

19 Ivo H. Daalder and James M. Lindsay, *America Unbound: The Bush Revolution in Foreign Policy* (Washington, DC: Brookings Institution, 2003), p. 147.

20 Philippe Sands, *Lawless World: America and the Making and Breaking of Global Rules* (London: Allen and Lane, 2005), p. 186.

21 Alex J. Bellamy, *Fighting Terror: Ethical Dilemmas* (London: Zed Books, 2008), p. 92.

22 The thesis put forward by Sands, *Lawless World*.

23 On drone attacks in Pakistan see Bruce Riedel, *Deadly Embrace: Pakistan, America, and the Future of the Global Jihad* (Washington, DC: the Brookings Institution Press, 2011), pp. 125–7, 135; and Mary Ellen O'Connell, 'Unlawful Killing with Combat Drones: A Case Study of Pakistan 2004–2009', *Notre Dame Legal Studies Paper* 9(43), http://ssrn.com/abstract=1501144 (accessed 4 April 2011). O'Connell estimates that the ratio killed is about 20 al-Qaeda leaders for 750–1,000 unintended victims.

24 G. John Ikenberry (2009) 'Liberal Internationalism 3.0: America and the Dilemmas of Liberal World Order', *Perspectives on Politics*, 7(1): 71–87.

8 Islam

1 Barack Obama, 'Remarks by the President on a New Beginning', Speech Before Cairo University, 2 June 2009, http://www.whitehouse.gov/the_press_office/Remarks-by-the-President-at-Cairo-University-6-04-09/ (accessed 23 September 2010).

2 'Islam: A Shifting Focus. New Data on the Second-Biggest Faith', *The Economist*, 8 October 2009.

3 The information is from various sources, and we cannot vouch for their accuracy; however, the point is not total accuracy, but 'good enough' general knowledge. Answers: (1) 1.57 billion or about 23 per cent of the global population of 6.8 billion. (2) Almost two thirds of Muslims live in Asia. (3) Indonesia (203 million), followed by Pakistan (174 million) and India (160 million). (4) At least 85 per cent of Muslims worldwide are thought to be Sunni. (5) It is estimated to be approximately 2.5 million, but exact figures are impossible because religious questions cannot be asked on the Census.

(6) 2.7 per cent. (7) Russia has the biggest Muslim population (16.5 million or nearly 12 per cent of the total population); Albania is the only country in Europe with a Muslim majority. (8) There are 1,900 mosques in the United States. (9) There are 2,100 mosques in France, 150 in Switzerland (but new minarets are banned), and 1,500 in the UK. (10) Between 2010–30 it is estimated that the global Muslim population will grow at twice the rate of the non-Muslim population (becoming 26.4 per cent of the world's total population); this rate will be slower, however, than the growth rate of the global Muslim population over the past 20 years. Sources: 'Islam: A Shifting Focus', *The Economist*; Henry Smith, 'The Prophet's People', *New Statesman*, 15 February 2010; John L. Esposito (ed.), *The Oxford Dictionary of Islam* (Oxford: Oxford University Press, 2003); Pew Forum, 'Global Muslim Population to Increase 35 Percent in the Next 20 Years', 31 January 2011, http://www.goddiscussion. com/.../pew-forum-global-muslim-population-to-increase-35-percent-in-next-20-years/ (accessed 29 March 2011) and Pew Forum, 'Mapping The Global Muslim Population' October 2009, http://www.pewforum.org/ uploadedfiles/Orphan_Migrated_Content/Muslimpopulation.pdf (accessed 29 March 2011); Bobby Ghosh, 'Islam in America', *Time*, 30 August 2010.

4   Amartya Sen, *Identity and Violence: The Illusion of Destiny* (London: Allen Lane, 2006), pp. 170–4.

5   Sen, *Identity and Violence*, pp. xiii, xvi, 12, 20, 176–8, 185.

6   Sen, *Identity and Violence*, pp. 77, 164.

7   Bernard Brodie, *Strategy in the Missile Age* (Princeton, NJ: Princeton University Press, 1959), p. 369.

8   Samuel Huntington, *The Clash of Civilisations and the Remaking of World Order* (New York: Simon & Schuster, 1996).

9   This is discussed in Gabriele Marranci, *The Anthropology of Islam* (London: Berg, 2008), pp. 367–73.

10 Marranci, *Anthropology of Islam*, p. 372.

11 Gabriele Marranci, 'Sociology and Anthropology of Islam: a Critical Debate', in Bryan S. Turner (ed.), *Sociology of Religion* (Chichester: Wiley-Blackwell, 2010), p. 368.

12 Talal Asad, *Genealogies of Religion: Discipline and Reasons of Power in Christianity and Islam* (Baltimore, MD: The Johns Hopkins University Press, 1993), p. 30. See also Marranci, *Anthropology of Islam*.

13 Asad, *Genealogies of Religion*, p. 28.

14 Sherifa Zuhar, *Precision in the Global War on Terror: Inciting Muslims Through the War of Ideas* (US Strategic Studies Institute: Carlisle, 2008), http://www. StrategicStudiesInstitute.army.mil/ (accessed 1 April 2011), p. 10, quoting As'ad Abukhalil (n. 17); Zuhar says the actual term was coined by Maxime Rodinson, *Le fascination de l'Islame* (Paris: La Decouverte, 1989).

15 Marranci, *Sociology and Anthropology*, p. 364.

16 Zuhur, *Precision in the GlobalWar on Terror*, p. 96.

17 Edmund Frettingham, describing arguments of Lewis and Huntington: *Security and the Construction of 'Religion' in International Politics* (Unpublished PhD: Aberystwyth University, 2009), p. 51.

18 Charles Krauthammer, 'The Bloody Borders of Islam', *Free Republic*, 6 December 2002, http://www.freerepublic.com/focus/news/838321/ (accessed 10 March 2011).

19 Asad, *Genealogies of Religion*, p. 54.

20 Bryan S. Turner, 'Islam, Diaspora, and Multiculturalism', in Akbar S. Ahmed and Tamara Sonn (eds), *The Sage Handbook of Islamic Studies* (London: Sage, 2010), p. 26. Turner is basing his argument about greater unity among British Muslims on the basis of the 2004 study *British Muslims' Expectations of the Government* sponsored by the Islamic Human Rights Commission and the Joseph Rowntree Charitable Trust.

21 The paragraph below is based on Theodore Dalrymple (2010) 'Fun-loving Muslims', *New Humanist*, 125(4): 32–3; this is based on his *The New Vichy Syndrome: Why European Intellectuals Surrender to Barbarism* (New York: Encounter Books, 2010).

22 Edward Said, *Orientalism: Western Conceptions of the Orient* (London: Penguin, 1979), and *Culture and Imperialism* (New York: Vintage Books, 1993).

23 Zuhur, *Precision in the GlobalWar on Terror*, p. 87.

24 See, for example, Robert Irwin, *Dangerous Knowledge: Orientalism and its Discontents* (Woodstock & NewYork: The Overlook Press, 2006).

25 Kenan Malik, *The Meaning of Race: Race, History and Culture inWestern Society* (Houndmills: Macmillan, 1996), p. 156.

9 Governance

1 Commission on Global Governance, *Our Global Neighbourhood* (Oxford: Oxford University Press, 1995), p. 2. For a more comprehensive definition, see Mark Webber, Stuart Croft, Lolyn Howorth, Terry Terriff, and Elke Krahmann (2004) 'The Governance of European Security', *Review of International Studies*, 30(1): 3–26, see p. 8.

2 Conor Gearty, 'Human Rights in an Age of Counter-Terrorism', *Oxford Amnesty Lecture*, 23 February 2006, http://www2.lse.ac.uk/humanRights/articlesAndTranscripts/Oxford_Amnesty_Lecture.pdf (accessed 11 April 2011).

3 David Cole and Jules Lobel, *Less Safe, Less Free: Why America is Losing the War on Terror* (NewYork: The New Press, 2007), p. 31.

4 Conor A. Gearty (2005) 'Human Rights in an Age of Counter-Terrorism: Injurious, Irrelevant or Indispensable?', *Current Legal Problems*, 58(1): 25–46, see p. 31.

5 Simon Geoffry, 'The Rules of the Game are Changing', *The Guardian*, 5 August 2005.

6   Michael Ignatieff, 'Is The Human Rights Era Over?', New York Times, 5 February 2002.

7   Gabriela Echeverria and Elizabeth Wilmshurst, Briefing Paper: Torture: An Overview of the Law (London: Chatham House, 2006).

8   See David Cole, Justice at War: The Men and Ideas that Shaped America's War on Terror (New York: New York Review Books Publication, 2008).

9   Mark Danner, Torture and Truth: America, Abu Ghraib and the War On Terror (London: Granta Books, 2005), see p. 115.

10 David Luban (2005) 'Liberalism, Torture and the Ticking Bomb', Virginia Law Review, 91(6): 1425–61, see p. 1456.

11 Philippe Sands, Lawless World: America and the Making and Breaking of Global Rules (London: Penguin, 2005), pp. 153–4.

12 David Forsythe, 'US Foreign Policy and Human Rights in an Era of Insecurity', in Margret Crahan, John Goering, and Thomas Weiss (eds), Wars on Terrorism and Iraq: Human Rights, Unilateralism, and US Foreign Policy (New York: Routledge, 2004), p. 81.

13 Tony Blair, 'Prime Minister's Press Conference', 5 August 2005. www.directgov.co.uk.

14 Elizabeth Wilmshurst, 'Extraordinary Rendition: A Summary of the Chatham House International Law Discussion Group Held on the 27 March 2008' (London: Chatham House, 2008).

15 Quoted in Clive Stafford Smith, 'Government's Rendition Bully Tactics', Guardian, 18 April 2010. See also, 'Developments in the European Union', Minutes of Evidence Taken Before the Foreign Affairs Committee, 13 December 2005, http://www.publications.parliament.uk/pa/cm200506/cmselect/cmfaff/c768-i/c76802.htm (accessed 4 April 2011).

16 Human Rights Watch, World Report 2006 (New York: Human Rights Watch and Seven Stories Press, 2006), see p. 9.

17 Sands, Lawless World, see p. 165.

18 Tom Bingham, The Rule of Law (London: Allen Lane, 2010), see p. 137.

19 Binyam Mohamed, 'A Victory for Open Justice and the Rule of Law', Guardian, 26 February 2010.

20 This is Michael Byers' view, see his (2002) 'Terrorism, The Use of Force and International Law After 11 September', International and Comparative Law Quarterly, 51(2): 401–14, see p. 412.

21 'Chilcot Inquiry: Iraq Papers Show Lord Goldsmith's Warning to Tony Blair', Guardian, 30 June 2010, http://www.guardian.co.uk/uk/2010/jun/30/chilcot-inquiry-lord-goldsmith-blair (accessed 15 November 2010).

22 Wilmshurt's resignation letter was submitted to the Chilcot Inquiry. See http://www.iraqinquiry.org.uk/media/44211/20100126pm-wilmshurst-final.pdf (accessed 4 April 2011).

23 Gearty, 'Human Rights'.

10 Democracy

1 Michael Doyle (1983) 'Kant, Liberal Legacies, and Foreign Affairs', Part 1 and Part 2, *Philosophy and Public Affairs*, 12(3): 205–35 and 12(4): 323–53.

2 Natan Sharansky with Don Dermer, *The Case for Democracy: The Power of Freedom to Overcome Tyranny and Terror* (New York: Public Affairs, 2004), p. xxv. In his inaugural address for his second term, George W. Bush proclaimed: 'The best hope for peace in our world' is the 'expansion of freedom in all the world'. 'Inaugural Address by President George. W. Bush', *U.S. Newswire*, 21 January 2005.

3 William Eubank and Leonard Weinberg (2001) 'Terrorism and Democracy: Perpetrators and Victims', *Terrorism and Political Violence*, 13(1): 155–64, see p. 160.

4 Michael Freeman (2008) 'Democracy, Al Qaeda and the Causes of Terrorism: A Study of U.S. Foreign Policy', *Studies in Conflict and Terrorism*, 31(1): 40–59, see p. 40.

5 See Robert Pape (2003) 'The Strategic Logic of Suicide Terrorism', *American Political Science Review*, 97(3): 343–61.

6 Feisal Devji, *Landscapes of the Jihad: Militancy, Morality, Modernity* (Ithaca, NY: Cornell University Press, 2005), pp. xvi, 95, 184.

7 Lewis, quoted in Michael Freeman, 'Democracy, Al Qaeda and the Causes of Terrorism', p. 40.

8 International Monetary Fund, *World Economic Outlook Database* (Washington, DC: International Monetary Fund, 2010), http://www.imf.org/external/data.htm (accessed 24 March 2011).

9 Freedom House, *Freedom in the World 2011: The Authoritarian Challenge to Democracy* (Washington, DC: Freedom House, 2011). Freedom House describes itself as an 'independent watchdog' though critics claim it is not sufficiently independent of US foreign policy interests.

10 Fareed Zakaria, *The Future of Freedom* (New York: W.W. Norton, 2003), p. 136.

11 Samuel P. Huntington, *The Third Wave: Democratization in the Late Twentieth Century* (Norman: University of Oklahoma Press, 1991), p. 65, quoted in Larry Diamond (2010) 'Why Are There No Arab Democracies?' *Journal of Democracy*, 21(1): 91–112.

12 Larry Diamond, 'Why Are There No Arab Democracies?', see p. 98.

13 Fred Halliday, 'Libya's Regime at 40: A State of Kleptocracy', *Open Democracy*, 7 March 2011. http://www.opendemocracy.net/article/libya-s-regime-at-40-a-state-of-kleptocracy, p.6 (accessed 24 March 2011).

14 'Blair Hails New Libya Relations', BBC, 25 March 2004, http://news.bbc.co.uk/2/hi/uk_news/politics/3566545.stm (accessed 29 March 2011).

15 'The Iraq War Did Not Force Gadaffi's Hand', *The Financial Times*, 9 March 2004.

16 Gregory Cause III (2005) 'Can Democracy Stop Terrorism?' *Foreign Affairs*, 84(5): 62–76, see p. 71.

17 *Pew Global Attitudes Survey*, 2 December 2010. Responses to 'Is It Good that Islam Plays a Large/Small Role in Politics', Muslim-only responses to 'large role' being a good think in brackets: Egypt (95), Indonesia (95), Pakistan (88), Nigeria (88), Lebanon (70), Turkey (45), Jordan (53). Conducted between 12 April and 7 May 2010. Available at http://pewglobal.org/2010/12/02/muslims-around-the-world-divided-on-hamas-and-hezbollah (accessed 10 October 2010).

18 Described by Robert Malley, of the International Crisis Group, as 'morally callous and politically counter-productive'. See: 'Flotilla Attack the Deadly Symptom of a Failed Policy', *International Crisis Group*, http://www.crisisgroup. org/en/publication-type/media-releases/2010/flotilla-attack-the-deadly-symptom-of-a-failed-policy.aspx (accessed 24 March 2011).

19 For critical scrutiny of the democratic peace thesis, see, for example, the Frankfurt research project that led to the publication Anna Geis, Lothar Brock, and Harald Mueller (eds), *Democratic Wars: Looking at the Dark Side of Democratic Peace* (Houndmills: Palgrave Macmillan, 2006); see also Tim Dunne (2009) 'Liberalism, International Terrorism and Democratic Wars', *International Relations*, 23(1): 107–14.

20 Quoted in Nicholas Pelham and Max Rodenbeck, 'Which Way for Hamas?', *New York Review of Books*, 5 November 2009.

21 Thomas Carothers (2003) 'Promoting Democracy and Fighting Terror', *Foreign Affairs*, 82(1): 84–97.

22 Cause, *Can Democracy Stop Terrorism?*, p. 69.

23 On the last points, see Amaryta Sen, *The Argumentative Indian: Writings on Indian Culture, History and Identity* (London: Penguin Books, 2006), pp. xiii, 39–42, 287–93.

24 Susan Buck-Morss, *Thinking Past Terror: Islamism and Critical Theory on the Left* (London: Verso, 2006), p. 102.

11 Security

1 'Stuff happens' was the phrase used by Rumsfeld on the looting in Iraq after the 'liberation'. 'Freedom's untidy, and free people are free to make mistakes and commit crimes and do bad things', Rumsfeld said. 'They're also free to live their lives and do wonderful things. And that's what's going to happen here.' Sean Loughlin, 'Rumsfeld on Looting in Iraq: "Stuff Happens"', *CNN Washington Bureau*, 11 April 2003.

 2 'The War With Iraq Is Not In America's National Interest', Paid Advertisement: Appearing on the Op-Ed Page of the *New York Times*, 26 September 2002. Available at http://www.bear-left.com/archive/2002/0926oped.html (accessed 4 April 2011).

 3 Philip Bobbitt, *Terror and Consent: The Wars for the Twenty-First Century* (London: Penguin Books, 2009).

4 Bobbitt, *Terror and Consent*, p. 12; the market state is defined on p. 4n.

5 Bobbitt, *Terror and Consent*, pp. 45–63.

6 Bobbitt, *Terror and Consent*, pp. 62–3.

7 This twinning of the 11s was first done, we believe, by John Kerry: John Kerry, 'U.S. Policy Towards the Middle East', Speech: Carnegie Endowment for International Peace, 16 March 2011. Available at http://kerry.senate.gov/press/speeches/speech/?id=CB945E57-2F36-4BAA-A751-600A15135389 (accessed 5 April 2011).

8 These matters are discussed within the idea of a historic 'Great Reckoning' in Ken Booth, *Theory of World Security* (Cambridge: Cambridge University Press, 2007), pp. 395–426.

9 Brian Michael Jenkins, *Will Terrorists Go Nuclear?* (Amherst: Prometheus Books, 2008), pp. 323–53.

10 Quoted by Schumpeter, 'Beyond Economics', *The Economist*, 12 February 2011.

11 See Doug Stokes and Sam Raphael, *Global Energy Security and American Hegemony* (Baltimore, MD: The Johns Hopkins University Press, 2010).

12 Robert Fisk, 'Nine Years, Two Wars, Hundreds of Thousands Dead – and Nothing Learnt', *The Independent*, 11 September 2010.

13 Frazer Egerton, *Jihad in the West: The Rise of Militant Salafism* (Cambridge: Cambridge University Press, 2011).

14 David Cole and Jules Lobel, *Less Safe, Less Free: Why America is Losing the War on Terror* (New York: New Press, 2007), see pp. 3–5.

15 Cole and Lobel, *Less Safe, Less Free*, p. 7.

16 Ken Booth and Nicholas J. Wheeler, *The Security Dilemma: Fear, Cooperation and Trust in World Politics* (Houndmills: Palgrave Macmillan, 2008), pp. 265–72.

17 An invaluable source tracking attitudes and offering a comprehensive definition is the Pew Research Centre, 'Islamophobia: Survey Reports', *Pew Global Attitudes Survey*, http://pewglobal.org/subjects/islamophobia (accessed 1 April 2011).

18 This is the view of Theodore Dalrymple, *The New Vichy Syndrome: Why Western Intellectuals Surrender to Barbarism* (New York: Encounter Books, 2009).

19 Andrew Anthony, 'Sayeed Warsi. A Matter of Prejudice', *The Observer*, 23 January 2011.

20 Jean Bethke Elshtain, *Women and War* (Brighton: Harvester Press, 1987).

21 Andrew J. Bacevitch, 'Obama Wants Us to Forget the Lessons of Iraq', *The New Republic*, 31 August 2010, http://www.tnr.com/blog/foreign-policy/77356/obama-wants-us-to-forget-the-lessons-iraq (accessed 2 April 2011). See also, Frank Rich, 'How Obama Failed to Give Voice to the US Legacy of Anger and Grief', *The Observer*, 12 September 2010.

22 'The Wounded Platoon', BBC 2, 25 August 2010. Originally on *Frontline: PBS*, 'The Wounded Platoon', 18 May 2010. http://www.pbs.org/wgbh/pages/frontline/woundedplatoon (accessed 2 April 2011).

23 Alan Dershowitz, 'Rape as Terrorism', *Huffington Post Politics*, 28 February 2007. Available at http://www.huffingtonpost.com/alan-Dershowitz/rape-as-terrorism_b_42309.html (accessed 2 April 2011).

24 Aryn Baker, 'Afghan Women and the Return of the Taliban', *Time Magazine*, 29 July 2010. Comments in the rest of the paragraph are based on Priyamvada Gopal, 'Not Another Morality Tale', *The Guardian*, 4 August 2010.

25 Booth, *World Security*, pp. 110–11.

26 Ahdaf Soueif, 'We Have Come Together to Reclaim Our Country', *The Guardian*, 29 January 2011.

27 Susan Buck-Morss, *Thinking Past Terror: Islamism and Critical Theory on the Left* (London: Verso, 2006).

12 Endings

1 Bernard Brodie, *War and Politics* (London: Cassell, 1973), p. 1.

2 National Intelligence Council, *Global Trends 2025: A Transformed World* (Washington, DC: US Government Printing Office, 2008). Available at http://www.dni.gov/nic/PDF_2025/2025_Global_Trends_Final_Report.pdf (accessed 6 April 2011).

3 Jennifer Rizzo, '"Flickers" of al Qaeda in Libyan Opposition, US NATO Leader Says', *CNN National Security*, 29 March 2011. Available at http://articles.cnn.com/2011-03-29/us/libya.opposition.analysis_1_james-stavriades-moammar-gadhafi-al-qaeda-or-one?_s=PM:US (accessed 3 April 2011).

4 For an excellent account of the crisis and ideas about the way forward, see Ali Allawi, *The Crisis of Islamic Civilisation* (New Haven, CT: Yale University Press, 2009).

5 Ken Booth, *Theory of World Security* (Cambridge: Cambridge University Press, 2007), pp. 441–5.

6 Michael Howard (2006) 'A Long War?', *Survival*, 48(4): 7–14, see p. 13.

7 Tom Englelhardt, *The American War of War: How Bush's Wars Became Obama's* (Chicago, IL: Haymarket Books, 2010), p. 22.

8 Martha Crenshaw (1991) 'How Terrorism Declines', *Terrorism and Political Violence*, 3(1): 69–87, see p. 79.

9 Audrey Kurth Cronin, *How Terrorism Ends: Understanding the Decline and Demise of Terrorist Campaigns* (Princeton: Princeton University Press, 2010), p. 40.

10 Both quotations in Cronin, *How Terrorism Ends*, p. 36.

11 Cronin, *How Terrorism Ends*, p. 206.

12 Cynthia Enloe, *The Morning After: Sexual Politics at the End of the Cold War* (Berkeley: University of California Press, 1993).

Epilogue

1 Albert Camus, *The Plague* (London: Penguin Books, 2001), pp. 237–8.

Appendix

1 We are very grateful to Alexander Pound at the University of Queensland for his assistance with these datasets. Any interpretive errors are the responsibility of the authors.

2 Rather than work with a single definition of terrorism, GTD uses 'properties' of a terrorist incident. This includes the following three: '*The incident must be intentional* – the result of a conscious calculation on the part of a perpetrator; *The incident must entail some level of violence or threat of violence* – including property violence, as well as violence against people; *The perpetrators of the incidents must be sub-national actors.*' This database does not include acts of state terrorism. Global Terrorism Database, START, http://www.start.umd.edu/gtd/ (accessed 14 March 2011).

3 UCDP 'One-Sided Violence Codebook Version 1.3 – September 4, 2008', http://www.pcr.uu.se/digitalAssets/19/19256_UCDP_One-sided_violence_Dataset_Codebook_v1.3.pdf (accessed 8 March 2011).

4 Global Terrorism Database, START, http://www.start.umd.edu/gtd/ (accessed 21 March 2011).

5 RAND data on the 2001–08 period are highly corroborative: 52, 350. http://www.rand.org/nsrd/projects/terrorism-incidents.html (accessed 31 March 2011).

Bibliography

We would like to thank Alexander Pound for preparing this bibliography.

Allawi, Ali A. (2009), *The Crisis of Islamic Civilization*, Yale: Yale University Press.

Allison, Graham (2004), *Nuclear Terrorism: The Ultimate Preventable Catastrophe*, New York: Times Books.

Antoun, Richard T. (2008), *Understanding Fundamentalism: Christian, Islamic and Jewish Movements*, Lanham, MD: Rowman & Littlefield.

Armstrong, Karen (2001), *The Battle for God: Fundamentalism in Judaism, Christianity and Islam*, London: Harper Collins.

Asad, Talal (1993), *Genealogies of Religion: Discipline and Reasons of Power in Christianity and Islam*, Washington, DC: Johns Hopkins Press.

Asad, Talal (2007), *On Suicide Bombing*, New York: Columbia University Press.

Aslan, Reza (2010), *How to Win a Cosmic War: Confronting Radical Religion*, London: Arrow Books.

Bacevich, Andrew (2005), *The New American Militarism: How Americans are Seduced by War*, New York: Oxford University Press.

Bandura, Albert (1998), 'Mechanisms of Moral Disengagement', in Walter Reigh (ed.), *Origins of Terrorism*, Washington, DC: Woodrow Wilson Center Press.

Bellamy, Alex (2008), *Fighting Terror: Ethical Dilemmas*, London: Zed Books.

Bergen, Peter (2004), *Holy War Inc.*, New York: The Free Press.

Bergen, Peter (2010), *The Longest War: The Enduring Conflict between America and Al-Qaeda*, New York: The Free Press.

Bingham, Tom (2010), *The Rule of Law*, London: Allen Lane.

Bobbitt, Phillip (2009), *Terror and Consent: The Wars for the 21st Century*, New York: Random House.

Booth, Ken (1979), *Strategy and Ethnocentrism*, London: Croom Helm.

Booth, Ken (2007), *Theory of World Security*, Cambridge: Cambridge University Press.

Booth, Ken (2008), 'The Human Face of Terror: Reflections in a Cracked Looking-Glass', *Critical Studies on Terrorism*, 1 (1): 65–79.

Booth, Ken and Dunne, Tim (eds) (2002), *Worlds In Collision: Terror and the Future of Global Order*, Houndmills: Palgrave.

Booth, Ken and Wheeler, Nicholas (2008), *The Security Dilemma: Fear, Cooperation and Trust in World Politics*, Houndmills: Palgrave Macmillan.

Borradori, Giovanna (2003), *Philosophy in a Time of Terror: Dialogues with Jürgen Habermas and Jacques Derrida*, Chicago, IL: Chicago University Press.

Bourke, Joanna (2005), *Fear: A Cultural History*, London: Virago.

Brachmen, Jarret M. (2009), *Global Jihadism: Theory and Practice*, London: Routledge.

Brodie, Bernard (1959), *Strategy in the Missile Age*, Princeton, NJ: Princeton University Press.

Brodie, Bernard (1973), *War and Politics*, Basingstoke: Macmillan.

Buck-Morss, Susan (2006), *Thinking Past Terror: Islamism and Critical Theory on the Left*, London: Verso.

Burke, Jason (2004), *Al-Qaeda: The True Story of Radical Islam*, London: Penguin Books.

Byers, Michael (2002), 'Terrorism, the Use of Force and International Law after 11 September', *International and Comparative Law Quarterly*, 51(2): 401–14.

Carruthers, Thomas (2003), 'Promoting Democracy and Fighting Terror', *Foreign Affairs*, 82(1): 84–97.

Carruthers, Thomas (2004), *Critical Mission: Essays on Democracy Promotion*, Washington, DC: Carnegie Endowment for International Peace.

Cause III, Gregory (2005), 'Can Democracy Stop Terrorism?' *Foreign Affairs*, 84(5): 62–76.

Clarke, Richard A. (2004), *Against All Enemies: Inside America's War on Terror*, New York: Free Press.

Cole, David (2008), *Justice at War: The Men and Ideas that Shaped America's War on Terror*, New York: New York Review Collection.

Cole, David and Lobel, Jules (2007), *Less Safe, Less Free. Why America is Losing the War on Terror*, New York: The New Press.

Cox, Michael (2005), 'Empire by Denial: The Strange Case of the United States', *International Affairs*, 81(1): 15–30.

Crelinsten, R.D. (2002), 'Analysing Terrorism and Counterterrorism: A Communication Model', *Terrorism and Political Violence*, 14(2): 77–122.

Crenshaw, Martha (1991), 'How Terrorism Declines', *Terrorism and Political Violence*, 3(1): 69–87.

Cronin, Audrey Kurth (2007), 'Ending Terrorism: Lessons for Defeating Al-Qaeda', *Adelphi Paper*, 47(394).

Cronin, Audrey Kurth (2009), *How Terrorism Ends: Understanding the Decline and Demise of Terrorist Campaigns*, Princeton, NJ: Princeton University Press.

Daalder, Ivo H. and Lindsay, James M. (2003), *America Unbound: The Bush Revolution in Foreign Policy*, Washington, DC: Brookings Institution.

Dalrymple, Theodore (2010), *The New Vichy Syndrome: Why European Intellectuals Surrender to Barbarism*, New York: Encounter Books.

Danner, Mark (2005), *Torture and Truth: America, Abu Ghraib and the War On Terror*, London: Granta Books.

Dershowitz, Alan (2002), *Why Terrorism Works: Understanding the Threat, Responding to the Challenge*, New Haven, CT: Yale University Press.

Devji, Faisal (2005), *Landscape of the Jihad: Militancy, Morality and Modernity*, Ithaca, NY: Cornell University Press.

Diamond, Larry (2010), 'Why Are There No Arab Democracies?', *Journal of Democracy*, 21(1): 91–112.

Doyle, Michael (1983), 'Kant, Liberal Legacies, and Foreign Affairs', Part 1 and Part 2, *Philosophy and Public Affairs*, 12(3): 205–35 and 12(4): 323–53.

Dunne, Tim (2009), 'Liberalism, International Terrorism and Democratic Wars', *International Relations*, 23(1): 107–14.

Dunne, Tim and Mulaj, Klejda (2010), 'America after Iraq', *International Affairs*, 86(6): 1287–98.

Egerton, Frazer (2011), *Jihad in the West: The Rise of Militant Salafism*, Cambridge: Cambridge University Press.

Elshtain, Jean Bethke (1987), *Women and War*, Brighton: Harvester Press.

Elshtain, Jean Bethke (2002), 'How to Fight a Just War', in Ken Booth and Tim Dunne (eds), *Worlds In Collision: Terror and the Future of Global Order*, Houndmills: Palgrave Macmillan.

Elshtain, Jean Bethke (2003), *Just War Against Terror. The Burden of American Power in a Violent World*, New York: Basic Books.

Englelhardt, Tom (2010), *The American War of War: How Bush's Wars Became Obama's*, Chicago, IL: Haymarket Books.

Enloe, Cynthia (1993), *The Morning After: Sexual Politics at the End of the Cold War*, Berkeley: University of California Press.

Eubank, William and Weinberg, Leonard (2001), 'Terrorism and Democracy: Perpetrators and Victims', *Terrorism and Political Violence*, 13(1): 155–64.

Falk, Richard (1988), *Revolutionaries and Functionaries: The Dual Face of Terrorism* (New York: E.P. Dutton).

Falk, Richard A. (2003), *The Great Terror War*, New York: Olive Branch Press.

Feldman, Noah (2008), *The Fall and Rise of the Islamic World*, Princeton, NJ: Princeton University Press.

Foot, Philippa (2001), *Natural Goodness*, Oxford: Oxford University Press.

Forsythe, David (2004), 'US Foreign Policy and Human Rights in an Era of Insecurity', in Margret Crahan, John Goering, and Thomas Weiss (eds), *Wars on Terrorism and Iraq: Human Rights, Unilateralism, and US Foreign Policy*, New York: Routledge.

Freedman, Lawrence (2005), 'War in Iraq: Selling the Threat', *Survival: Global Politics and Strategy*, 46(2): 7–49.

Freeman, Michael (2008), 'Democracy, Al Qaeda and the Causes of Terrorism: A Study of U.S. Foreign Policy', *Studies in Conflict and Terrorism*, 31(1): 40–59.

Frettingham, Edmund (2009), *Security and the Construction of 'Religion' in International Politics*, Unpublished PhD: Aberystwyth University.

Furedi, Frank (2008), *Invitation to Terror: The Expanding Empire of the Unknown*, London: Continuum Books.

Gardner, Dan (2008), *Risk: The Science and Politics of Fear*, London: Virgin.

Gearty, Conor (2006), 'Human Rights in an Age of Counter-Terrorism', *Oxford Amnesty Lecture 23 February 2006*. Available at http://www2.lse.ac.uk/humanRights/articlesAndTranscripts/Oxford_Amnesty_Lecture.pdf. (accessed 11 April 2011).

Geis, Anna, Brock, Lothar, and Mueller, Harald (eds) (2006), *Democratic Wars: Looking at the Dark Side of Democratic Peace*, Houndmills: Palgrave Macmillan.

George, Alexander (ed.) (1991), *Western State Terrorism*, Cambridge: Polity Press.

Gerges, Fawaz (2005), *The Far Enemy: Why the Jihad Went Global*, Cambridge: Cambridge University Press.

Goodin, Robert (2006), *What's Wrong with Terrorism*, Cambridge: Polity Press.

Greenberg, Karen (ed.) (2005), *Al Qaeda Now: Understanding Today's Terrorists*, Cambridge: Cambridge University Press.

Greenberg, Karen and Dratel, Joshua (eds) (2005), *The Torture Papers: The Road to Abu Ghraib*, New York: Cambridge University Press.

Guelke, Adrian (2006), *Terrorism and Global Disorder*, London: I.B. Tauris.

Guelke, Adrian (2009), *The New Age of Terrorism and the International Political System*, London: I.B. Tauris.

Halliday, Fred (2010), *Shocked and Awed: How the War On Terror and Jihad Have Changed the English Language*, London: I.B. Tauris.

Hillyard, Paddy (1993), *Suspect Community*, London: Pluto Press.

Hoffman, Bruce (2006), *Inside Terrorism*, 2nd ed., New York: Columbia University Press.

Horgan, John (2005), *The Psychology of Terrorism*, New York: Routledge.

Howard, Michael (2006), 'A Long War?', *Survival*, 48(4): 7–14.

Huntington, Samuel (1996), *The Clash of Civilisations and the Remaking of World Order*, New York: Simon & Schuster.

Hurd, Ian (2005), 'The Strategic Use of Liberal Internationalism: Libya and the Use of UN Sanction, 1992–2003', *International Organisation*, 59(3): 495–526.

Ikenberry, G. John (2011), *Liberal Leviathan: The Origins, Crisis and Transformation of the American World Order*, Princeton, NJ: Princeton University Press.

Ikenberry, G. John (2011), 'Liberal Internationalism 3.0: America and the Dilemmas of Liberal World Order', *Perspectives on Politics*, 7(1): 71–87.

Irwin, Robert (2006), *Dangerous Knowledge: Orientalism and its Discontents*, Woodstock & New York: The Overlook Press.

Jackson, Richard, Jarvis, Lee, Gunning, Jeroen, and Smith, Marie Breen (2011 in press), *Terrorism: A Critical Introduction*, Houndmills: Palgrave Macmillan.

Jenkins, Brian (2008), *Will Terrorists Go Nuclear?*, New York: Prometheus Books.

Jervis, Robert (2003), 'Understanding the Bush Doctrine', *Political Science Quarterly*, 118(3): 365–88.

Jervis, Robert (2006), 'Reports, Politics and Intelligence Failures: The Case of Iraq', *The Journal of Strategic Studies*, 29(1): 3–52.

Jurgensmeyer, Mark (2000), *Terror in the Mind of God: The Global Rise of Religious Violence*, Berkeley: University of California Press.

Kampfner, John (2003), *Blair's Wars*, London: Free Press.

Lacey, Paul (2010), *The Unequal World We Inhabit: Quaker Responses to Terrorism and Fundamentalism: Swarthmore Lecture, 2010*, London: Quaker Books.

Lacquer, Walter (2003), *No End to War: Terrorism in the Twenty-First Century*, New York: Continuum.

Lynch, Timothy and Singh, Robert (2008), *After Bush: The Case for Continuity in American Foreign Policy*, Cambridge: Cambridge University Press.

Malik, Kenan (1996), The Meaning of Race: Race, History and Culture in Western Society, Houndmills: Macmillan.

Marranci, Gabriele (2008), The Anthropology of Islam, London: Berg.

Marranci, Gabriele (2009), Understanding Muslim Identity, Rethinking Fundamentalism, Houndmills: Palgrave Macmillan.

Marranci, Gabriele (2010), 'Sociology and Anthropology of Islam: a Critical Debate', in Bryan S. Turner (ed.), Sociology of Religion, Chichester: Wiley-Blackwell.

Mearsheimer, John (2001), The Tragedy of Great Power Politics, New York: Norton.

Mueller, John (2006), Overblown: How Politicians and the Terrorism Industry Inflate National Security Threats and Why We Believe Them, New York: The Free Press.

Mueller, John (2010), Atomic Obsession: Nuclear Alarmism from Hiroshima to Al Qaeda, Oxford: Oxford University Press.

National Commission on Terrorist Attacks Against the United States (2004), The 9/11 Commission Report: Final Report of the National Commission on Terrorist Attacks Against the United States, Washington, DC: US Government Printing Office.

Pape, Robert (2003), 'The Strategic Logic of Suicide Terrorism', American Political Science Review, 97(3): 343–61.

Pape, Robert (2005), Dying to Win: The Strategic Logic of Suicide Terrorism, New York: Random House.

Pedahzur, Ami (2005), Suicide Terrorism, New York: Polity Press.

Pollock, Kenneth M. (2002), The Case for Invading Iraq, New York: Random House.

Ranstorp, Magnus (2007), Mapping Terrorism Research: State of the Art Gaps and Future Direction, Abingdon: Routledge.

Reus-Smit, Chris (2004), American Power and World Order, Cambridge: Polity Press.

Richardson, Louise (2006), What Terrorists Want: Understanding the Enemy, Containing the Threat, New York: Random House.

Riedel, Bruce (2011), Deadly Embrace: Pakistan, America, and the Future of the Global Jihad, Washington, DC: Brookings Institution Press.

Robin, Corey (2004), Fear: The History of a Political Idea, Oxford: Oxford University Press.

Roy, Oliver (2006), Globalised Islam: The Search for a New Ummah, London: Hurst.

Sageman, Marc (2008), Leaderless Jihad: Terror Networks in the Twenty First Century, Philadelphia: University of Pennsylvania Press.

Said, Edward (1979), Orientalism: Western Conceptions of the Orient, London: Penguin.

Said, Edward (1993), Culture and Imperialism, New York: Vintage Books.

Sands, Philippe (2005), Lawless World: America and the Making and Breaking of Global Rules, London: Allen and Lane.

Scarry, Elaine (1985), The Body in Pain: The Making and Unmaking of the World, New York: Oxford University Press.

Schmidt, Alex and Jongman, Albert (1988), Political Terrorism: A New Guide to Actors, Authors, Concepts, Databases and Literature, Amsterdam: Transaction Books.

Sen, Amartya (2006), Identity and Violence: The Illusion of Destiny, London: Allen Lane.

Sen, Amaryta (2006), The Argumentative Indian: Writings on Indian Culture, History and Identity, London: Penguin Books.

Sharansky, Natan with Dermer, Don (2004), The Case for Democracy: The Power of Freedom to Overcome Tyranny and Terror, New York: Public Affairs.

Silke, Andrew (2003), 'Retaliating Against Terrorism', in Andrew Silke (ed.), *Terrorists, Victims and Society: Psychological Perspectives on Terrorism and its Consequences*, Chichester: John Wiley & Sons.

Sjoberg, Laura and Gentry, Caron (2007), *Mothers, Monsters, Whores: Women's Violence in Global Politics*, London: Zed.

Stohl, Michael (1979), *The Politics of Terrorism*, New York: M. Dekker.

Stokes, Doug and Raphael, Sam (2010), *Global Energy Security and American Hegemony*, Baltimore, MD: The Johns Hopkins University Press.

Suskind, Ron (2006), *The One Percent Doctrine: Deep Inside America's Pursuit of its Enemies Since 9/11*, London: Simon & Schuster.

Tilly, Charles (2007), *Democracy*, Cambridge: Cambridge University Press.

Tirman, John (2009), 'Diplomacy, Terrorism, and National Narratives in the United States–Iran Relationship', *Critical Studies on Terrorism*, 12(3): 527–39.

Turner, Bryan S. (2010), 'Islam, Diaspora, and Multiculturalism', in Akbar S. Ahmed and Tamara Sonn (eds), *The Sage Handbook of Islamic Studies*, London: Sage.

Turner, Bryan S. (ed.) (2010), *The New Blackwell Companion to the Sociology of Religion*, Chichester: Wiley-Blackwell.

Walton, Stuart (2004), *Humanity: An Emotional History*, London: Atlantic Books.

Waltz, Kenneth N. (2002), 'The Continuity of International Politics', in Ken Booth and Tim Dunne (eds), *Worlds in Collision: Terror and the Future of Global Order*, Houndmills: Palgrave Macmillan, pp. 348–53.

Walzer, Michael (1984), 'Liberalism and the Art of Separation', *Political Theory*, 12(3): 315–30.

Walzer, Michael (2000), *Just and Unjust Wars*, New York: Basic Books.

Webber, Mark, Croft, Stuart, Howorth, Lolyn, Terriff, Terry, and Krahmann, Elke (2004), 'The Governance of European Security', *Review of International Studies*, 30(1): 3–26.

Wight, Colin (2009), 'Theorising Terrorism: The State, Structure and History', *International Relations*, 23(1): 100–3.

Wilkinson, Paul (2006), *Terrorism Versus Democracy: The Liberal State Response*, London: Routledge.

Wolfendale, Jessica (2007), 'Terrorism, Security and the Threat of Counterterrorism', *Studies in Conflict and Terrorism*, 30(1): 75–92.

Woodward, Bob (2004), *Plan of Attack*, London: Simon & Schuster.

Wright, Lawrence (2007), *The Looming Tower*, London: Vintage.

Zakaria, Fareed (2003), *The Future of Freedom*, New York: W.W. Norton.

Zuhur, Sherifa (2008), *Precision in the Global War on Terror: Inciting Muslims Through the War of Ideas*, Carlisle: US Strategic Studies Institute:

Zulaika, Joseba (2009), *Terrorism: The Self Fulfilling Prophecy*, Chicago, IL: University of Chicago Press.

Zulaika, Joseba and Douglass, William (1996), *Terror and Taboo: The Follies, Fables and Faces of Terrorism*, New York: Routledge.

Index